Reframing Yeats

Historicizing Modernism

Historicizing Modernism challenges traditional literary interpretations by taking an empirical approach to modernist writing: a direct response to new documentary sources made available over the last decade.

Informed by archival research, and working beyond the usual European/American avant-garde 1900–45 parameters, this series reassesses established readings of modernist writers by developing fresh views of intellectual contexts and working methods.

Series Titles:

Reframing Yeats

Genre, Allusion and History

Charles I. Armstrong

Bloomsbury Academic
An imprint of Bloomsbury Publishing Plc

B L O O M S B U R Y
LONDON • NEW DELHI • NEW YORK • SYDNEY

Bloomsbury Academic

An imprint of Bloomsbury Publishing Plc

50 Bedford Square	1385 Broadway
London	New York
WC1B 3DP	NY 10018
UK	USA

www.bloomsbury.com

BLOOMSBURY and the Diana logo are trademarks of Bloomsbury Publishing Plc

First published 2013
Paperback edition first published 2015

British Library Cataloguing-in-Publication Data
A catalogue record for this book is available from the British Library.

ISBN: HB:	978-1-4411-8316-3
PB:	978-1-4742-2285-3
ePDF:	978-1-4411-3971-9
ePub:	978-1-6235-6353-0

Library of Congress Cataloging-in-Publication Data
A catalog record for this book is available from the Library of Congress

Typeset by Newgen Imaging Systems Pvt Ltd, Chennai, India

To Inger

Contents

Series Editor's Preface

This book series is devoted to the analysis of late-nineteenth to twentieth-century literary Modernism within its historical context. *Historicizing Modernism* thus stresses empirical accuracy and the value of primary sources (such as letters, diaries, notes, drafts, marginalia or other archival deposits) in developing monographs, scholarly editions and edited collections on Modernist authors and their texts. This may take a number of forms, such as manuscript study and annotated volumes; archival editions and genetic criticism; as well as mappings of interrelated historical milieus or ideas. To date, no book series has laid claim to this interdisciplinary, source-based territory for modern literature. Correspondingly, one burgeoning sub-discipline of Modernism, Beckett Studies, features heavily here as a metonymy for the opportunities presented by manuscript research more widely. While an additional range of 'canonical' authors will be covered here, this series also highlights the centrality of supposedly 'minor' or occluded figures, not least in helping to establish broader intellectual genealogies of Modernist writing. Furthermore, while the series will be weighted towards the English-speaking world, studies of non-Anglophone Modernists whose writings are ripe for archivally based exploration shall also be included here.

A key aim of such historicizing is to reach beyond the familiar rhetoric of intellectual and artistic 'autonomy' employed by many Modernists and their critical commentators. Such rhetorical moves can and should themselves be historically situated and reintegrated into the complex continuum of individual literary practices. This emphasis upon the contested self-definitions of Modernist writers, thinkers and critics may, in turn, prompt various reconsiderations of the boundaries delimiting the concept 'Modernism' itself. Similarly, the very notion of 'historicizing' Modernism remains debatable, and this series by no means discourages more theoretically informed approaches. On the contrary, the editors believe that the historical specificity encouraged by *Historicizing Modernism* may inspire a range of fundamental critiques along the way.

Matthew Feldman
Erik Tonning

Acknowledgements

Many people and several institutions have helped make this book possible. Margaret Mills Harper first encouraged me to pursue the study of Yeats, at a time when other alternatives seemed easier. She has been a great inspiration and support ever since. My friends and colleagues in the Nordic Irish Studies Network have also provided important assistance and academic company: I would especially like to thank Ruben Moi, Anne Karhio and Seán Crosson. Colleagues at the universities of Bergen and Agder have also provided long-term encouragement, in addition to valuable tips: Stuart Sillars and Roy Eriksen have been especially generous with their time. Thanks are also due the following individuals, for valuable advice or backing: Daniel Albright, Jonathan Allison, Per Buvik, Matthew Campbell, Kent Cartwright, Jon Cook, Deborah Fleming, Tadhg Foley, Matthew Gibson, Asbjørn Grønstad, Oddvar Holmesland, Coppelia Kahn, Youngmin Kim, Birgitte Kleivset, Ed Larrissy, Elizabeth Bergmann Loizeaux, Neil Mann, Paul Muldoon, Claire Nally, James Pethica, Young Suck Rhee, Timothy Saunders, Goran Stanivukovic, Lars-Håkan Svensson, John Wilhelm Vinje, Øyvind Vågnes, Tom Walker and Susanne Wolford. Erik Tonning and Matthew Feldman have been exemplary editors, helping me both through acts of support and criticism. I would also like to thank family and friends for all their help and encouragement. I am especially indebted to my wife, Inger Margrethe Stoveland, to whom this book is dedicated.

I would like to thank library staff at the following institutions for their assistance with work on this study: University of Agder; University of Bergen; National University of Ireland-Galway; University Library, Cambridge; Manuscripts Reading Room, National Library of Ireland; and the Manuscripts and Archives Research Library, Trinity College Dublin. I am also grateful to the Department of Foreign Languages at the University of Bergen and the Faculty of Humanities and Pedagogy at the University of Agder for financial assistance, and would like to thank the editorial staff at Bloomsbury for their kind assistance.

Chapter 5 is a revised version of 'Ancient Frames: Classical Philosophy in Yeats's *A Vision*', in Neil Mann, Matthew Gibson and Claire Nally (eds), *W. B. Yeats's 'A Vision': Explications and Contexts.* Clemson: Clemson University Digital Press, 2012, 90–102. I am grateful to Wayne K. Chapman and Clemson University Digital Press for permission to publish this extract from a book that promises to be an invaluable resource for future scholarship on *A Vision*.

A section of Chapter 10 has been published as 'A Master's Monument: Shakespeare's Sonnets in the Poetry of W. B. Yeats', *Early Modern Culture Online*, 1, 2010, 21–34. Another part of the same chapter is based upon 'The Monstrosity of Form: Patterns in the Yeatsian Lyric', published by *The Yeats Journal of Korea*, 37, (spring 2012), 61–72. I am grateful to the editors of these journals, who have kindly granted permission to publish the material included in this chapter.

List of Abbreviations

References to Yeats's published writings make, as far as possible, use of the multivolume collected edition, published by Scribner and Macmillan. References to his plays and poems are also accompanied by the page numbers of the relevant Variorum editions. References to the 1925 version of *A Vision* make use of the thirteenth volume of the collected works, while the revised 1937 version of the same work is referred to by way of Macmillan's 1962 edition.

AVB   *A Vision.* London: Macmillan, 1962 (1937).

CL   *The Collected Letters of W. B. Yeats.*

CL1   *Volume I, 1865–1895,* edited by John Kelly and Eric Domville. Oxford: Clarendon Press, 1986.

CL3   *Volume III, 1901–1904,* edited by John Kelly and Ronald Schuchard. Oxford: Clarendon Press, 1994.

CL Intelex   *The Collected Letters of W. B. Yeats,* general editor John Kelly. Oxford University Press (Intelex Electronic Edition) 2002; letters cited by accession number.

CW   *The Collected Works of W. B. Yeats.*

CW1   *Volume I: The Poems,* second edition, edited by Richard J. Finneran. New York: Scribner, 1997.

CW2   *Volume II: The Plays,* edited by David R. Clark and Rosalind E. Clark. New York: Scribner, 2001.

CW3   *Volume III: Autobiographies,* edited by William H. O'Donnell, Douglas N. Archibald, J. Fraser Cocks III, and Gretchen L. Schwenker. New York: Scribner, 1999.

CW4   *Volume IV: Early Essays,* edited by Richard J. Finneran and George Bornstein. New York: Scribner, 2007.

CW5   *Volume V: Later Essays,* edited by William H. O'Donnell with Elizabeth Bergmann Loizeaux. New York: Scribner, 1994.

CW6   *Volume VI: Prefaces and Introductions,* edited by William H. O'Donnell. New York: Macmillan, 1989.

CW8   *Volume VIII: The Irish Dramatic Movement*, edited by Mary FitzGerald and Richard J. Finneran. New York: Scribner, 2003.

CW9   *Volume IX: Early Articles and Reviews,* edited by John P. Frayne and Madeleine Marchaterre. New York: Scribner, 2004.

CW10   *Volume X: Later Articles and Reviews: Uncollected Articles, Reviews, and Radio Broadcasts Written After 1900*, edited by Colton Johnson. New York: Scribner, 2000.

CW12   *Volume XII: John Sherman and Dhoya,* edited by Richard J. Finneran. New York: Macmillan, 1991.

CW13   *Volume XIII: A Vision (1925),* edited by Catherine E. Paul and Margaret Mills Harper. New York: Scribner, 2008.

Ex   *Explorations,* selected by Mrs. W. B. Yeats. London: Macmillan, 1962.

Mem   *Memoirs: Autobiography – First Draft: Journal,* transcribed and edited by Denis Donoghue. London: Macmillan, 1972.

MTPQ   *The Making of 'The Player Queen',* edited by Curtis Bradford. DeKalb: Northern Illinois University Press, 1977.

Myth   *Mythologies.* London: Macmillan, 1959.

NPMM   *New Poems: Manuscript Materials,* edited by J. C. C. Mays and Stephen Parrish. Ithaca and London: Cornell University Press, 2000.

RMM   *The Resurrection: Manuscript Materials,* edited by Jared Curtis and Selina Guinness. Ithaca and London: Cornell University Press, 2011.

SS   *The Senate Speeches of W. B. Yeats,* edited by Donald R. Pearce. Bloomington: Indiana University Press, 1960.

TMM   *The Tower (1928): Manuscript Materials,* edited by Richard J. Finneran with Jared Curtis and Ann Saddlemyer. Ithaca and London: Cornell University Press, 2007.

VP   *The Variorum Edition of the Poems of W. B. Yeats,* edited by Peter Allt and Russell K. Alspach. New York: Macmillan, 1966 (1957).

VPl   *The Variorum Edition of the Plays of W. B. Yeats*, edited by Russell K. Alspach, assisted by Catharine C. Alspach. London and Basingstoke: Macmillan, 1979 (1966).

Introduction: 'Ancient Salt'

In a polemical outburst late in his career, William Butler Yeats defended his use of traditional forms: 'If I wrote of personal love or sorrow in free verse, or in any rhythm that left it unchanged, amid all its accident, I would be full of self-contempt because of my egotism and indiscretion, and I foresee the boredom of my reader' (*CW5* 213). Some readers of poetry have been inclined to complain of the boredom they feel encountering forms that have been handed down through the centuries; for Yeats the situation is quite the reverse. Tradition is crucial: 'I must choose a traditional stanza, even what I alter must seem traditional' (*CW5* 213). A prodigiously strong investment in the past comes to view, even while Yeats admits that it can involve an element of subterfuge; at times when he actively intervenes in order to contribute something new, his writings just 'seem' traditional – that is, they just appear to be in line with time-sanctioned practice. There is thus a peculiar 'fusion of autonomy and obedience' in how Yeats relates to the forms and authors of the past,[1] and an important part of that engagement comes about through a concern with literary technique – as seen in the references to stanza forms and poetic rhythms.

This outburst stems from an introduction to a planned edition of Yeats's collected poetry (to which Chapter 2 of this study will return at greater length). A little later on in the same introduction, Yeats makes use of an interesting metaphor to further articulate his position: 'Talk to me of originality and I will turn on you with rage. I am a crowd, I am a lonely man, I am nothing. Ancient salt is best packing' (*CW5* 213). Why this particular image? The primary reference is to salt's preservative powers: without salt, foodstuffs deteriorate. This is made plain in a slightly earlier use of the same metaphor: 'all that is personal soon rots; it must be packed in ice or salt' (*CW5* 213). One might call this a strategic use of tradition: if Yeats keeps company with the best of what is thought and written, then his writings are more inclined to endure. More tacitly, the references to salt (which is bitter rather than sweet) and ice (which is cold rather than warm) may be taken as alluding to a sense of abstemiousness: the author must cultivate an austere position of aesthetic indifference, resisting the temptation of personal gratification. There is a slight echo of Yeats's poem 'The Fisherman', which contrasts the cultivation of contemporary popularity with the writing of poetry for an idealized (and fictional) reader; there Yeats expresses a wish to write a poem 'maybe as cold / And passionate as the dawn' (*VP* 348; *CW1* 149). At yet another level the salt metaphor evokes the quotidian routine of travel and packing. A tourist may choose a modern suitcase, but Yeats the poet carries nourishing goods that need to be stowed in a meticulous and more timeless manner.

Travel is here a spatial trope for survival in time.[2] The poet, one might say, is an expert on time travel. That is not all, however; the activity of packing also brings with it associations of manual labour. In the poem 'Adam's Curse', Yeats claims a poet's work is harder than that of someone who must 'go down upon your marrow-bones / And scrub a kitchen pavement, or break stones / Like an old pauper, in all kinds of weather' (*VP* 204–5; *CW1* 78). Implicitly, then, both of these passages suggest that poetry can bear comparison to hard, physical labour. One might hazard that it is the technical challenge of the poem that provides a craftsman-like parallel to such labour. And indeed the notion of packing might suggest a physical container – like a crate, or packing-paper – that safeguards the transported object. Yeats's metaphor thus implies that the historical act of transfer involves a distinction between an inner content and a framing external form, tradition being linked to the latter. The implicit paradox here is of course that the very ingredient that ensures longevity is itself transparent or almost invisible – it plays a predominantly supplementary role and is (in the case of ice) susceptible to disappear. Perhaps one should not push the metaphor too far in this direction: after all, most metaphors involve secondary associations that are not significantly related to the intended meaning. Yet the link between literary permanence and historical change is a complex one, and more often than not scrupulous analysis will uncover that the connection between the two involves such paradoxes.

This book aims to provide a new sense of the formal and historical specificity of a selection of W. B. Yeats's writings over a wide range of genres. The issue of genre itself is the most important frame to be addressed, but it is not the only one. As already suggested by the explication of Yeats's 'ancient salt' metaphor, another important mode of 'reframing' in this study will be a close analysis of Yeatsian negotiations with history through literary form; if the framing container, or preservative ingredient, of Yeats's content is tradition itself (or at least a combination of tradition and its forgeries), then an in-depth understanding of his writings must address how his writings relate to earlier traditions.

Both 'tradition' and 'genre' can be described as instances of 'transtextuality'. The French theorist Gérard Genette has used this term to refer to everything that brings a text 'into relation (manifest or hidden) with other texts'.[3] He distinguishes five different forms of transtextuality.[4] *Intertextuality* involves the co-presence of one text within another, for instance through quotation, allusion or plagiarism. *Paratextuality* refers to those devices that mediate between a text and its reader (including prefaces, dedications, titles and so on). Genette also includes manuscript materials left behind by an author – materials which he categorizes as 'pre-texts' – under this concept.[5] *Metatextuality* concerns how one text can function as a commentary to another. *Hypertextuality* involves relations of superimposition of one text upon another, such as parody and pastiche. Finally, *architextuality* denotes the relationship between a text and the type of discourse that it exemplifies. Genre is an instance of architextuality, and will provide the main example of transtextuality discussed in this study. But other forms, too, will be addressed: paratextuality, for instance, will be evident in the attention given to Yeats's introductory texts (to *A Vision* and a planned edition of his collected works) and framing songs (in *The Resurrection*). The way paratextuality interrogates and implies a context – Genette goes so far as to say that 'in principle, every context serves as a paratext' – will also be a recurring theme.[6] Jonathan Culler has referred to 'the framing of signs' as the way in which signs are 'constituted (framed) by various discursive practices, institutional arrangements, systems of value, semiotic mechanisms,'[7] and his understanding of this operation will be explicitly drawn upon later in this study.

Both Genette and Culler refer to Jacques Derrida's ambitious work on the frame. The latter's analysis of Immanuel Kant's *Critique of Pure Judgement*, in *The Truth of Painting*, draws attention to how the frame (or the closely related 'parergon') – which constitutes the border between the interior and exterior of a work of art – becomes a challenge to interpretation. As Derrida points out, the existence of such a border is a premise for the strictly aesthetic approach of Kant and his many followers: 'Aesthetic judgment *must* properly bear upon intrinsic beauty, not on finery and surrounds. Hence one must know [. . .] how to determine the intrinsic – what is framed – and know what one is excluding as frame *and* outside-the-frame.'[8] According to Derrida, traditional criticism chooses either the inside of the frame or the outside of it, and as a result cannot truly face up to the intricate connection between the terms included in classical conceptual pairs such as text/context and form/content.

In contemporary Yeats scholarship, the bifurcation noted by Derrida is paralleled in a fairly consistent division between approaches that privilege form and close reading, on the one hand, and more historical and biographical approaches on the other. This study will seek to mediate between these opposing methodologies, according to one of the trajectories Marjorie Levinson has described as characteristic of New Formalism in literary studies. Levinson distinguishes between two different strains of New Formalism. There is, she claims,

> a practical division between (a) those who want to restore to today's reductive reinscription of the historical reading its original focus on form (traced by these critics to sources foundational for materialist critique – e.g., Hegel, Marx, Freud, Adorno, Althusser, Jameson) and (b) those who campaign to bring back a sharp demarcation between history and art, discourse and literature, with form (regarded as the condition of aesthetic experience as traced to Kant – i.e., disinterested, autotelic, playful, pleasurable, consensus-generating, and therefore both individually liberating and conducive to affective social cohesion) the prerogative of art. In short, we have a new formalism that makes a continuum with new historicism and a backlash new formalism.[9]

Although the particular theorists mentioned by Levinson will not feature centrally in this study, it will utilize other theoretical figures – such as Michel de Certeau, Hayden White, Jacques Rancière and Jonathan Culler – to articulate a position that hopefully will not deserve the tag 'backlash new formalism'. The way in which Helen Vendler's recent study *Our Secret Discipline: Yeats and Lyric Form* (2007) provides an in-depth analysis of several crucial lyric genres in Yeats will provide a formalist inspiration, but only to a certain point; arguably, Vendler's meticulous readings are not overly concerned with the historical development of the genres she addresses.[10] Where Vendler's formalism seems somewhat oblivious of historicism, another outstanding representative of contemporary Yeats scholarship, R. F. Foster, presents something akin to the opposite case: Foster's outstanding two-volume tome on the life of Yeats is a consummate achievement of historically oriented biography, but contains readings of Yeats's texts that only to a limited extent take into account those texts' status as literary works of art. These criticisms of Foster and Vendler will be fleshed out in Chapters 3–4 and 10, respectively – chapters with special emphasis on what Genette would call metatextual aspects of Yeats's *oeuvre*.

The relationship between form and content is important for the understanding of genre. Can genres be purely formal, or exclusively based on content? Amy J. Devitt has written off the former alternative, but in a way that also seems to imply that the latter, content-oriented approach is problematical:

> Although the classifications named by genre labels would seem to be based on common formal patterns, form alone cannot define genres. Theoretically, equating genre with form is tenable only within a container model of meaning, for it requires a separation of generic form from a particular text's context.[11]

Since many genres (especially of a non-literary kind) involve interaction not only between form and content, but also for instance with typical contexts and modes of reception, it is indeed tempting to define genres as *necessarily* involving a wider range of factors. Yet the fact remains that many literary forms are exclusively formal (or almost exclusively so) – even if one may believe that the form in question has a more significant role to play than that of being a mere container. Should the sonnet not be considered a genre, merely because it embraces a wide range of themes (far beyond the love and politics characteristic of sonnetic subgenres)? To be sure, the sonnet neither comes supplied with a ready-made context, nor asks its readers for a prescribed form of action. Yet despite its limited range of characteristics, it seems impractical from the view of poetry criticism to deny the sonnet the status of a genre. It seems more sensible to accept the idea of more or less purely formal genres. Further, the role of the reader, and historical audiences more generally, may be important for the establishment and development of genres, but this is not something that can always be defined or identified within narrow limits.

In *Kinds of Literature,* Alastair Fowler argues for an inclusive definition of genre: for him, there is no necessary combination of both 'internal and external characteristics'.[12] Fowler insists that 'all genres are continuously undergoing metamorphosis' – and adds that this, 'indeed, is the principal way in which literature itself changes'.[13] One form of change that he devotes particular attention to is generic modulation, whereby a specific genre evolves into a more abstract, general and inclusive term. Thus the genre of tragedy becomes 'the tragic' and comedy becomes 'the comic'. In this process, a noun is replaced by an adjective, and there is a shedding of formal (or what Fowler calls 'external') aspects: 'modal terms never imply a complete external form. Modes have always an incomplete repertoire, a selection only of the corresponding kind's features, and one from which overall external structure is absent.'[14] Such modulation – which inevitably leads to the modular adjective being linked up with new generic nouns – is relevant with regard to Yeats's development of his ideal of tragic poetry, which will be addressed in Chapter 7 of this study, as well as a 'sonnetic' grouping of poems that will be discussed in Chapter 10.

Both tragedy and the sonnet are genres that may sometimes slip out fashion, but nevertheless have an outstanding historical resilience. Longevity is certainly an overt ideal for Yeats: in 'The Circus Animals' Desertion', he expresses a desire to present 'Character isolated by a deed / To engross the present and dominate memory' (*VP* 630; *CW1* 356). One reason why Yeats is such a compelling author is his head-on engagement with our cultural heritage. From the stand-off between Christianity and paganism in *The Wanderings of Oisin* to the *Supernatural Songs* late in his career, he never shuns central questions of civilization and belief. He also engages with major spiritual and literary figures: in *Eminent Domain,* Richard Ellmann charts Yeats's interaction with some of his most distinguished contemporaries, claiming that the 'best writers expropriate best, they disdain petty debts in favour of grand, authoritative larcenies.'[15] Even if Yeats does not always give a fair account of his most influential forerunners – as in his caricatures of Keats, for instance – his acts of literary appropriation nevertheless always involve fascinating subtexts of self-reflection and renunciation. This book will return to 'grand, authoritative' engagements with writers such Shakespeare and Plato, as well as his engagement with major cultural institutions such as Greek tragedy and the Bible. Ellmann's study anticipates Harold Bloom's theory of the anxiety of influence by claiming that writers 'move upon other writers not as genial successors but as violent expropriators, knocking down established boundaries to seize by the force of youth, or of age, what they require. They do not borrow, they override.'[16] Ellmann also insists upon a noticeably muscular description of literary interaction when he claims that an author may not have 'sufficient strength' to expropriate the work of a particularly eminent precursor.[17] On Bloom's reading of (chiefly Romantic) influence in Yeats, the poet could only acknowledge these debts by obfuscating them: 'Yeats is perhaps the most eloquent misrepresenter in the language. Wherever Yeats's debts were largest, he learned subtly to find fault.'[18] Both Bloom's downplaying of Yeats's debts to Victorian predecessors and his more general theory have later been criticized widely.[19]

Yeats's relationship to Romanticism and his tendency to be rather free with his own influences will be recurring motifs in the chapters that follow. At the same time, however, I will also make a plea for both more detailed and more exploratory accounts of literary influence. Yeats may have disdained owning up to what Ellmann calls 'petty debts', but sometimes exchanges taking place in less eminent domains are what make the whole process of literary influence and composition add up. Here the Genettian categories of intertextuality and metatextuality tend to be imbricated in Yeats's oeuvre: his metatextual comments on his own work can at times comes across as more or less manipulative attempts to establish authorial control, by steering the intertextuality of allusion away from undesired or unflattering company over to grander or more appropriate affinities. Thankfully, some Yeats criticism has lately followed a revisionary tack here, unearthing surprising or unacknowledged sources for his work; thus, for instance, the case has recently been made for the theatrical influence of figures such as Ibsen, Maeterlinck and Kokoscha on Yeats.[20] In this study, the main arguments for allusions unendorsed by the author himself will be made on behalf of Oliver Wendell Holmes (in Chapter 2) and W. S. Gilbert (in Chapter 8).

According to Genette, as we have seen, allusions of this sort belong to the category of intertextuality and as such they are to be fundamentally distinguished from issues concerning generic belonging, which are categorized under architextuality. Although such a distinction is valid for analytical purposes, and in many cases can be used without much trouble, it does sometimes break down.[21] As John Frow has pointed out, 'reference to a text implicitly invokes reference to a full set of potential meanings stored in the codes of the genre.'[22] Although it doubtless had strategic uses early on, the critical vogue of Julia Kristeva's concept of intertextuality – often used blandly as a catch-all for transtextual relationships per se, even neglecting Kristeva's own avant-garde critique of subjectivity – has arguably caused a neglect of such distinctions.[23] Just as a use of a particular genre often can evoke a particular author, so the allusion to an author is frequently accompanied by a tacit reference to the specific contribution that author made to a relevant genre: the individual and the collective intertwine. In addition, closer scrutiny often reveals that the individual pole of this relation is actually more articulated than it might seem at first sight. Here Wayne K. Chapman's work on Yeats's use of Renaissance sources and modes includes a significant insight. Stressing that the Irishman's relation to this period always involved 'the transformation and synthesis of one's materials,'[24] he argues that the relationship is better described as adaptation than imitation in a narrow sense:

> Interwoven by association and perpetuated by mental habits which alter over time, lines of influence converge in individual works, cluster at various stages of Yeats's career, and run their course in the canon. The English Renaissance exerted a *powerful* influence on him, yet its authors were often interpreted in relation to the great Romantics (and vice versa).[25]

The term 'adaptive complex' is used by Chapman to cover the multiplicity of such relations. He also points out that influences often come in pairs, and launches the concept of 'dyad' to refer to 'any two recurrently linked sources of content and/or form in an adaptive complex.'[26] In general, any allusion to an author (or several authors) and reference to (or use of) a genre frequently fuse in a complex act of transtextuality.

Literary and historical eras are located at a level of generality between individual authors and literary genres. Though concepts such as Romanticism, Victorianism and the Renaissance (or Early Modern period) are historical constructs, and thus inevitably subject to revision, they help bring into focus historical forces that critics neglect at their own peril. Hans-Georg Gadamer best articulates how historical placement impacts all interpretation, in that each interpretative act is bound by a certain 'horizon of understanding' that both limits and enables:

> Every encounter with tradition that takes place within historical consciousness involves the experience of tension between the text and the present. The

hermeneutic task consists not in covering up this tension by attempting a naïve assimilation of the two but in consciously bringing it out. This is why it is part of the hermeneutic project to project a historical horizon that is different from the horizon of the present. Historical consciousness is aware of its own otherness and hence foregrounds the horizon of the past from its own.[27]

Gadamer uses the term *Wirkungsgeschichte* (sometimes translated as 'history of effect') to articulate how one's framing of the past is not something suddenly constructed ex nihilo, but rather bases itself on an accumulated tradition of previous interpretations. Such a perspective will prove particularly relevant when this study examines how Yeats responds to authors and texts located in a relatively distant past; his interpretations of Shakespeare, ancient Greek philosophy and the Bible do not involve simple one-on-one encounters, but rather interact with a larger 'adaptive complex' (to use Chapman's term) that features Romantic, Victorian and other intermediate links.

Yeats's complex investments in earlier time periods lie at the heart of his vexed relationship with literary Modernism. Early constructions of the latter stressed links with nineteenth-century Symbolism. Thus Edmund Wilson, in *Axel's Castle* (1931), claimed that the work of Yeats, James Joyce, T. Eliot and Gertrude Stein 'has been largely a continuance or extension of Symbolism.'[28] Later, a more particularized historical approach brought a more exclusive focus on Ezra Pound and writers intimately associated with Imagism and Vorticism: Symbolism was now sidelined as precisely part of the Victorian heritage resisted by the modernists, and as such Yeats's link with Modernism became problematic, too. Michael Levenson's *A Genealogy of Modernism* (1984) is a preeminent example of this tendency, and one can see many critics still being successfully tempted to follow suit; for how could an author so respectful of tradition truly be part of a movement that is all about innovation and experiment? It is no accident that Yeats frequently had harsh words concerning not only free verse, but also the poetry of T. S. Eliot and the writings of many other modernists whom he felt were replacing time-honoured sanctities with passing fads. Yet, as Daniel Albright has pointed out, Yeats's position is complex: 'Yeats fights Modernism as hard as he can, only to find himself acknowledging that he is Modernist to the marrow of his bones.'[29]

Even while close attention to Yeats's texts reveals a complex relationship to the foremost literary movement of his age, Modernism itself has increasingly had to submit to a process of revaluation and restructuring in recent decades. Levenson acknowledges as much:

> What once seemed the exclusive affair of 'modern masters', the 'men of 1914' (as Wyndham Lewis called them), now stands revealed as a complex of inventive gestures, daring performances, enacted also by many who were left out of account in the early histories of the epoch, histories offered first by the actors themselves and later produced within an academic discourse, willingly guided by the precedents of the eminent artists.[30]

Much of this revisionism has concerned figures and issues that have been marginalized on grounds related to gender, class and race. In this respect, it is perhaps inevitable that

Yeats – as a white male with strong sympathies with the Protestant Ascendancy and right-wing movements of the 1930s – is not a privileged recipient of renewed centrality. Nevertheless, more inclusive accounts of Modernism have also, on occasion, led to a more nuanced understanding of Yeats's place in the modernist narrative. The work of James Longenbach can be taken as an outstanding exemplar of this: Longenbach has stressed the radicality of Yeats's turn, in a movement that began during the first decade of the twentieth century, to a 'more expansive and aggressive music'.[31] As a result, the early Yeats now already appears to be almost a fully fledged modernist, and as such is in less need of the outside help of Ezra Pound in order to obtain – or borrow – a modernist idiom in his key volumes in the 1920s. Further, Longenbach has also presented a close reading of the three winters Pound and Yeats spent working intensely together at Stone Cottage in Sussex. The upshot is a reversal of the traditional story; while 'Pound has so often been credited with producing the Yeats of *Responsibilities*', Longenbach concludes that a 'more careful reading of their relationship shows that Yeats was far more influential in producing the Pound of *Lustra*.'[32]

Such a reversal of received wisdom is striking enough in itself, but also susceptible to contestation. Longenbach's revisionary account of Modernism may be accused of being unfair to Pound – he for instance claims that Eliot, too, was a larger influence on Pound than vice versa – and no doubt his understanding of these relationships will be more readily accepted and digested among Yeatsians than other scholars of modernist literature. More generally digestible, perhaps, is Longenbach's suggestion that Modernism itself is a construct that changes according to which criteria we use to define it: 'At large, modernism is divided against itself, impossible to oppose neatly to Romanticism or Postmodernism, difficult to associate cleanly with any particular aesthetic practice or ideological position.'[33] Modernism, in other words, is not a monolithic entity but changes according to whatever horizons of understanding we deploy in interpreting it. If one defines the movement as a pure cult of literary autonomy or formalist aesthetics, then Yeats will not figure at the centre of it – although his formative influence on Pound and the later Eliot might assure him a honourable mention. On the other hand, a reading of Modernism on the basis of genre will necessarily lead to the construction of a very different kind of entity – as will be suggested in my final chapter. According to Steven Matthews, Yeats's relation to contextual frameworks actually makes his work in some respects more ambivalent and polysemic – more modernist, if such characteristics are to remain defining features of the movement – than that of other, key figures of Modernism: 'The unresolved, open-ended nature of his own historical location opens his work to reappropriation within a greater variety of contexts, perhaps, than that of his modernist successors Pound and Eliot.'[34]

Yeats's relationship to Modernism is one of several recurring concerns in this book. The three first chapters address the borderline between Yeats's literary work and different conceptions of life. As an overture, Yeats's differentiation between the poet and the man who sits down to breakfast (in the 1938 introduction to a planned Scribner's edition of his collected works) will be subjected to a close reading in Chapter 2. Using theories of everyday life (stemming from Henri Lefebvre, Michel de Certeau and others), Yeats's pronouncement will be linked with the contemporary connotations of breakfast and the quotidian – as well as related references in other parts of Yeats's oeuvre. At the end of this chapter, a supplementary interpretation of Yeats's quote as a combative (if obscure and passing) allusion to Oliver Wendell Holmes' *The Poet at the Breakfast-Table* (1872) is presented.

Chapter 3 turns to biography and the quest for a 'true', more historical Yeats behind the idealizing accretions of his poetical persona. Here the existing biographies of the Irish poet will be investigated, with special emphasis given to Foster's two-volume work. Precisely because it is an inestimable resource for all who study or are interested in Yeats, the underlying premises of Foster's biography deserve to be probed: my reading will tease out some of the narrative and structural foundations of his biography, as well as the way in which it is engaged in a form of mimetic competition with Yeats himself.

Continuing to explore versions of the connection between life and literature, Chapter 4 moves the focus over to Yeats's own autobiographical practice. Countering approaches that place an overwhelming emphasis on Yeats's personal circumstances, this chapter brings the genre of autobiography to the fore: Yeats's autobiographical writings are situated historically in relation to both preceding Victorian practices and the contemporary, modernist experimentation with the genre of his own day.

The next three chapters focus on Yeats's prose and drama, with special emphasis on his encounters with major literary monuments of ancient times. Chapter 5 is titled 'Ancient Frames in *A Vision*'. Here Yeats's use of classical Greek philosophers such as Plotinus, Plato and Heraclitus in the two versions of his esoteric tract *A Vision* (1925, 1937) is examined. In contrast with earlier readings of the use of Greek philosophy in Yeats's writings, the stress is here on the necessity of looking at how these philosophical concerns both (a) may or may not affect the entire interpretation of *A Vision* as a text, and (b) are themselves subject to given generic and contextual frames.

Differing understandings of the frame also take centre stage in the next chapter, which looks at how the framing of transtextual phenomena – paratexts and genres – complicate the meaning of Yeats's play *The Resurrection*. The play is situated in the context of Yeats's generic development as a dramatist, with particular reference to his adaptive transformation of the Japanese Noh theatre and his place in a tradition of Biblical plays that includes Oscar Wilde's *Salomé*. Thematically, the way in which *The Resurrection* overlays Biblical narrative with Yeats's esoteric system of thought (as presented in *A Vision*) is questioned, with special attention being given to the play's framing songs and articulation of space.

Chapter 7 is devoted to the intersection of the genre of tragedy and the concept of 'the tragic' in Yeats's *oeuvre*. Building on excellent existing scholarship on how these concepts are relevant to Yeats's project, this chapter analyses them with special emphasis on genre and Alastair Fowler's concept of generic modulation. A sketch is given of how Yeats's thought on the tragic develops through his career, from the 1910 essay 'The Tragic Theatre', via an investigation of the manuscripts and versions of the play *The Player Queen*, to Yeats's late poetry. As such, the itinerary traced in this generically inclusive chapter – devoted to essays, drama, poetry and autobiographical prose – marks a transition from the focus on drama and prose, in the middle part of this book, to an emphasis on Yeats's poetry in the three next chapters.

As a writer, Yeats embodies a peculiar combination of the popular and the elitist. In Chapter 8, the transtextual influx of popular voices into Yeats's poetry is discussed on the basis of readings of two poems: 'Easter, 1916' and 'Among School Children'. The reading of the former addresses Yeats's reliance on traditional, nationalist ballads, displaying a particular nexus between genre and history in this much-discussed poem. The second part of this chapter demonstrates the presence of a surprising echo of Gilbert and Sullivan's *Princess Ida* – and thus, by extension, also of Tennyson's 'The Princess' – which casts new light on 'Among School Children' by bringing it into the ambit of nineteenth-century debates on women's education. This chapter also uses the work of Mikhail Bakhtin to address how non-literary genres can be said to interact with literature.

While most of this book is devoted to verbal relationships between Yeats, on the one hand, and precursors and pre-existing genres on the other, Chapter 9 looks at how his poetry positions itself in an intermedial relation to external images. The first part of this chapter scrutinizes the iconography of 'Leda and the Swan', arguing that it sets to work a particularly fluctuating kind of historicity, which constantly asks for new frames of understanding. As a verbal representation that bases itself on visual representations of Greek mythology, 'Leda and the Swan' is a rather indirect example of the genre of ekphrasis. Subsequently a genre-centred reading of another ekphrastic poem, 'The Municipal Gallery Re-visited', delves into the way in which Yeats seemingly attempts to appropriate not only paintings and the entire institution of the gallery in question, but also modern Irish history, to his own aesthetic ends.

Chapter 10 raises a number of questions about the genre of the sonnet in Yeats's poetry, responding to Helen Vendler's work on the sonnet in *Our Secret Discipline*. Vendler's findings are compared to her understanding of the Shakespearean sonnet as presented in *The Art of Shakespeare's Sonnets* (1997). Pointing at Victorian and *fin du siècle* contexts for Yeats's use of the genre, the chapter argues for a more historically informed contextualization of the Yeatsian sonnet. Building on Vendler's idea that several poems in Yeats's *oeuvre* are intrinsically linked the genre of the sonnet even while not appearing to be sonnets, the latter part of this chapter raises fundamental issues concerning the use of inclusive definitions of genre on the basis of family resemblances.

The concluding coda revisits the main findings of this study, and also returns to the question of how Yeats's deployment of genres – with particular attention to his more innovatory gestures in this regard – place him in relation to movements such as Modernism and Romanticism. Substantial parts of this study will, however, primarily be concerned with acts of criticism, through interpretation of individual works and themes, rather than overarching issues relating to poetics or historiography. Methodological and strategic issues concerning source material will therefore be of some importance. Recent academic work on Yeats has been dominated by (a) the preparation of scholarly editions of his works and manuscripts, and (b) the interpretation of his works on the basis of biographical background and/or his explicit references to source materials. In a recent essay devoted to Yeats's relationship to his father, Douglas Archibald has paid tribute to

the vast amount of excellent scholarship done at the end of twentieth century and beginning of the twenty-first: biography, especially William Murphy on JBY [i.e.

the poet's father, John Butler Yeats] and R. F. Foster on WBY [i.e. William Butler Yeats]; the information gathered in the Macmillan/Scribner *Collected Works* and the Oxford *Letters*; a large array of critical and specialized studies. We know a lot more than we did 50 years ago, some of it corrective, and we have been made to think about it all in different ways.[35]

The scope and value of this work is unquestionable, and the current study – like most other contemporary work on Yeats – would be infinitely worse off without it. Arguably, however, much of this work has been devoted to a thorough mapping of the known and documented biographical sources and backgrounds of Yeats's career, making this a fitting time to explore new emphases and points of vantage. This study will attempt to break new ground, by nudging Yeats out of the most familiar contexts and into surprising or neglected frameworks.

Yeats's editors have given us access to incredible textual resources; in contrast, for example, to scholars of Oscar Wilde, Yeatsians now have access to wonderfully thorough editions of his collected works, letters and manuscripts. As a consequence, a broader range of Yeats's texts and pre-texts is more readily available than ever before, making it harder to interpret any of his works in splendid isolation. A critic may wish to read a classic poem such as 'Sailing to Byzantium' without paying any attention to Yeats's drafts, its publishing history, or related textual material (including, for instance, Yeats's comments on Byzantium in *A Vision*), but now more than ever this is a difficult exercise to pursue.[36] At the same time, however, the interaction between the various parts of Yeats's literary and extra-literary *oeuvre* can be pursued with varying degrees of critical vigilance. Sometimes this exercise can acquire an illusory straightforwardness, given the fact that Yeats himself provided extensive introductions, notes and other metatextual comments that sought to explicate his own literary works. In other cases more ingenuity is needed, as the relations between some parts of his *oeuvre* may be more indirect or tacit. Like most other books on Yeats, this one too will make extensive cross-sectional use of available material. As mentioned before, there will however also be times when the obvious, critically accepted options will be questioned or avoided. Apart from the need for criticism to provide new knowledge, this basically has two reasons: (a) we cannot always trust Yeats's own interpretations of his work, and (b) the generic differences between various literary and extra-literary forms – between texts and paratexts – entails that such traffic is not at all times equally straightforward. My attempt at reframing Yeats thus involves, on occasion, a questioning of the validity or exhaustiveness of sources. Is a biographical fact a sufficient explanation for a textual phenomenon, providing both its motivation and meaning? And does, say, Yeats's claim about a genre at one particular stage of his career have universal validity for our understanding of this genre throughout his writings? Thus the very glut of historical and biographical information now available also calls for renewed critical vigilance and scrutiny that will hopefully continue beyond the present volume.

2

Yeats at Breakfast

This chapter will reframe Yeats by inspecting his writings from an unusual point of view. Paradoxically, what is 'unusual', in this context, is precisely the ordinary. For rather than treating him as a poet of High Numinosity, this reading will approach Yeats in terms of recent critical and theoretical interest in ordinariness. One of the most compelling and influential explorations of the ordinary in contemporary thought and culture concerns the notion of the *everyday*. As the word itself indicates, the everyday involves a sense of repetition and of being bound to routine or habitual activities linked to particular periods of time. As such the term embraces phenomena that risk being neglected in favour of the exceptional and the unique. The everyday is mere background noise: that which we ignore and overlook in order to focus our attention on matters that are supposedly more exacting or elevated. This 'background' therefore frames literary works and other work of importance, inhabiting the position Derrida has granted the concept of the *parergon*: 'a form which has as its traditional determination not that it stands out but that it disappears, buries itself, effaces itself, melts away at the moment it deploys its greatest energy.'[1] In its most common usage, the everyday stands in contrast to the sacred and to the festival – it concerns the humdrum, down-to-earth unfolding of life that occurs at the periphery of the high points of the calendar or the most central precincts of power. As such, it would indeed seem to be of negligible importance. Yet if we are to believe the Canadian philosopher Charles Taylor, innocuousness does not equate with irrelevance in this case: 'ordinary life', he writes,

> has become one of the most powerful ideas in modern civilization. It underlies our contemporary 'bourgeois' politics, so much concerned with issues of welfare, and at the same time powers the most influential revolutionary ideology of our century, Marxism, with its apotheosis of man the producer. This sense of the importance of the everyday in human life [. . .] colours our whole understanding of what it is truly to respect human life and integrity.[2]

If the everyday has general human importance, it also increasingly has a specific role to play in the arts. A recent book by Yuriko Saito, *Everyday Aesthetics*, spells out the challenge that the notion of the everyday presents for our understanding of art. She points out that 'Environmental art, happenings, performance, chance music, installation, conceptual art, and interactive art' all are forms of expression 'meant to break out of the confinement' of traditional aesthetics.[3] In literature, a similar movement has been spearheaded internationally by the work of the French novelist Georges Perec, whose novel *Life: A User's Manual* for instance provides an exhaustive – and also, for its readers, frequently exhausting – catalogue of the events and contents of a large apartment block in Paris. Perec's project is not without its precedents, one of the most important of which would be James Joyce's *Ulysses*. Another important example of everyday life suffusing the modern novel is to be found in the work of Virginia Woolf,[4] and it is instructive to see Woolf and William Butler Yeats seeming to agree – in Woolf's diary rendition of a dinner conversation from 1930 – that poetry and prose go separate ways on this issue. In Woolf's diary, Yeats is cited as saying that he and contemporaries like Walter de la Mare 'can only write small fireside poems. Most of emotion is outside their scope.' Woolf's rejoinder was that all the rest then was 'left to the novelists.'[5] The novel, according to this view, has a large remit: while poetry deals with a small, circumscribed part of modern experience, narrative prose unfolds on a much larger and more inclusive canvas.

We are not told how Yeats responded to this generically imperialistic gesture, but later evidence would seem to suggest he was not averse to agreeing with the gist of it. In the 1936 introduction to Scribner's planned edition of his collected poems – also cited at the beginning of our introductory chapter – he granted that while a 'novelist might describe his accidence, his incoherence', the poet 'must not, he is more type than man, more passion than type' (*CW5* 204). The inconsequential details of a novelist's life may be apposite topics for his writings, but the same is not the case for the poet. In the introduction, this differentiation follows Yeats's famous insistence that the poet transforms the givens of his empirical life into something rich and strange, once it enters the crucible of art: 'A poet writes always of his personal life', Yeats insists, 'in his finest work out of its tragedies, whatever it may be, remorse, lost love or mere loneliness; he never speaks directly as to someone at the breakfast table, there is always a phantasmagoria.' An indirect address is part of the result of art's transformative process, whereby personal givens are depersonalized and distanced. Yeats goes on to state that 'even when the poet seems most himself [. . .] he is never the bundle of accident and incoherence that sits down to breakfast; he has been re-born as an idea, something intended, complete' (*CW5* 204).

As part of the opening of the introduction to the author's collected works, this passage was to have an important part in Yeats's *oeuvre*. Owing to the fact, however, that the planned edition was never published, it occupies a rather idiosyncratic position; rather than being placed at the head of Yeats's collected poems, it appears among his later essays. As Gérard Genette's reflections on the 'location' of textual prefaces make clear, though, this is far from a unique situation:

'Location' means the possibility, over time and particularly from one edition to another, of a change in location, which sometimes involves a change in status. A preface, authorial or allographic [i.e. either written by the author or by someone else], may become after the event a chapter in a collection of essays: see Valéry's prefaces in *Variété,* Gide's in *Incidences,* Sartre's in *Situations,* and Barthes's in *Essais critiques*; indeed, after the event a preface may become a chapter in a collection of prefaces, either all autographic, such as James's in *The Art of the Novel* (posthumous collection of 1934), or all allographic, such as Borges's in his *Prólogos* of 1975, In all these cases, the preface comes to have two sites, the original and the one in the collection; the original site, however, may be abandoned in a later edition.[6]

A whole volume of Yeats's collected works is devoted to allographic prefaces: *Prefaces and Introductions* is thus subtitled 'Uncollected Prefaces and Introductions by Yeats to Works by Other Authors and to Anthologies Edited by Yeats' (see *CW6*). There one finds Yeats's prefaces to works such as his 1889 edition of *The Stories of Carleton,* a 1925 translation of Villiers de l'Isle-Adam's symbolist masterpiece *Axël,* and a 1936 edition of selected poems by his friend Dorothy Wellesley – to mention just three examples. The introduction discussed here, however, is an 'authorial' or 'autographic' one (since it introduces Yeats's own works), and is characterized by a certain peculiarity of location: its original site was not so much 'abandoned in a later edition' as never actually launched at all. Despite this anomaly, however, it may be said to play its part in the framing of Yeats's entire poetical *oeuvre,* providing the reader with guidelines for how to approach and interpret the literary texts. As such, it plays the kind of role a generic marker does for an individual text: it initiates an informal contract of sorts with the reader, telling that reader what kind of status the literary object(s) or text(s) will have. And yet, despite this privileged position, the passage tends to be taken for granted; it is easily remembered, and indeed often cited, but has not been subject to detailed analysis. What happens, though, if one tries to delve beyond the surface here?

The first response might be one of bemused fascination. This effect is not primarily due to the aesthetic insularity of Yeats's poetics here – however forbidding and even perhaps chilling that tendency might be – since, after all, it is well known from his other writings. No, what stands out in this passage is the repeated reference to breakfast: first we are told that the poet 'never speaks directly as to someone at the breakfast table', and then that he is not identical with 'the bundle of accident and incoherence that sits down to breakfast.' Why breakfast? Where on earth did this reference to the morning meal come from?

The given context of these passages suggests that what distinguishes breakfast from the business of poetry is two things: first, the communicative situation (where intersubjective, informal dialogue is contrasted with the more impersonal encounter of reading), and secondly, the link between breakfast and contingency of all sorts. But such an explanation does not fully satisfy. For these particular characteristics can be found in any number of other phenomena, and do not suffice to motivate the specific reference made to breakfast. It is instructive to compare this passage to Yeats's disparagements of the realist tendency in modernist poetry:

In the third year of the War came the most revolutionary man in poetry during my life-time, though his revolution was stylistic alone – T. S. Eliot published his first book. No romantic word or sound, nothing reminiscent, nothing in the least like the painting of Ricketts could be permitted henceforth. Poetry must resemble prose, and both must accept the vocabulary of their time; nor must there be any special subject-matter. Tristram and Isoult [sic] were not a more suitable theme than Paddington Railway Station. The past had deceived us: let us accept the worthless present. (*CW5* 95)

This is from Yeats's radio broadcast on modern poetry. In his roughly contemporaneous introduction to the *Oxford Book of Modern Verse*, Eliot's style is characterized as having 'an unexaggerated plainness that has the effect of novelty' (*CW5* 191). Modern poetry is compared to the realist novel, creating an effect 'as if the poet could at any moment write a poem by recording the fortuitous scene or thought, perhaps it might be enough to put into some fashionable rhythm – "I am sitting in a chair, there are three dead flies on a corner of the ceiling"' (*CW5* 194–5).

In line with Jacques Rancière's analysis of the history of modern art, one can say that Yeats is objecting to a break with poetry's traditional, representational regime. Old hierarchies are dismissed: 'everything is now on the same level, the great and the small, important events and insignificant episodes, human beings and things. Everything is equal, equally representable.'[7] Like Yeats, Rancière links this change with the practice of the realist novel. For the Frenchman, the process involves a breakdown of traditional dividing lines: 'there is no longer any boundary separating what belongs to the realm of art from what belongs to the realm of everyday life.'[8] Yeats's protest against the everyday partakes in a more encompassing anxiety about this change of artistic norms. Yet one must presume that the varying choice of imagery, in differing contexts, is not randomly selected. In other words, there must be further grounds for excluding breakfast – rather than, say, dead flies – as something peculiarly unpoetic in the Scribner introduction. In the latter text, Yeats imbues breakfast with a symbolical power of its own, making it stand for all that is irrelevant in a poet's life. Breakfast is a sign for the whole sphere of the everyday – insofar as the everyday concerns that which is humdrum, routine and evanescent in human life. In this context, one might be inclined to share Henri Lefebvre's belief in that 'Any feature of daily life, including objects, words and gestures can give expression to it as a totality.'[9] Yet if any feature of the everyday is an equally valid representative of it, this makes it even more unclear why Yeats chose to focus specifically on breakfast. In fact, the motif of breakfast can highlight some of the specific aspects of the everyday excluded by Yeats's poetic ideal. Once I have shown this, I will go on to establish some dimensions of the everyday that nevertheless are embraced by his poetics, before concluding with a brief comparison between his various positions on this matter and those of other prominent thinkers of the everyday. Finally, this chapter will speculate on a different, more intra-literary, way – through intertextuality (in the Genettian sense) – of making sense of this throwaway reference.

In Yeats's poetry, one of the defining features of morning is that it is the time of day subsequent to night – and few poets have been more devoted to dreams and the night. 'Dream' is one of Yeats's key words, insistently repeated both in his drama and his poetry. The oneiric is always close at hand, from the early 'The Man who Dreamed of Faeryland' to the career-concluding admission, in the grand retrospect of 'The Circus Animals' Desertion', that 'It was the dream itself enchanted me' (*VP* 630; *CW1* 355).

From this vantage point, breakfast is an interruption of the poet's proper business of engaging with his own dream world, and the phatic chit-chat of the morning repast constitutes a rather jarring contrast to the inner theatre of the night. Yet the collision between these two domains is not a major factor, in this form, in Yeats's poetry; instead he chooses to completely sidestep the domestic trappings of the morning meal in favour of more solitary activities that take place in the freedom of nature. In Yeats's poetry, morning is typically the encounter with the dawn in natural surroundings – though not related to agriculture or any sort of work. Thus 'Towards Break of Day' may contrast the dream with the 'first cold gleam of day', but does so only to dwell upon a white stag, mountains, and 'a waterfall / Upon Ben Bulben side / That all my childhood counted dear' (*VP* 398; *CW1* 187). In the third section of 'The Tower', Yeats does not even bother to establish a contrast, magisterially choosing 'upstanding men / That climb the streams until / The fountain leap, and at dawn / Drop their cast at the side / Of dropping stone' (*VP* 414; *CW1* 203). The same nexus between dawn, nature and the leisurely activity of fishing recurs in 'The Fisherman', where Yeats presents his preferred reader as a 'freckled man who goes / To a grey place on a hill / In grey Connemara clothes / At dawn to cast his flies' (*VP* 347; *CW1* 148). On the basis of this evidence, it becomes clear that neither Yeats's ideal poet nor his ideal reader is to be found sitting docilely by the breakfast table: both have serious business elsewhere. One recalls Mrs. Cheveley's observation, in *An Ideal Husband*: 'In England people actually try to be brilliant at breakfast. That is so dreadful of them! Only dull people are brilliant at breakfast.'[10] If Yeats's poet or reader of choice shows up for breakfast at all, they will presumably be very late – like Yeats himself, in George Moore's memory of a visit to Coole Park, refusing to let conventional social niceties get in the way of his poetry:

[. . .] Lady Gregory came to meet me with news of Yeats. He was still composing; we should have to wait breakfast for him; and we waited till Lady Gregory, taking pity on me, rang the bell. But the meal we sat down to was disturbed not a little by thoughts of Yeats, who still tarried. The whisper went round the table that he must have been overtaken by some inspiration, and Lady Gregory, fluttered with care, was about to send the servant to inquire if Mr Yeats would like to have his breakfast in his room. At that moment the poet appeared, smiling and delightful, saying that just as the clocks were striking ten the metre had begun to beat, and abandoning himself to the emotion of the tune, he had allowed his pen to run till it had completed nearly eight and a half lines [. . .].[11]

Under Moore's satirical gaze, the poet is someone who does not fear insulting his hostess. Lady Gregory was, however, an exceptional hostess for Yeats, being uniquely fitted to bestow patience, wealth and encouragement upon him. Other hostesses would necessarily be more demanding, and this perhaps encroaches upon something of the tricky nature of the conventions surrounding mealtimes for Yeats. Given the fact that the Victorians developed breakfast into a ritual where the mistress of the house, in the words of Andrea Broomfield, 'was to showcase orderliness, punctuality, diligence, and efficiency along with presenting the food,'[12] it is not unlikely that Yeats's desire to distance poetry from breakfast involves a certain gender element. There is little direct evidence of this, even if Yeats at times certainly includes less than flattering references to scullery maids. One might also think of an anecdote in *A Vision*, where one of Yeats's fictional characters despairs over a 'realist' version of *Romeo and Juliet* that contains mere 'kitchen gabble' (*AVB* 33). A gender-specific comment occurs in *Per Amica Silentia Lunae*, where Yeats finds time enough to interrupt his esoteric musings to ask: '[. . .] how to forgive [. . .] that woman who murmurs over the dinner-table the opinion of her daily paper?' (*CW5* 31). Here the everydayness of what is being held at an arm's remove is underscored by the reference to a 'daily paper'. Journalism's obvious dedication to the contingencies of the passing moment is stressed, and significantly linked to unclear 'murmurs'.

All in all, breakfast as a motif presents itself as the meeting place of a weave of connotations, bringing together the feminine and empty forms of communication with the concept of the everyday. Later on in *Per Amica*, Yeats is at pains to emphasize that poetry occurs in an altogether different sphere: 'I am in the place where the Daemon is, but I do not think he is with me until I begin to make a new personality, selecting among those images, seeking always to satisfy a hunger grown out of conceit with daily diet' (*CW5* 31). Breakfast is a fruitful embodiment of the lower realms of Yeats's poetic universe not only due to its own status, then, but also because it provides an apt contrast to the heavenly nourishment available for more transcendent hungers. As an artist, he deals with the symbols of the imagination, rather than the raw, empirical material of the world – and the relationship between these two spheres is one of mutual opposition or negation: 'Every artist is a starving man', Yeats wrote in the draft of an unpublished dialogue, 'who creates imaginary drink and food, which content him while the want lasts.'[13]

The morning meal is tacitly cast, then, as something that provides *no food for thought*. As such, it is a far cry from the night-time repast of 'All Soul's Night', where Yeats and his cohorts imbibe an expensive muscatel. Spirits, we are told in this poem, are of so fine a constitution that they 'drink from the wine-breath / While our gross palates drink from the whole wine' (*VP* 471; *CW1* 232). This motif of a midnight repast being linked with epiphanic insight is anecdotally echoed in *A Vision*, where Yeats remembers: 'Someone has said that Balzac at noonday was a very ignorant man, but at midnight over a cup of coffee knew everything in the world' (*AVB* 162; *CW13* 78).[14] The use of Balzac in this context is interesting, as the Frenchman himself insisted that his own personally brewed coffee constituted not only an elixir of inspiration, but also a gateway that led beyond the confines of middle-class mediocrity. In his short essay 'The Pleasures and Pains of Coffee', Balzac explains how coffee presents an alternative to what he calls 'the relaxed, meandering, simple-minded, and cryptogamous life of the retired bourgeoisie.'[15]

'Meandering' is a relevant adjective in this context, as Yeats's vision of the poet – in contrast with the Balzacian bourgeoisie – as someone highly concentrated, rather than characterized by distraction and a wandering attention, is implicit in the Scribner preface's evocation of 'something intended, complete' cited earlier. For breakfast is not only a meal digested by someone whose wits may be not fully collected; it is arguably also a phenomenon essentially characterized by a lack of focus.[16] As such, breakfast is closely linked to the notion of the quotidian as presented in Michael Sheringham's study

Everyday Life. Sheringham writes that 'The everyday is what we sally forth into when we wake, before we direct ourselves to some specific sector or more specialized activity.'[17] As a meal, breakfast further lacks the sacramental associations of dinner or supper, where the whole family is gathered together as both a real and symbolical unity. Not infrequently, breakfast will be a less synchronized affair, where each individual appears at whatever time suits him or her – sometimes being very late indeed, as indicated by Moore's Coole Park anecdote. In addition, the reading of the morning newspapers – reviled by Yeats as purveyors of superficial and fragmented information – distracts from, and complicates, any profound form of communication.[18]

The picture I have been sketching so far is a rather unequivocal one, of Yeats as an adamant denier of the realm of the everyday and all that goes with it. Certainly, there is no denying that his work never severed a fundamental link with French Symbolism, a movement which in the writings of poets such as Baudelaire and Mallarmé tended to see poetry as a sacramental endeavour, usurping the ground of religion and distancing itself from the instrumental values of modern society. A similar tendency is evident in British Aestheticism, stretching all the way back to Arthur Hallam's concern, in 1831, about how 'higher feelings' were increasingly being displaced by the 'palpable interests of ordinary life'.[19] In a 1909 diary entry, Yeats approvingly cites Hallam's claim that the 'heterogeneous' destroys genius, going on mischievously to claim: 'I have certainly known more men destroyed by the desire to have wife and child and keep them in comfort than I have seen destroyed by drink and harlots' (*CW3* 358).[20] Yet such attempts to *épater le bourgeois* do not tell the whole story: Yeats always cuts a complicated figure, and other tendencies in his writings pull in other directions. Interestingly, food and domesticity provide important motifs in his early drama, explicitly being brought up in order to be eschewed or transgressed. Set in the time of the famine, Yeats's first play *The Countess Cathleen* has demonic merchants trying to barter souls in exchange for gold that will enable the starving populace to 'eat, drink, and be merry' (*VPl* 39; *CW2* 35). In *The Land of Heart's Desire*, Mary Bruin is tempted by a faery child to leave behind the family hearth and the 'common light of common hours' for a more elusive, transcendental desire (*VPl* 185; *CW2* 68). As its title intimates, *The Pot of Broth,* a play in large part co-written with Lady Gregory, circles around a humble meal, and how a wily tramp uses the gullibility of his hosts – fooled into believing that a magic stone can convert plain water into a miraculous repast. The stone, he insists, is 'better than beef and mutton, and currant cakes and sacks of flour' (*VPl* 242; *CW2* 112). In a more programmatic mode, *The King's Threshold* provides an anticipation of both Bobby Sands and Kafka's *Hungerkünstler,*[21] as the poet Seanchan goes on a hunger strike in order to protest the loss of his traditional, artistic privileges to the new dispensation of King Guaire. The power of the poet, one might say, lies precisely in his power not to break his fast. At one point, Seanchan's enthusiastic defence of the virtues of poetry is dismissed by the king's chamberlain as a mere symptom of his physical privation: 'If you would but eat something, you'd find out / That you have had these thoughts from lack of food, / For hunger makes us feverish' (*VPl* 290; *CW2* 137). Thus Yeats's later distancing of poetry from the everyday routine of breakfast is anticipated by an early collision between domesticity and inspiration in his dramatic works. In the less elevated precincts of these earthy plays, the dividing line between the two takes place within the literary text rather than in its margins.

Nevertheless, the separation of poetry and the quotidian is not quite this permanent and inflexible in Yeats's *oeuvre* as a whole. In poetic diction, for instance, he may deny everyday chatter, but he still espouses a kind of ordinariness, trying – as he put it on one occasion – 'to make the language of poetry coincide with that of passionate, normal speech' (*CW5* 212). One of the reasons why turns of phrase from Yeats's poetry have become such a natural part of public and everyday language in the English-speaking world is that he combines memorability with a relatively direct ordinariness. Similarly (as we shall also see in Chapter 8), his investment in traditional Irish poetry pulls him towards that which is common rather than elevated: 'the folk song is still there', he claims, 'but a ghostly voice, an unvariable possibility, an unconscious norm' (*CW5* 214). The same pull towards quotidian language is registered in his work for the stage. In a 1906 note to the play *On Baile's Strand*, Yeats claims that all the songs of his plays 'are sung so as to preserve as far as possible the intonation and speed of ordinary passionate speech, for nothing can justify the degradation of an element of life even in the service of an art' (*VPl* 526). The latter principle would seem to be squarely at loggerheads with much of Yeats's symbolist heritage, and as such it represents a somewhat anomalous – but nonetheless significant – Yeatsian defence of life against the trespasses of art.

Another impulse pulling Yeats towards the everyday, is the concerted effort to make his domestic life at Thoor Ballylee a central part of his later poetic identity. One never finds the early Yeats's writing of his lodgings in Woburn Buildings in London, but once he has established his residence in the west of Ireland the everyday life connected to a specific place becomes a suitable topic for poetic treatment. The latter move should not, however, be read simply as a combining of the quotidian and the artistic in one articulated whole. Rather, Yeats tries to raise the everyday unto the level of the artistic. This is evident in his account of Vladimir Soloviev's notion of the spiritualization of the soil, which in 'If I were Four-and-Twenty' is interpreted as involving 'all the matter in which the soul works, the walls of our houses, the serving up of our meals, and the chairs and tables of our rooms, and the instincts of our bodies' (*CW5* 41). Our everyday acts, places and bodies are to be transformed by less tangible, transcendent forces. Such spiritualization of the quotidian can, for instance, be seen in Yeats's use of the sword gifted to him by a Japanese reader. As he writes in the third section of the 'Meditations in Time of Civil War', 'Sato's gift, a changeless sword, / By pen and paper lies, / That it may moralize / My days out of their aimlessness' (*VP* 421; *CW1* 206). Here the Japanese tradition of not distinguishing clearly between ordinary and artistic objects is set to work by Yeats, but the aim is still to get rid of the distraction or 'aimlessness' of everyday activities (such as breakfast) that disturbed him so much. If all things can tempt Yeats from the laborious craft of verse, then a transfiguration of the everyday is required in order to make his writing a natural and worthy part of his existence.

Transfigurations of the everyday are also the topic of some of the more epiphanic moments in Yeats's *oeuvre*. In the fourth section of 'Vacillation', for instance, a casual instance of leisure becomes a moment of insight, as a visit to a coffee shop yields a sudden and surprising feeling of blessedness. One may speculate whether Yeats here had asked for a specially brewed cup of Balzac's own blend of coffee. Much earlier in his career, 'The Lake Isle of Innisfree' builds upon a similar instance of an epiphanic vision in an urban context. The associative trigger that set off the poem took place in an urban setting that is only revealed in other texts by Yeats – as for instance in his early prose piece *John Sherman*, where we are told of the protagonist's day-dream of the lake being sparked by 'a faint trickling water' that 'came from a shop window' on the Strand 'where a little water-jet balanced a wooden ball upon its point' (*CW12* 56–7). In such cases the everyday provides the occasion or setting for a vision, yet the vision itself leaves the messy details of the everyday behind. Yuriko Saito has claimed that this is a necessary consequence of all artistic treatment of the quotidian: 'by making the ordinary extraordinary and rendering the familiar strange, while we gain aesthetic experiences thus made possible, we also pay the price by compromising the very everydayness of the everyday.'[22] Yeats is thus in rather large and also good company here. Even such a consistent and outstanding champion of the everyday as the French theorist Henri Lefebvre wanted to conceive 'of life as a work of art'.[23]

Yeats's different responses to the everyday can be compared with the cognate conceptions of others. While seeming far removed from the influential accounts of everyday life given by recent French thinkers such as Lefebvre and Michel de Certeau, Yeats at times shares with them a vision of an everyday life suddenly made luminous and meaningful, through its integration into art. Still the urban, left-wing tenor of these thinkers – linked with a stress on consumer activism in de Certeau – is far removed from Yeats's thought. The Irishman's tendency to seemingly only unreservedly embrace the everyday when it is a rural phenomenon, hallowed by centuries of use and custom, is more akin to the romantic version of the ordinary that has been criticized by Richard Kirkland. For Kirkland, the everyday is characterized by a 'rural, countrified version of history' that elides political division into a notion of timeless tradition.[24] Yet much in Yeats's writings seems to pull away even from such a delimited and purified conception of the quotidian. In so far as the everyday is life without focus or any one aim, a state of distraction that is difficult to grasp only because it is inherently unformed, it is for Yeats a raw state of being that the responsible artist must reshape and reconfigure into a work of art. By thus consistently dismissing the everyday – as well as his quintessentially everyday beings, the breakfasting, middle-class women who chat over their morning paper – Yeats's poetics is effectively out of line with much of what has followed after him in literature and the arts. Yet his unflagging commitment to the craft and discipline of verse, a commitment in some ways inextricably linked with this aversion, remains a compelling legacy. When all is said and done, we might indeed be better off with Yeats the bard than we would have been with Yeats at breakfast.

The morning meal may thus be read as a cipher of all that Yeats had to deny, in order to make of himself the great craftsman whose poetry still lives on today. Yet this is a gesture strikingly at odds with important figures who have come after him; what would the poetry of Louis MacNeice, Philip Larkin or Seamus Heaney be, without an intense and pervasive immersion in the everyday? One of the major limiting factors to Yeats's influence on recent poetry is precisely his stark denial of such things as journalism, mealtimes and flies in the corner of the ceiling. In this respect, the claim that 'even when the poet seems most himself [. . .] he is never the bundle of accident and incoherence that sits down to breakfast' marks an act of denial that rebounds on the poet himself. By closing the door to the more inclusive subject matter made available by a break with the traditional representational art (as theorized by Rancière), Yeats effectively shut himself off from one of the most vital impulses of twentieth- and twenty-first century poetry.

However, it is still the case that Yeats's contrast between the complete and ideal poetic self and the breakfasting self may be doing several things at once, some rather different from what has transpired so far in this chapter. For instance, what if one reads this contrast as an allusion to Oliver Wendell Holmes's *The Poet at the Breakfast-Table* (1872)? This follow-up volume to Holmes's popular successes *The Autocrat at the Breakfast-Table* (1858) and *The Professor at the Breakfast-Table* (1859) was subtitled 'His Talks with his Fellow-Boarders and the Reader'. Although Holmes had passed away by the time Yeats visited America, he would still have been remembered. The Irishman lectured at Holmes's Harvard on both of his first two American tours, on 1 December 1903 and 5 October 1911.[25] Familiarity with Holmes is demonstrated by a 1909 letter to Lady Gregory, in which Yeats casually refers to a poem by Holmes in order to demonstrate the mess of his domestic arrangements: 'When I got home last night my dress trousers had gone all over like the dog cart in some poem of Wendell Holmes that was so well made that it lasted many years & then fell to powder – all parts had been equally strong' (Letter to Lady Gregory, 9 December 1909; *CL Intelex* 1238).[26]

Almost 30 years later, Yeats would seem to be alluding to Holmes's *The Poet at the Breakfast-Table* in order to convey another instance of unwanted, domestic messiness. Although none of Holmes's books figure in the collected remains of Yeats's library, it is quite conceivable that he either had read *The Poet at the Breakfast-Table* or heard about it. Certainly, the contents of this book make it a fitting foil for the ideals of Yeatsian poetics. Casual, conversational and almost ingratiatingly familiar with its readers, *The Poet at the Breakfast-Table* is not a text that risks challenging or shocking anyone. The poet reports the words and impressions gleaned from the other residents of the New England boarding-house, and is himself not so much a visionary magus as a sympathizing go-between, providing a wry but affectionate glance at polite society. Yet not all its content would be equally alien to Yeats. The hostess is a rather characterless landlady, who early on in the narrative provides a characteristic interruption of the poet's thoughts: 'I wanted to write out my account of the other boarders, but a domestic occurrence – a somewhat prolonged visit from the landlady, who is rather too anxious that I should be comfortable – broke in upon the continuity of my thoughts and occasioned – in short, I gave up writing for that day.'[27] Holmes's poet goes on to imagine Shakespeare being interrupted, during the composition of *Hamlet*, by a landlady asking 'William, shall we have pudding to-day, or flapjacks?' Holmes thus shows how domesticity and literary values pull in different directions, with an implicit gendering that concurs with the subtext of Yeats's passage.

Yeats's own youthful exposure to Victorian doubt is also mirrored by the worries of two characters – the widow and the young astrologer of Holmes's narrative – who struggle with the challenges to 'eternal truths' in a 'fearful time'.[28] Despite giving vent to nineteenth-century uncertainty about the tenets of Christianity, though, *The Poet at the Breakfast-Table* is keen to stay plumb in the middle of 'the highway of human experience'.[29] One of the ways in which Holmes's narrative differs from Yeatsian poetics, is in stress on everyday conversation. In the opening to the 'Anima Hominis' section of the essay *Per Amica Silentia Lunae* – a text that in many respects anticipates the Scribner introduction – it is precisely a sense of alienation with informal intercourse in a social setting that sparks off a search for a deeper sense of identity. In that essay Yeats envisages coming home 'after meeting men who are strange to me, and sometimes even after talking to women,' subsequently going over 'all I have said in gloom and disappointment' (*CW5* 4). Here too there is a passing mention of a meal – he refers to the 'mixed humanity' of his 'fellow-diners' – and the description of the salutary alternative as a 'heroic condition' that is 'complete' would also seem to anticipate the reference to the poetic self as 'an idea, something intended, complete' (*CW5* 4, 204). Holmes's poet may ironically describe conversation as 'at the best [. . .] only a thin sprinkling of felicities set in platitudes and commonplaces,'[30] but he remains devoted to record precisely what he disparages – and thus implicitly endorses that which is most alien to Yeats's poetic self.

Irony is also present in how Holmes's poet describes his youthful interest in esoteric pursuits:

I have never lost my taste for alchemy since I first got hold of the *Palladium Spagyricum* of Peter John Faber, and sought – in vain, it is true – through its pages for a clear, intelligible, and practical statement of how I could turn my lead sinkers and the weights of the tall kitchen clock into good yellow gold, specific gravity 19.2, and exchangeable for whatever I then wanted, and for many more things than I was then aware of.[31]

This is far removed from the earnest – if always complex, and frequently sceptical – dealings Yeats had with alchemy. Similarly, Holmes's avuncular poet-narrator pokes fun at his own literary pretentions, yet nevertheless insists – when addressing his readers early on in the book – upon his own poetical vocation: 'I am talking, you know, as a poet; I do not say I deserve the name, but I have taken it.'[32] This kind of attitude would presumably have presented itself to Yeats as a presumptuously complacent dilettantism. More to the point, Holmes's dialogue supports an expressive view of poetry that is squarely at odds with the ineradicable impersonality present in Yeats's poetics: 'The works of other men live, but their personality dies out of their labours; the poet, who reproduces himself in his creation, as no other artist does or can, goes down to posterity with all his personality blended with whatever is imperishable in his song.'[33] Where this view seeks to perpetuate a worldly self, Yeats's poet looks to be re-born as a self beyond the world.

It seems that we are dealing with a clear contrast – but why, then, leave out any explicit reference to Holmes himself? Why make the allusion so understated that no commentator has been able – or bothered – to identify it? This may have something to do with Holmes's lack of renown, and lack of centrality as a figure in the Yeatsian pantheon. Perhaps he is merely a go-between here, as a mediator between Yeats and figures of more eminent domains? We may be dealing with an adaptive complex involving a dyad, or perhaps even a triad, of figures. One possibility is that Holmes is representing a specifically American brand of expressivism. We are given a nudge in this direction, if we inspect a text closely related to the Scribner introduction to Yeats's poetry. In the related introduction to his essays, he contrasts his own emphasis on tradition with another, more recent – and more deracinated – approach. The latter comes about when tradition is no longer available as a living heritage:

> When that is no longer possible we are broken off and separate, some sort of dry faggot, and the time has come to read criticism and talk of our point of view. I thought when I was young – Walt Whitman had something to do with it – that the poet, painter and musician should do nothing but express themselves. (*CW5* 219)

As a young man, Yeats had described Walt Whitman as 'the greatest teacher of these decades' (to an unidentified correspondent, 11 March 1887; *CL1* 9), but it did not take long for him to leave the belief in the unity between poet and poem behind.

Yeats often spoke of Whitman in the company of his critical champion, Ralph Waldo Emerson. As Oliver Wendell Holmes was counted among a coterie of poets – the Fireside poets – inspired by Emerson, and indeed also published a laudatory monograph on the latter in 1884, it is a distinct possibility that Emerson is also included in the ambit of this allusion. This would contradict the reading made by Patrick J. Keane, when he aligns Emersonian self-reliance with the self of Yeats's poetry.[34] There is certainly some evidence that the later Yeats was less than enthusiastic about Emerson. Already in the 1905 article 'America and the Arts', Emerson was deemed to be 'of a lesser order' than Poe, Thoreau and Whitman, 'because he loved the formless infinite too well to delight in form' (*CW10* 119). This early criticism was linked to Yeats's own desire to move from what he saw as a too receptive and feminine yearning after the infinite, to a more shaping and masculine approach. Later on in his career, Yeats's criticism of Emerson takes a somewhat different form, even as it becomes stronger. In 'Ireland after Parnell' section (1922) of the autobiographical volume *The Trembling of the Veil*, he claims that the influence of Emerson and Whitman was responsible for George Russell not attaining a more profound vision:

> I sometimes wonder what he would have been had he not met in early life the poetry of Emerson and Walt Whitman, writers who have begun to seem superficial precisely because they lack the Vision of Evil; and those translations of the Upanishads, which it is so much harder to study by the sinking flame of Indian tradition than by the serviceable lamp of Emerson and Walt Whitman. (*CW3* 200)

The following volume of *The Trembling of the Veil*, 'Hodos Chameliontos' (also 1922), specifies that the so-called Vision of Evil plays a significant role in the establishing of a deeper self. Genius, Yeats writes, 'is a crisis that joins the buried self for certain moments to our trivial daily mind' (*CW3* 217). The claimed superficiality of Emerson and Whitman – and, presumably, of Oliver Wendell Holmes – is the result of their being unable to attain the 'birth' and 're-creation' of man that 'terror' makes possible. Here they are, in Yeats's scheme of things, unlike Dante and Villon:

> Had not Dante and Villon understood that their fate wrecked what life could not rebuild, had they lacked their Vision of Evil, had they cherished any species of optimism, they could but have found a false beauty, or some momentary instinctive beauty, and suffered no change at all [. . .]. (*CW3* 217)

Without the struggle with evil, Emerson – like his two fellow American poets – would lack the incentive to transcend the self of superficial appearances and conversation, and the attainment of a deeper, more complete self could not take place.

It is evident, then, that Yeats's denunciation of breakfast has far-flung echoes in his writings. It can be read as part of a problematical, and in part self-contradictory, eschewal of everyday life. Contextualized in a different way, it can also be interpreted as an intertextual gesture, distancing Yeats's poetics from the writings of Oliver Wendell Holmes – and also, perhaps, from the related careers of Walt Whitman and Ralph Waldo Emerson. The meaning of the passage to some extent shifts according to how one decides to frame it. Fundamentally, though, regardless of one's approach, what seems to be at stake here is a question concerning the connection between poetry and life. The quoted 'Hodos Chameliontos' passage on Dante and Villon refers to 'what life could not rebuild': the deeper self or soul is beyond life. As such, it is presumably also beyond many of the biographical particulars linked to a poet's daily existence. For Helen Vendler, though, the onus is on the biographer to ignore such a distinction: 'Yeats said that the poet is not the bundle of accident and incoherence that sits down to breakfast, but the interplay between that man and the poet is, or ought to be, the stuff of biography.'[35] She makes this remark in connection with a criticism of a biography that, in her opinion, does not make sufficient links between Yeats's life and literature. In doing so, however, she seems to imply that Yeats's distinction implies a reservation against precisely such mixing. Seen in this light, the disjunction between poet and breakfast is not, primarily, one between the poetic and everyday – nor does it involve a marking of difference between Yeats and an American programme of poetic self-realization. And certainly, as will be shown in Chapter 10 of this study, Vendler's own criticism can be used to demonstrate the riskiness inherent in making too quick and speculative links between Yeats's poetics and matters concerning nationality. But is the border between biography and literary *oeuvre* any less challenging? The next two chapters will address problems concerning how we write about Yeats's life, in terms of literary biography, as well as about Yeats's own autobiographical practice.

3

Patterns of Biography

In both his life and his work, Yeats is a cultivator of masks. Significantly, Richard Ellmann entitled his critical biography of the poet *Yeats: The Man and the Masks*. What happens, though, when one counters the poet's own masks with other images of him? Take for instance the following anecdote, involving one of the more prosaic examples of Yeats's proclivity for self-invention: pausing by a mirror on the stairs of the Savile Club, the by then famous author drily but self-ironically informed his companion that 'One must adjust the image'.[1] A recent eminent biographer has utilized this episode to throw light on his own mission: whoever writes of Yeats's life, R. F. Foster claims, is faced with 'the challenge of getting behind the adjustments'.[2] Does this mean that whereas the poet occludes and makes things up, the fact-finding scribe hot on his heels must reveal what goes on behind the trembling of the poet's autobiographical veil? Can biography perhaps grant us access to a form of real life behind the myths and fictions? Yeats was not dismissive of the biographical hunger for facts and background knowledge. 'I have no sympathy', he once expostulated, 'with the mid-Victorian thought to which Tennyson gave his support, that a poet's life concerns nobody but himself.'[3] Tennyson was famously shocked by how Froude's indiscreet biography of Carlyle divulged extreme marital problems, and – at least partially as a result of this – he chose to appoint his son as his authorized biographer.[4] For Yeats, who considered lack of discretion to be one of his own most characteristic faults (see *Mem* 227), the poet's life is not to be walled away from the precincts of poetry. In Yeats's case the poetry and the life may not be one simple and indissoluble thing, but they certainly are related and overlapping entities. If the Russian Formalist Boris Tomashevskij had to make an allowance for the relevance of a 'mythical biography' to accompany and supplement the reading of the poetry of a writer like Byron, a similar case can certainly be made for Yeats, too.[5]

Life and literature are, then, interconnected. Once one has allowed the relevance of biography in the reading of Yeats, though, there is still a need for a caveat. For although there has been a return to biography and contextual readings of literature in recent decades, there are many reasons to hold back from any simple return to the kind of positivistic objectivism that has in the past reduced the impact and validity of historical and biographical criticism. Yeats's life is more than a set of easily grasped facts, and it is also something much more complex than a solid and determinable background to his writings. In what follows, I would like to question the imbrication of poetry, life writing and biography in Yeats's texts. In the next chapter, I will put the focus squarely on the genre of autobiography. Here, though, this problem will be approached through the prism of the recent glut of biographies on Yeats, with particular emphasis on R. F. Foster's two-volume work.

Foster's two volumes have been very well received, and deservedly so. Together they form a widely encompassing work, which not only gives a very detailed account of Yeats's week-to-week engagements and interests but also manages to pay heed to important, large-scale developments in his career and life. This is a biography that already seems likely to become as influential within the study of Yeats as Richard Ellmann's classic work long has been within Joyce scholarship. Yet this should blind us to the fact that even in such an indispensable landmark study there remain unanswered questions and problematic emphases. A pertinent approach is suggested by the simple question: What kind of a biography is this? For there are, after all, various ways of framing the life of a poet. In the preface to his second volume on Yeats's life, Foster himself circumscribes the field somewhat, by intimating that his is not a *critical* biography of the kind written by Terence Brown.[6] Yet here the differing approaches of Foster's two volumes might give us pause. For, as Bernard O'Donoghue has suggested, the second volume attains a far closer relationship to Yeats's poetry than the first volume does, and owes much of its power to that closeness.[7] While the first tome struggles with a characteristic failing of much historicist work on literature, in that it allows Yeats's entrepreneurial activities to dwarf his poetry, the depiction of the last 24 years of the poet's career achieves a better balance. Thus it is no accident that while Foster admits in the preface to the first volume that it 'may often contain less about poetry and its making than might be expected,' no similar defensive manoeuvre is needed the second time around[8]: *The Arch-Poet* is indeed more of a critical biography than *The Apprentice Mage*, and this difference is arguably linked with Foster's understandable predilections as an accomplished historian. The later poetry is quite simply more public, more directly embroiled in the political debates of the day, than Yeats's early efforts.

An example of Foster's more comfortable, and extensive, treatment of the poems in the second volume, is provided by his reading of 'In Memory of Eva Gore-Booth and Con Markiewicz'. Foster not only places this text firmly in its poetical context, praising it for 'striking the keynote' for *The Winding Stair* collection 'as ringingly as "Sailing to Byzantium" did for *The Tower*',[9] but also goes on to make a detailed – if relatively short – argument about the underlying meaning of this enigmatic poem. Unsurprisingly, perhaps, Foster's reading emphasizes Yeats's public role in the national life of Ireland at the time, effectively interpreting the poem as a political performative. Contrary to other readings, Foster casts the elegy as being primarily an indictment of Gore sisters' betrayal of their Ascendancy heritage. According to his view, the cryptic final lines – 'We the great gazebo built, / They convicted us of guilt; / Bid me strike a match and blow' (*VP* 475–6, ll. 30–2; *CW1* 237–8) – primarily make a political statement: '"we" embraces WBY and his chosen Ascendancy ancestors; and the people who convicted "us" of guilt are not the "sages" but the Gore-Booth sisters themselves, who denounced the Anglo-Irish world from whence they came.'[10]

Although Foster's interpretation deftly marshals different textual sources to make its point, it remains too sketchy and unfinished to function as a full-scale reading of the poem. He does not account in any depth for the motivation of the agent who wants to 'strike a match and blow', nor does he even comment upon the fact that 'the great gazebo' surely refers just as much to time itself (lines 26–7 exclaim: 'Arise and bid me strike a match / and strike another till time catch') as to the proud Anglo-Irish mansion of Lisadell evoked in the opening lines of the poem. For Foster the apocalyptical destruction of time is beside the point: the Yeats he wants to capture is a poet who acts *within* time, and – more specifically – almost exclusively within the time of a specific Anglo-Irish history. Foster is also to a large degree uninterested in individual participants (other than Yeats) in this history, unless they play an emblematic role linked to class or religion. Thus he does not explore the complicated nexus of topography and memories linking Yeats and Countess Markiewicz,[11] opting instead to only use the latter figure as a depersonalized metonym for the poet's troubled relationship with the Ascendancy.

A certain partisanship is present, then, as an underlying factor in Foster's reading of Yeats's life and career. If John Banville is correct in calling this biography a 'triumph' of 'empathy', then that empathy is both very concentrated and also comes at a certain cost.[12] The Yeats we meet in this book is very much Foster's own version of him, and it is hard to avoid the feeling that there is a certain kind of prejudice, a historicist prejudice, informing his biography. But then one would have to add that this is a prejudice in the hermeneutical sense: a necessary precondition for framing – for selecting and filtering – the otherwise chaotic mass of available information. As Hans-Georg Gadamer has repeatedly stressed, this kind of prejudice is not only limiting but also enabling – and every form of understanding must, at least within the human sciences, take it on board.[13] It is an ineluctable part of historicity of understanding – or, as one can glean from Richard Holmes, in many ways a very different writer, 'self-identification' may be 'the first crime of biography', but it is also 'an essential motive for following in the footsteps, for attempting to re-create the pathway, the journey, of someone's else's life through the physical past.'[14]

The detail and broad, contextual sweep of Foster's historical knowledge is one of the major strengths of this biography, making it an invaluable tool for many Yeats scholars. When René Wellek and Austin Warren's classic *Theory of Literature* proposes that biography 'is a part of historiography', one has the sense of a door slamming shut – a sense of that literary biography is being denied entrance to the elevated precincts of more specialist literary criticism.[15] The historical slant of Foster's biography is arguably a different kettle of fish altogether, as it has already been of demonstrative value for literary critics. In Foster's work, Yeats's subtly varying alliances and positionings in the Irish and English society of the time, with inevitable emphasis on issues concerning the Anglo-Irish ascendancy and Irish independence, come across in a nuanced manner, clearly useful for the critic as well as the historian. Foster's historicist prejudice is, in such matters, a rich prism that gives us a many-coloured view on the poet's writings. However, while there is no reason to fault a biographer for giving us a limited and time-bound truth, one can still question and ponder the premises underlying the particular kind of truth with which he or she supplies us. Before turning to Yeats's own views on the connection between life and literature, it might prove instructive to scrutinize how Foster accounts for (a) divisions between different phases in Yeats's career, and (b) the interplay between specificity and holistic unity that characterizes the genre of biography.

It is of course immediately evident that Foster divides Yeats's life into two main phases. The first volume of his biography, *The Apprentice Mage*, describes the first 50 years, while the second – *The Arch-Poet* – traces the succeeding 24. Even if it covers a smaller amount of time, Foster still refers to the content of the second volume as 'the second half of his life',[16] in effect signalling that he does not consider the bipartite structure an arbitrary one. In a larger perspective, there seems to be something almost mechanically compelling about the tendency to divide a writer's career into early and late periods. The same is repeatedly done with Wordsworth and Tennyson, for instance, though in the case of Wordsworth in particular, critics have recently tended to approach this kind of dichotomy with increasing wariness. Exactly where, for instance, does the early and innovative phase of Wordsworth's career end? There are numerous answers to this question, many of which may be reasonable enough – but none of which are exactly compelling.

Similarly, contrasting Foster's approach with that of other biographers can lead to a more flexible and open-ended view on the dynamics of the Irish poet's literary career. For where Foster follows Francis Hackett in claiming that 1915 is a watershed, a point at which his subject 'had achieved Yeats',[17] other feasible options are available. Richard Ellmann, for instance, chooses to locate a turning point when Yeats was informed of Maud Gonne's marriage to John MacBride in 1902: 'Yeats', he claims, 'until his thirty-seventh year, had remained in his love affair a wide-eyed boy'.[18] This date has the advantage of being not only close to the turn of the century, but also of being at the chronological mid-point of the poet's life. For Ellmann, though, it also has the added attraction of creating a fault-line between Yeats the symbolist and Yeats the more economical and spare modernist: 'The world which Yeats builds up in the 'nineties' is unlike what would come later in that it (i.e., the world of Yeats's early poetry) is 'not really an independent world at all, but a skilful evasion, neither here nor there'.[19]

Ellmann's rather dismissive account of Yeats's early poetry has provoked a significant riposte – from Ellmann himself. His later, 1954 study *The Identity of Yeats* seeks among other things to combat those who 'were inclined to dismiss his early work as aberrant, and to exalt his later work as an entirely different thing'.[20] Nevertheless, the critical view of Yeats's early symbolist verse has continued to hold sway in most quarters. In Terence Brown's more recent critical biography, the major divisions are tacit, but generally the author seems to distinguish between three Yeatses: (1) the early symbolist, (2) the mature modernist and (3) the rather strained experimentalist of the final years. This *trivium* of Yeatses is not new, however, being, for instance, anticipated by Ellmann's evocation of 'the frustrated, unsuccessful lover of the early verse, [. . .] the hounded public figure of the middle period, [and] the time-struck, age-worn old man of the later work'.[21]

Although Yeats's troubled relationship with Maud Gonne has long been central to the trajectory of biographical accounts of his life, the last decades have seen a change in emphasis with regard to critical renderings of his love life. Brenda Maddox' *George's*

Ghosts: A New Life of W. B. Yeats provides an achronological account, starting in 1917 and focusing on Yeats's marriage with Georgie Hyde-Lees. Only after unfolding the first few years of this marriage does she go back to Yeats's first years, subsequently paying special attention to Yeats's mother (usually a rather neglected figure in biographical accounts).[22] Ann Saddlemyer's recent biography of Yeats's wife is at least partially motivated by a similar desire to be fair to what has frequently been presented as more of a convenient than passionate marriage. Both of these books are part of a new trend in biography writing, whereby biographers such as Claire Tomalin, Ann Thwaite and Brenda Maddox have given accounts of the lives of women who have played an important, if hitherto marginalized, role in the careers of famous writers.[23]

Foster's biography is cognizant of these developments, and takes special care to depict Yeats's marriage and occasional details of his family life. Bernard O'Donoghue has argued that the resulting image of Georgie Yeats's dedication, perseverance and ultimate frustration makes her, rather than her husband, the hero of Foster's story. Such a conclusion might lead one to believe that the division between Foster's two volumes is related to Maddox's chronological sleight-of-hand: that before and after 1915 is roughly synonymous with life before and after Georgie Yeats's decisive entry into Yeats's life. Although Foster is at pains to emphasize that his subject was no saint, this is to underestimate the historical and public – rather than private – tenor of his approach. The events of 1916 loom large – larger even than Yeats's marriage – and as a result Foster pays especially close attention to the interesting publication history of the poem 'Easter, 1916'.[24] The result is a lucid explication of Yeats's reservations concerning the republican movement, which neither dismisses nor trivializes his motives. There is a connection here with Foster's own position as a revisionary Irish historian, embracing Irishness as a topic while at the same time displaying scepticism with regard to some of its alleged myths. Arguably, this causes him to align Yeats with his own political views. The poet's life is seen in light of what Foster elsewhere has called

> the transformation of Ireland's international position and domestic experience in the last thirty years – the exact period which saw the final abandonment of the introverted, autarchical national view in culture and economics inherited from early Sinn Féin.[25]

If Yeats's life provides us with a 'palimpsest of Irishness',[26] then it is this particular Irishness that provides the normative and guiding view of Yeats in Foster's account. When Foster refers to Yeats's investment in 'the long war about defining Irish identity',[27] both the continuation of that 'war' after Yeats's own lifetime, as well as Foster's own engagement in it, is implicated. It is Yeats the broad-minded Protestant, advocate of a cosmopolitan and liberal form of nationalism, who is endorsed. Catholic resistance to this form of Irishness is firmly opposed, while Yeats's interest in fascism during his last few years is – even if not excused – accounted for as an aberration of limited scope.[28]

Yeats is thus both appropriated and endorsed as a political figure. The events of 1916 provide the main reason for 'why things turned out differently' from his 'expectations'.[29] These events are a fulcrum around which the Yeats of this narrative recreates his poetical persona. But Foster's biography is by no means exclusively focused on this one major event alone. It is the density and richness of detail that primarily sets this book apart from other accounts of Yeats's life: Foster's chronological, blow-by-blow account bravely ventures forth where others biographies have feared to tread. Ellmann, for instance, excused his rather schematic account of the poet's early life on the following grounds:

> Of all periods of Yeats's life the years from 1889 to 1903 are the most difficult to follow. He has so many interests and activities during this time, with so little obvious relation between them, that a strictly chronological account would give the impression of a man in a frenzy, beating on every door in the hotel in an attempt to find his own room.[30]

Where Ellmann summarizes and organizes material under thematic headings, Foster generally sticks to the sequential unfolding of events when working with this time-period. Foster has self-consciously emphasized this difference, insisting that while Ellmann's biography is 'a masterpiece of intellectual analysis and psychological penetration, to which all Yeatsians are for ever indebted', the fact remains that 'we do not, alas, live our lives in themes, but day by day.'[31]

Ellmann himself argued that chronology was indispensable for biography,[32] so one might argue that Foster is trying to beat his American predecessor at his own game. Still, there is cause to demur. Not only does Ellmann's narrative of Yeats's life in fact often keep a chronological sequence, but it is also true that the disputed period of Yeats's life (from 1889 to 1903) is one where Foster's own biography struggles to keep the specifically *literary* side of this life in view. As mentioned earlier, Foster's first volume largely jettisons Yeats the poet for Yeats the administrator and impresario. In addition, one might add that, though Foster stresses 'the chronological and contingent nature' of his narrative,[33] absolute chronology is more of an ideal than a fully attained actuality in his two volumes. This is evident in those long passages of *The Apprentice Mage* that deal almost exclusively with controversies connected with the Abbey Theatre; also, towards the end of *The Arch-Poet*, day-by-day sequentiality is at times overridden by in-depth discussions of long-term developments. At one stage, for example, a detailed account of how the life and career of Yeats's Abbey Theatre associate Lennox Robinson was to unfold after his marriage to Dolly Travers Smith interrupts Foster's account, only for the narrative voice to rein in the proceedings with the words 'All this lay in the future in the autumn of 1927.'[34] A more significant deviation from chronology is evident in Foster's depiction of Yeats's relationship to Iseult Gonne. Despite causing Georgie Yeats considerable strain, Yeats was intensely solicitous of Maud Gonne's daughter in the time following his own marriage. Foster largely vindicates Yeats's seemingly obsessional interest in the welfare of this young woman – to whom he had unsuccessfully proposed, shortly prior to his engagement with Georgie Hyde Lees – and consistently anticipates her later problems in life (particularly in relation to her troubled marriage to Francis Stuart) in order to win the reader over to the poet's side from the onset. It is as if Foster is constantly making sure that the reader should not become too critical of his subject's ethics, with regard to this particularly delicate relationship with a vulnerable young woman.

Thus Foster seems in some ways to be closer to Ellmann than he himself admits. Both wish to use chronology as a fundamental structuring device, yet find good reasons to deviate from it when they are compelled to do so. In addition, there is also the sense that Foster's biography on Yeats is *emulating* Ellmann rather than competing with him – but emulating his life on Joyce rather than the shorter and less definitive one on Yeats. And in a later interview it is indeed claimed that the chronological approach of the Joyce biography was in fact the 'model' for Foster's own practice.[35] Fundamentally, of course, a completely sequential unfolding of a life would be largely unreadable. It would also neglect the fact that we do not live our lives in a series of distinct and immediate present moments, but rather employ various mediating devices to create some sense of continuity and permanence. Certainly Foster analyses and compares not only days, but also weeks, months and years of the poet's life. This is not biographical pointillism, and the focus on detail and sequentiality is relative rather than absolute. There is generally a strong narrative drive to Foster's account – a sense that Yeats's life is a story to be told – that tends to override the desire to merely register a series of facts.

But what, one might ask, is the rationale – apart from the pleasure we all take in telling and listening to stories – for such narrative cohesion? Is there a sense in which Yeats's life story is necessarily just that: a story? Or is Foster a purely empiricist chronicler – one of the 'erudite scholars' that Michel de Certeau claims, due to a 'devotion to "facts"', can only 'gather elements necessary for their research' without reflecting on how 'these are framed and mobilized with an order of knowledge of which they are unaware and which functions unbeknownst to them?'[36] Here Foster does not provide many hints.[37] Perhaps his strong emphasis on the term 'pattern' can point us in the right direction. The word crops up at crucial junctures both at the very beginning and at the very end of the biography. Most insistently, the final words of the epilogue contrast 'the contingencies and inconsistencies of fate' with what can 'be turned into pattern',[38] arguing that Yeats was not the victim of circumstances beyond his control precisely because of his ability to shape his own life. In a later work, Foster has referred to Yeats's 'self-fashioning', as well as more broadly reformulated the effects of this ability as 'Yeats's spectacular imposition upon events and people around him and after him.'[39] Although it is not quite as forceful an instance, Foster also makes use of the term 'pattern' in the introduction to the first volume. In this case it is employed to justify the biographer's two-part division of the poet's life: Yeats 'was not wrong', Foster claims, 'in believing that the years up to 1914 fixed the patterns by which he lived his astonishing life.'[40]

In both of these uses, 'pattern' is what enables a transcendence of a mere catalogue of facts and incidents. Foster appears, in part at least, to be drawn to Yeats for much the same reason he was previously attracted to the life of Sir Randolph Churchill: both have a self-transformative power, a self-imposed fluidity which leads Foster to claim that Winston Churchill's father 'makes – and unmakes – sense from day to day'.[41] Pattern is precisely what allows some broader and more comprehensive account of the resulting plethora of actions and thoughts. The forcefulness of the politician and the poet, in constructing examples of such a pattern, thus provide the historian with a precedent or lesson for his own activity. This should come as no surprise: Michel de Certeau has claimed that *all* history is, by virtue of 'intellectually controlling the connection of a particular will to the forces facing it [. . .] itself the subject on which it endlessly writes'.[42] The historian finds himself, and makes sense of his own endeavour, in his subject matter.

Yet Foster leaves the justification and precise articulation of the term 'pattern' hanging. I have previously alluded to hermeneutics in trying to account for the positive power of Foster's historicist prejudice, and here too one might be tempted to compare his approach to that sanctioned by German hermeneutical thinkers. In Foster's insistence upon 'pattern' there seems to be an allusion to how detail and design interact in his biography. This resembles the hermeneutical circle of part and whole as it has been elaborated by thinkers such as Schleiermacher, Dilthey and Gadamer. Yet there is arguably one important difference. These hermeneutical thinkers all build on a Romantic heritage where unity and wholeness not only has the final word, but also the first word: an organic sense of unity is claimed to be the common denominator for all understanding, and all understanding springs out of a prehension of unity that precedes any experiential confirmation whatsoever.[43] In Foster's case, there seems to be less explicit emphasis on unities, as he draws on a more empiricist tradition of historiography. But even in his text there is clear recourse to the supposed integrity of the individual life. Apart from the passages already cited, one might look at the reference in the second volume to 'the great design' of Yeats's life.[44] Foster also makes use of the traditional analogy of life and book: when Lady Gregory is about to die, he describes the interim as 'the last chapter of the most important friendship' of Yeats's life.[45]

As in the case of chronological detail, such references – and many others like them – show that Foster does have recourse to a sense of unity beyond the merely accidental assemblage of facts. Yet it is a loosely conceived unity, where the movement from detail to whole is always provisional and tenuous. Something similar occurs in the interaction between individual life and more general history in his text. Foster wishes to stress the arbitrary and accidental way in which Yeats's life is buffeted by the incidental and unpredictable events of history, and yet he also wants to argue that Yeats made himself into an emblematic figure for Ireland: Yeats's *representative* status seems important, and this is surely no accident – given that the author's most celebrated earlier work is a history of Ireland. In an essay included in *The Irish Story*, Foster has claimed that 'we must place [. . .] Yeats [. . . .] firmly in his own times, and perhaps see him [. . .] as an emblematic figure as well as an individual genius'.[46] The reason for granting this emblematic status is a little vague, though, as Foster gestures towards 'how directly' important problems of current historiography of Yeats's times 'intersect with Yeats and his life'.[47] But he also goes further than this, claiming that 'Yeats's experience contributes central illumination' to these problems.[48] The use of the term 'central' is a bit ambiguous here, as it is unclear whether Yeats provides illumination because of his centrality as a publicly expressive figure, or whether he illuminates the centre, the kernel as it were, from his own position (which in itself might be deemed somewhat marginal compared to that of Parnell and other politicians).

In the introduction to the first volume of the biography, Foster is more circumspect. There he argues that Yeats's

> extraordinary life deserves to be studied for its relationship to his work; it also needs to be studied for its influence on his country's biography. [. . .] His best-known poetry defines for many people the Irish identity which was forged in revolution. But he represented, in the intersections and traditions of his own life, a complex tangle of historical allegiances as well as personal relationships. A historically grounded biography can attempt to survey this, without necessarily adopting the nineteenth-century framework of the 'exemplary life' [. . .].[49]

Although the reference to 'his country's biography' suggests a surprisingly intense homology between the micro-narrative of biography and macro-narrative of national history, it is hard to avoid a sense of evasion here. It is not obvious why Foster feels the need to at least partially distance himself from the kind of history writing that he espoused earlier, by insisting that it is exclusively characteristic of a past century. An earlier essay on Parnell had, for instance, approvingly made use of an emblematic anecdote which was described as 'in its way a Carlylean moment: a sudden conjunction of the personal and the "world-historical".'[50] Perhaps the need to keep this nineteenth-century *topos* at an arm's length derives from the vexed problem of 'centrality' – hardly a simple or uncontentious issue – which was rather cursorily addressed in *The Irish Story*. It is also possible that Foster is wary of the ideological baggage involved in this kind of history writing. Paula R. Backscheider, for one, has questioned 'The Great Man Theory of biography', especially for the way in which this theory has been fostered by a tradition that almost invariably treats a *male* individual as 'role model, admirable product/exemplar of a nation, or important agent in history.'[51] This is a tradition and school of thought upon which Yeats, influenced by writers like Carlyle and Hegel – who were part of precisely this 'nineteenth-century framework' – also reflected. Yeats claimed that an individual could represent a people symbolically. Foster's account of Yeats's life certainly does not ignore this theme, referring at one stage to 'the mysterious connections between individuals and world history – in war, love, and art – which he [i.e. Yeats] continued to interrogate and which even the rewritten *A Vision* could never quite explain.'[52] What Foster does not do, however, is to subject this idea to any kind of clear and sustained criticism. It is part of Yeats's heritage, which he seems to take partially on board, and yet which he seemingly wants to avoid embracing fully.

This is by no means an isolated instance. On all the meta-biographical issues we have outlined, Yeats had strong and clearly expressed – if occasionally varying – views. Often during the process of reading Foster's biography one comes across such views, and it is hard to know whether they are being endorsed or held at a safe distance. Certainly this biographer is very preoccupied with Yeats's desire to write autobiography – far more so, in fact, than any other major biographer of the poet. It is striking, for instance, that Foster's choice of 1915 as the turning point of his biography is partially motivated by Yeats's decision to publish his first volume of memoirs around this time. For while the tumultuous events of 1916 are on one side of this watershed, the less dramatic – but nevertheless important – event of Yeats turning to autobiographical prose in 1914 is on the other. In the summer of 1914 the poet started writing what was to become *Reveries over Childhood and Youth*, a re-telling of his early years that originally echoed the title of his brother's painting *Memory Harbour*. By devoting the last few pages of the first volume to this act of retrospection, Foster manages to connect his own two-part division not only to political events but also to Yeats's personal life.

One important reason for Foster's focus on Yeats's autobiographical writings is his use of them as a foil for his own historical accuracy. It is implied that where Yeats's unreliable memories give us an entertaining myth, Foster will give us the sober – but still interesting – facts. The posthumously published book that was given the title of *Memoirs*, for instance, is described as 'a masterpiece of reordering and manipulation', a characterization which is said to be true of 'all his autobiographical writing'.[53] We are told that the self-portrait is far from being fully truthful, as the 'recollected personality is not the impetuous, charismatic figure who is reflected in his early letters, and who entranced the people who met him at the time'.[54] What do we get instead? According to Foster, Yeats's autobiographical writings must be read as partisan re-writings of the past for the uses of the present. Although the parallel to Nietzsche's *On the Uses and Disadvantages of History of Life* is not made, Foster's Yeats follows the German philosopher's dictum: '*If you are to venture to interpret the past you can do so only out of the fullest exertion of the vigour of the present*'.[55] For even in writing the *Memoirs*, essentially a more direct and unexpurgated version of his life up to 1898 than is present in any other work, Yeats does not produce anything close to an objective view: 'the circumstances of 1916 permeate the memory of the nineties'.[56] On other occasions George Russell is pulled in as a witness confirming how Yeats's autobiographical writings are buttressed by arbitrary contents and acts of selection.

It is hard to quibble with this criticism: no one would claim that Yeats is presenting the gospel truth, or rock-solid historical fact. But that is precisely the point: *no one* would claim it, for it is surely self-evident? One is reminded of Pierre Nora's opposition between memory and history:

> Memory, being a phenomenon of emotion and magic, accommodates only those facts that suit it. It thrives on vague, telescoping reminiscences, on hazy general impressions or specific symbolic details. It is vulnerable to transferences, screen memories, censorings, and projections of all kinds. History, being an intellectual, nonreligious activity, calls for analysis and critical discourse.[57]

To conflate Yeats's reveries with the scrupulosity of history might, therefore, be construed as something of a category mistake, making Foster's repeated insistence upon this matter more than a little surprising. Nora argues, however, that nothing is less typical than history's attempt to demystify memory: 'Memory is always suspect in the eyes of history, whose true mission is to demolish it, to repress it.'[58]

Still, Nora's opposites are perhaps not quite as absolute as such pronouncements would lead one to believe: history and memory overlap and interlink, in both overt and subterranean ways. As has already been noted, the historicist basis of Foster's biography is noticeable in how it emphasizes events and perspectives that fit into precisely a historicist template. Furthermore, the stress on the public, entrepreneurial energy of its protagonist marks the biography distinctively as a product of the age of the Celtic Tiger.[59] Presumably, a new version of Yeats's life written during or after the current economic recession would look rather different. An ungenerous reading could thus suggest that Foster has done something rather odd and even unprepossessing in criticizing Yeats's autobiographical writings for a tendency – a rootedness in its own present – that is also true of his own study. But this would overlook the fact that Foster is implicitly *emulating* Yeats's form of partisan recollection just as much as he is criticizing it. Foster does not simply dismiss the practice of his commemorative predecessor: Russell's criticism of Yeats's autobiographies is not allowed to stand unqualified, and one occasion Foster makes extensive reference to Russell's grudging admission that these texts do after all 'fill up the spiritual emptiness' that comes with more factual accounts.[60] We are, to be sure, left with no illusions about the fact that the 'objective retailing of old letters and diary extracts' was 'the opposite' of Yeats's 'own method'.[61] Foster insists, for instance, that Balzac's novels were an important influence on this method. Yet this also establishes some proximity to the biographer himself, since it constitutes an interesting echo of his own claim to have used Trollope and the Victorian political novel as something approaching a 'template' for his own biography of Lord Randolph Churchill.[62]

The validity of, and the rationale behind, Yeats's understanding of autobiographical memory is not explained or analysed. It is perhaps not the task of a biographer to judge these things too firmly – although biographers seldom have qualms about making such judgements about literary works when they feel inclined to do so. In any case, Foster is less than definitive about Yeats's autobiographical writings, and this leaves an odd sort of gap in his book. When there are so many parallels to his own practice, and such a sustained interest in the topic, one is led to expect a firm stance on this issue. One gets a sense that Foster has used Yeats's writings as a kind of sounding-board for his own commemorative practice – as an influence informing not only the content but also the form of his biography – but in a rather uneasy and implicit fashion. We are not dealing with a historian who is, in the words of Hayden White, a 'naive storyteller'[63] – the way in which Foster marshals Yeats's views on autobiography in his introductions is enough to dispel such a suggestion – but much remains tacit and unclear. Perhaps a closer look at how Yeats wrote about his own life will dispel something of the murkiness surrounding this question? The next chapter will focus precisely on those autobiographical writings.

4

Autobiographical Reverie

Hayden White has controversially claimed that history is closely related to poetry. Before starting to describe historical events, the historian must delimit his field. When establishing this preliminary demarcation or framework, he follows the dictates of poetry: 'In the poetic act which precedes the formal analysis of the field, the historian both creates his object of analysis and predetermines the modality of the conceptual strategies he will use to explain it.'[1] In *Metahistory*, White supported this thesis mainly on the basis of a reading of nineteenth-century historians, whom (it might be claimed) were far more inclined towards philosophical idealism – and perhaps also less adept in the modern study of an enormous range of historical sources – than a contemporary figure like Yeats's biographer R. F. Foster. Yet in the previous chapter we saw plenty of evidence that Foster's approach to biography entails an implicit preapprehension of unity of the kind that White describes. So the notion that his presentation of Yeats's life can be placed in a fruitful dialogue with the practice of poetry may not be all that far-fetched. Rather than connecting Foster's biography to White's rather heavy-handed tropical schema (in which respect *Metahistory* is more part of the history of structuralism than our living present), though, I will now turn to the object of Foster's own work. How, then, does Yeats himself confront the issues concerning life-writing that we have encountered so far?

The generic make-up of an autobiography may differ more or less radically from what one finds in a biography, but there are also significant differences between how different autobiographies relate to their 'architextual' basis. One obvious fact about Yeats's many forays into autobiography is that they are a piecemeal and protracted affair. Unlike Goethe, for example, whose *Dichtung und Wahrheit* presents a momentous and unified image of the author's own life, the Irishman never published his literary self-portraits in one single, comprehensive and continuous volume. Instead we have a farrago of diverse texts, with different subjects and a multiplicity of emphases, written over an extensive period of time. In part, this was a mode of composition that was forced upon him. Apart from Yeats's self-admitted inability to settle down to long spells of concentrated work, it seems safe to say that autobiography (in the traditional sense) was never his main interest, and therefore was something that he undertook in pauses from work of a higher priority. In addition, it was very much a money-making enterprise, and Yeats soon understood that a series of texts had more pecuniary potential than one definitive volume.

There are, however, also more substantial reasons for this intermittent approach. At a relatively early stage, after finishing the *Reveries* in 1914, Yeats foresees that he will only write autobiography in bits and pieces. A letter to his father, the painter John Butler Yeats, reveals a variety of motives:

> Yesterday I finished my memoirs; I have brought them down to our return to London in 1886 or 1887. After that there would be too many living people to consider and they would have besides to be written in a different way. While I was immature I was a different person and I can stand apart and judge. Later on, I should always, I feel, write of other people. I dare say I shall return to the subject but only in fragments. Some one to whom I read the book said to me the other day: 'If Gosse had not taken the title you could call it *Father and Son*.' I am not going to ask your leave for the bits of your conversation I quote. It is about 17,000 words, which is just the right size for Lolly's press, and will prepare for my quotations from your letters. (26 December 1914; *CL Intelex* 2571)

We shall return later to the significance of the intertextual reference to Gosse's classic autobiographical text. For now it must suffice to say that this allusion adds a note of flattery, as Yeats is straining to prepare his father for what would be a rather critical, if not exactly damning, view of J. B. Yeats's impact on the son's early years, which were characterized by a lack of stability as well as long absences from the father. The squeamishness about writing about 'too many living people' surely extends to the father,[2] although Yeats is to a certain extent overriding and subduing whatever qualms he may have in this particular case. Hence he has a need to reassure, a little later in the same letter: 'You need not fear that I am not amiable.' The living are too close, one could say, for the autobiographical author to have the necessary freedom. Yet this statement extends to Yeats himself: he is too close to *himself*, for autobiography to be possible. The only exception is when W. B. *est un autre*: when the self, such as the youthful self described in *Reveries*, is so distant as to become almost a different being.[3] This is a less dramatic admission of internal heterogeneity than that which Wordsworth presented, when he in *The Prelude* deemed his youthful memories so distant that 'sometimes when I think of them I seem / Two consciousness – conscious of myself, / And of some other being.'[4] Wordsworth's alienation comes across as both more alarming and disarming in this sudden admission of a surprising sense of distance from the self. This distance is so unheard of, it must be approached as an analogy rather than a fact: Wordsworth *seems* another being, even as the simile entails a remainder of sustained commitment to the self. Notwithstanding the impression one gains of that Yeats is unlike his Romantic forerunner in that he does not take himself by surprise, one might actually argue that it is the Irish poet who presents the most radical instance of personal distention of the two: 'While I was immature I was a different person and I can stand apart and judge.' Even if this might be construed as a rather naïve distancing of himself from his younger self, it is also more than that: an insistence upon the disjunction between the adult and the youth.

This disjunction is figured by the mask. In Yeats's other writings, the process of maturation is frequently linked to the process of choosing, and growing into, the features of an anti-self or mask. Here, however, the mask might seem instead to remove the remembering self from his past identity, splitting the entire life story in two. Yet the resulting disjunction does not spell out the entire truth about the relation between the mature and younger selves, as becomes evident in Yeats's account of the next autobiographical instalment, *Four Years*, in a letter from 22 December 1921:

> My dear Olivia [Shakespear], I send *Four Years* which is the first third of the complete memoirs. As they go on they will grow less personal, or at least less adequate as personal representation, for the most vehement part of youth must be left out, the only part that one well remembers and lives over again in memory when one is in old age, the paramount part. I think this will give all the more sense of inadequateness from the fact that I study every man I meet at some moment of crisis – I alone have no crisis. (*CL Intelex* 4039)

As in the earlier letter to his father, the relationship to his addressee plays an important role here. Yeats's important early relationship to Olivia Shakespear is alluded to in the reference to 'the most vehement part of youth': he is effectively excusing the inevitable omission of his affair with this married woman (she would appear, disguised as 'Diana Vernon', in the posthumously published *Memoirs*). But he is also once more fretting about the limitations of the autobiographical form. Whereas the letter to his father worried about obstacles to the expression of the whole truth about others, in this note to Shakespear discretion prevents full representation of Yeats's own life. The writer's own moments of crisis must be omitted, leading to a one-sided version of events.

The split in the subject we find here is not as absolute, perhaps, as the earlier one between a younger and more mature self. Still, there is a division between the public and the private self. In the unclear borderline between these two realms, gossip can find its place. There are certainly times when Yeats's autobiographical writings become dominated by personal anecdote of a less than trustworthy kind: in another letter to Shakespear he states that one of his autobiographical instalments 'needs the wild mystical part to lift it out of gossip' (7 June 1922; *CL Intelex* 4135). On yet another occasion he laments to her that editing has forced him to leave out what he calls – referring to a story relating to his early association with the Theosophical Society and Madame Blavatsky – 'my best Blavatsky tale' (1 August 1921; *CL Intelex* 3958). Many such anecdotes were not left out, though. Indeed, the numerous stories involving Lionel Johnson, Arthur Symons and the other members of the *Rhymers' Club* might be said to work more powerfully as isolated tableaux than as part of an instructive historical account. The way he presents these early influences tends towards a moralizing critique of the dangers involved in living a too unworldly life, and, as such, have some of the tone of Pater's 'Sebastian van Storck'.[5] Unfortunately, while recent biographers have queried Yeats's treatment of both his own life and that of his Irish contemporaries, his rather one-dimensional – if amusing – parody of Johnson and other related 1890s figures has largely been endorsed. The upshot is not only that a biographer like Terence

Brown – usually an instructive guide to Yeats's life – propagates a simplifying caricature of Walter Pater and his English followers,[6] but also that the appraisal of Yeats's early poetry (so wound up in the atmosphere of the 1890s) becomes un-nuanced.

The 'wild mystical part' that removes Yeats from such hasty verdicts should not be neglected, even if it is perhaps a bit harder to separate from the trivia and anecdotes than one might expect. Yeats's autobiographies both include, and are marked by, the contingencies of fate, but he always insists upon the notion that everything is part of one complete unity. Thus a letter to H. J. C. Grierson asserts of *The Trembling of the Veil*: 'my book is a whole, one part depending upon another, and all on its speculative foundation' (21 October 1922; *CL Intelex* 4196). The notion of a unified structure in which every part is reciprocally interdependent rests upon the traditional conception of an organic whole, inherited from Yeats's romantic precursors. Thinkers such as Coleridge, Goethe and Schelling all conceived of organicism as a way of combating the empiricism and increasingly mechanical thought of their day. Yeats himself tends to evoke organicism in a similar way (finding new combatants however),[7] although his stress here on the 'speculative foundation' does not fully reflect the richness and multifariousness of romantic versions of organicism. The romantics were typically in two minds about whether the centre or life-giving power at the heart of the organism was heterogeneous or homogeneous to the structure as a whole. Frequently it was envisaged as a spiritual, enlivening power emerging from without – like the faculty of Imagination collecting and ordering the manifold of sense data. Yet just as frequently the notion of a fundamental form of reciprocity – or what one today might call dialogism – at the heart of structure made it impossible to conceive of the central function as being in any way external to what after all is to be a unified whole or living body. The fault-line between the heterogeneous and homogeneous modes of conceiving organic unity also led to radically different conceptions of the body politic, veering from Coleridge and Hegel's rather draconian conceptions (where the individual must be willing to sacrifice him- or herself to the whole) to a form of anarchism (evident, for instance, in some of Friedrich Schlegel's early writings).[8]

Yeats's most outspoken political sympathies towards the end of his career would place him in the totalitarian and Hegelian end of this spectrum. Nonetheless, the early autobiographical writings divulge few traces of the increasingly conservative tenor of his later thought. In a self-reflective turn not unlike that of Proust, they do however dramatically enact the rites of passage that enabled the writer to write the text one is reading. While the romantics revolted against the empiricist and rationalist bent of their times, it is the positivism of Yeats's age that provides the antagonist for his own brand of organicism. In *Reveries*, we accordingly encounter a young man that grows tired of the factuality of the natural sciences, and later rejects the realistic detail of the impressionist school of painting. The portrait of the young man has its vanishing point in the growing awareness that something is lacking. While *Reveries* ends in a dejected note, *The Trembling of the Veil* soon – in its section titled *Four Years* – presents him fretting at the leash: 'A conviction that the world was now a bundle of fragments possessed me without ceasing' (*CW3* 163). Echoing Coleridge's search for a harmonization of head and heart at the outset of the *Biographia Literaria*, Yeats identifies his own nostalgic point of origin for the dissociation of sensibility: 'Had not Europe shared one mind and heart, until both mind and heart began to break into fragments a little before Shakespeare's birth?' (*CW3* 165). The future reconciliation of these opposites in a desired Unity of Being can only be achieved by finding some common point of unity, where the broken fragments of this vessel can be soldered together. Significantly, the concluding vision of *Four Years* unifies both the individual and the nation according to organicist tenets:

> a nation or an individual with great emotional intensity might follow the pilgrims, as it were, to some unknown shrine, and give to all those separated elements, and to all that abstract love and melancholy, a symbolical, a mythological coherence. (*CW3* 166)

In the ensuing autobiographical instalments, Yeats will grow increasingly sceptical about the attainment of this ideal at the collective (rather than individual) plane. But the general tendency – a desire for organic coherence – stands firm.

At this juncture we can identify a more thorough account of the fundamental cohesiveness that we, in the previous chapter, saw Foster loosely alluding to with the term 'pattern'. In *The Tragic Generation* Yeats uses the very same term to express how a sense of organic unity can provide a compositional basis for his own text: 'yet as I have set out to describe nature as I see it, I must not only describe events but these patterns into which they fall, when I am the looker-on' (*CW3* 253). For Yeats, a 'pattern' is something more than a mere index of regularity. Writing to his father, in a long missive dated 5 March 1916, he uses it to distinguish a living and active whole from its opposite – a loosely structured conglomerate of elements:

> In the last letter but one, you spoke of all art as imitation, meaning, I conclude, of something in the outer world. To me it seems that it often uses the outer world as a symbolism to express subjective moods. The greater the subjectivity, the less the imitation. Though perhaps there is always some imitation. You say that music suggests now the roar of the sea, now the song of the bird, and yet it seems to me that the song of the bird itself is perhaps subjective, an expression of feeling alone. The element of pattern in every art is, I think, the part that is not imitative, for in the last analysis there will always be somewhere an intensity of pattern that we have never seen with our eyes. In fact, imitation seems to me to create a language in which we say things which are not imitation. (*CL Intelex* 2880)

The patterning of Yeats's autobiographical writings thus implies something more than a mere copying of facts. It implies an internal structuring that shapes the events of the story into the organicism of a well-crafted plot. Paul Ricoeur's translation of the Ancient Greek *muthos* as 'emplotment' alerts us to how Yeats's desire for a 'mythological coherence' in the structures of self and nation communicates with his insistence upon how all art transcends mere mimeticism.[9] At heart, individuals, nations and plots all should be structured around one central fulcrum in order to have true coherence.

Here something of an explanation is offered for the kind of structural unity Foster presupposes in his biography. Yet one should be wary of bringing the different practices of punctilious biographer and wayward poet in too close proximity. Otherwise, one would have to claim that bad faith were the sole possible explanation for Yeats's refusal to write Sir Hugh Lane's biography, in 1915 – for in making this refusal he claims that he has 'not the training to marshal a mass of facts, and besides, I have made a vow with myself now, never to do anything again that is not creative literature.'[10] Taken at face value, Yeats's organicism would seem to imply that *all* structured or composed language transcends mimeticism and partakes in 'creative literature'. Yet he is always careful to distinguish his own autobiographical writings from more subdued and objectifying accounts, and presumably the generic distinction between biography and autobiography implicitly plays some role here. The letter to his father that compares his first autobiographical instalment to Gosse's *Father and Son* describes the former as 'less an objective history than a reverie' (26 December 1914; *CL Intelex* 2571) – and of course *Reveries Over Childhood and Youth* was to become its published title.

As we soon shall see, the autobiographical reveries are not all that removed from the supernatural process of 'dreaming back' that Yeats claimed, in *A Vision*, follows after our deaths. In any case, by describing his memoirs as akin to 'reveries', he is signalling a robust – if implicitly also defensive – denial of strict realism. Here there is precedent in George Moore's writings: Yeats described Moore's attack on his own circle in the *English Review* – titled 'Yeats, Lady Gregory and Synge' – as a report which to a large degree consisted of 'mere novel writing' (*Mem* 269). Moore himself claimed to have composed his autobiographical text 'as if I were writing a novel, and the people in my book are not personalities but human types' (*Mem* n5 269–70). Foster places special emphasis on such parallels, largely casting Moore as the inspiration for not only Yeats's decision to take up autobiography, but also his methods of writing. Emphases on anecdote and reverie can, true enough, be found in the three volumes that together constitute Moore's autobiographical tome on the Irish Revival, *Hail and Farewell*, and the self-indulgent admission that 'documentary evidence jars my style' is evocative of the method, if not quite the tone, of Yeats's autobiographies.[11] Yet although Yeats will to a certain degree use the form of reverie, or freely adapted memoir, as the kind of weapon he can use to fight his enemies on equal terms – Moore had stressed that 'We writers know how to get the knife under the other fellow's ribs'[12] – it is surely too simplistic to explain his choice of form as exclusively resulting from internal Irish battles.

If a critic such as Wayne Chapman can unravel a complicated adaptive complex lurking behind single lines of Yeats's poetry, then surely a wider range of reference than one single author (e.g. George Moore) is needed to contextualize Yeats's autobiographical works. To refer back to Genette's distinction, mentioned in the introduction to this study, between different kinds of transtextual relations: a text does not solely get its bearings on the basis of intertextuality (through, for instance, allusions to earlier works), but is also constituted by other relations – including what he calls 'architextuality'. Genette defines architextuality as 'the entire set of general or transcendent categories – types of discourse, modes of enunciation, literary genres – from which emerges each singular text.'[13] Genre is particularly relevant here: seen in a larger context, Yeats's memoirs can be understood as taking their place in the post-Victorian development of autobiography, at a point of crisis for the genre.[14] Harold

Nicolson once commented that Froude's use of satire constituted the first stirrings of 'the peculiar brand of sceptical detachment which we realize to be the main element in twentieth-century biography.'[15] To isolate Yeats and Moore from this development, and pass by their common ground with a landmark work such as Strachey's *Eminent Victorians*, runs the risk of not only overlooking relevant influences but also of marginalizing them as idiosyncrasies alien to some phantasmal and ahistorical fiction of biographical objectivity. Certainly the reaction against Victorianism should not be underestimated. Yeats's contemporary Virginia Woolf once characterized the 'the majority of Victorian biographies' as being 'like the wax figures now preserved in Westminster Abbey, that were carried in funeral processions through the street – effigies that have only a smooth superficial likeness to the body in the coffin.'[16] Woolf's own experiments with the forms of both biography and autobiography grew out of her frustration with the limitations of Victorian life narratives. This does not mean, though, that Victorian autobiography was a completely static or uniform phenomenon. Linda H. Peterson has shown how positivism challenged the unifying heritage of Biblically inspired autobiography during the Victorian age, and with Gosse's *Father and Son*, published in 1907, she claims this tradition was finally plunged into a decisive crisis. Gosse's text reflected a fundamental generic disarray, in which a patchwork of 'discrete scientific and literary interpretations' substituted for 'a comprehensive biblical system'.[17] Hence *Father and Son* does more than demonstrate a generational gap; it also marks, in Peterson's account, a crucial point of crisis in the development of the autobiographical genre.

In light of this, Yeats's comparison of *Reveries* to Gosse's text – in the letter cited earlier in this chapter – is more significant than it might seem at first sight. Not only do both texts feature Oedipal dramas of the familiar Victorian kind (although the irresponsible John Butler Yeats hardly fits in with the typical cliché of a Victorian father), they also share a sense of wanting to anchor their fragmented memories in some sort of memory harbour. In Peterson's reading, the challenge for Gosse is to ensure textual cohesion in the default of having a single interpretative paradigm sufficiently powerful to function on its own. His book 'empties the hermeneutic system' upon which the typical episodes of spiritual autobiography depend for their authority, and allows this authority to be 'dispersed to a variety of interpretive strategies'.[18]

Yeats, too, varies his autobiographical schemas, as he allows spiritual autobiography to interact with a more collective account of the history of a generation, while the development of a personal self overlaps with the development of a national identity. Yet his text is marked by a more fundamental form of fragmentation in how it unfolds a challenge to the organic notion of a unified life. In Peterson's account, a major division in Victorian autobiography is between the cohesiveness of a hermeneutical model and the more fragmented result of the analytical methodology of the scientifically informed approaches. Charles Darwin's *Autobiography* (1876) exemplifies the latter strand in how it allows some details to float free from the general movement of the life narrative, having the status of 'facts [that] remain random data'.[19] One could of course argue that Yeats's tendency away from chronology reflects an unacknowledged borrowing from this tradition, and that Yeats thus represses his own debt to the positivistic approach to autobiography – but that would be to surrender to the prejudice, often found in hermeneutical thought, that all sense of alienation or disjointedness has to be explained as the consequence of a scientific worldview. It seems more meaningful to follow Ian Fletcher in making a link to Walter Pater's understanding of personal experience. In a reading of Yeats's autobiographical practice, Fletcher has claimed that Pater influenced Yeats in how he 'distinguished the "moment" as the unit of experience, isolated, absolute, flexible, in protest against the "positive" fiction of a stable world.'[20] This emphasis would have a major impact on the modernist conception of the image, and it has also left traces in Yeats's memoirs. In the imaginary portrait of 'The Child in the House', Pater presented the authentic memory as being an isolated instant in a dream: 'the finer sort of memory, bringing its object to mind with a great clearness, yet, as sometimes happens in dreams, raised a little above itself, and above ordinary retrospect.'[21] Although Yeatsian reverie does not exclusively fix upon such commemorative epiphanies, it is open to upsetting chronology and narrative in order to fasten on the luminous detail. *Reveries over Childhood and Youth* begins, for instance, in the following fashion:

> My first memories are fragmentary and isolated and contemporaneous, as though one remembered some first moments of the Seven Days. It seems as if time had not yet been created, for all thoughts are connected with emotion and place without sequence. (*CW3* 41)

In these first memories there is little sense of there being an ordered sequence, 'for all these events seem at the same distance' (*CW3* 49). Although *Reveries* is soon marked by an increasing tendency towards narrative and protracted anecdote, the fragmentation persists in disturbing and disorienting the process even after Yeats's first years. A supernatural story from his youth is introduced as follows: 'At Ballisodare an event happened that brought me back to the superstitions of my childhood. I do not know when it was, for the events of this period have as little sequence as those of childhood' (*CW3* 88).

   In detailing such memories, Yeats is effectively breaking apart the organic whole of his life story in the very process of constructing it. The randomness of sudden revelations interrupts and addles his desire to construct an ordered, mythological whole. In their sudden and unmotivated manner, such memories have something epiphanic, and indeed also mythological, about them. Foster has pointed to another influence on Yeats's early forays into autobiographical prose, namely Joyce's *A Portrait of the Artist as a Young Man*, and it seems safe to say that the Joycean parallel is relevant to how Yeats's text straddles the mythological and the structurally modernist in its deployment of fragmentary structure. It certainly provides a counterweight to the influence of Balzac, and is a point of divergence between Yeats and his biographer; as was noted in the previous chapter, both Foster and Yeats look to the nineteenth-century novel for a kind of paradigm for their writings (in Trollope and Balzac, respectively), but it appears their ways part where the poet is also willing to take on the compositional challenge of integrating later modernist developments into the texture of his practice of life writing. Here indeed it is Foster, not Yeats, who to some extent cleaves to a 'nineteenth-century framework'.[22]

The disjointedness of isolated moments is also characteristic of some of Yeats's less-studied attempts at autobiography, particularly the intriguing diary entries written from 1909. Ian Fletcher decided to ignore not only these diaries, but also some other short biographical sketches by Yeats, on the grounds that these are not 'less important, but because they are less consciously historical, more disjunct, aphoristic, the raw material for composed autobiography'.[23] Yet given Yeats's penchant for the Paterian moment, it seems too simplistic to dismiss these as unfinished material merely waiting for a more artistic working over. The Irishman may desire *muthos*, but he is certainly also pulled towards a very modern form of fragmentation. This fragmentation is evident not only in the internal structure of some of his memoirs, but also – as we have seen earlier – in his tendency to publish discrete and shortish instalments of biographical writing. In the irregular stop–start rhythm of the writing of these instalments, one can locate an even more radical challenge to the form of cohesive life story that Foster and other biographers have tried to construct for Yeats. While their divisions of the life into two or three parts only articulate a unity from within, the poets' own more diversified approach arguably goes beyond unity.

Forerunners such as Pater and Joyce are no doubt important in terms of why Yeats fastens onto the isolated memory fragment, but one could argue that they only assist him towards uncovering what is actually an essential, though often overlooked, element in all reminiscence. For Claire Lynch, the 'fragmentary and anecdotal' quality of some of Yeats's autobiographical writings is due to their being 'structured as they might naturally occur in memory'.[24] More generally, Edward Casey has argued that details of memory frequently are so 'dispersed and disjointed' that 'we cannot claim that all remembered content has even an implicit narrative structure'.[25] An unorthodox autobiography such as *Roland Barthes par Roland Barthes* takes this kind of realization as part of its justification for its fragmentary form, and its desire to form something like 'a book of haiku'.[26] One should perhaps resist making Yeats into some kind of spontaneous phenomenologist of memory, though. Not only is historical contextualization important and necessary, in addition every account of a seemingly personal experience must at least partially be seen from the vantage point of a more comprehensive project of establishing and reinventing a poetical persona.

This process is related to yet another divergence from more traditional forms of biography. Towards the end of his life, Yeats's processes of reinvention were increasingly fuelled by the desire for a new simplicity. In order to write creatively, he felt he had to cleanse himself of old ties and worries. This desire is expressed in a generalized form towards the end of *Dramatis Personae*: 'A writer must die every day he lives, be reborn, as it is said in the Burial Service, an incorruptible self, that self opposite of all that he has named "himself"' (*CW3* 336). Especially his retiring from the Senate was linked to this cathartic desire. Thus a letter to Olivia Shakespear, dated 23 February 1928, anticipates the end of his tenure in the Senate in the following terms: 'Once out of Irish bitterness I can find some measure of sweetness and of light, as befits old age – already new poems are floating in my head, bird songs of an old man, joy in the passing moment, emotion without the bitterness of memory' (*CL Intelex* 5079). The beginning of this excerpt significantly echoes 'Sailing to Byzantium': 'Once out nature I shall never take / My bodily form from any natural thing' (*VP* 408; *CW1* 198). Although the sentiment of the letter is less lofty than this poem, it too evokes a form of poetical transcendence that links up in significant fashion with the ageing poet's desire to escape 'the bitterness of memory'.

A little later in the same year, a joyous Yeats tells John Masefield that 'now that I am free of the Senate [. . .] I am at peace. There is now no reason why my shade should walk after I am buried'.[27] This is a striking conflation between Yeats's personal life and his esoteric thought, showing that the notion of a protracted afterlife has more than a literal application. On a later occasion, Yeats repeated this view in a slightly modified way. As Foster writes: 'A year before Gregory's death WBY had told his mesmerized interviewer in London, "if you don't express yourself you walk after you're dead. The great thing is to go empty to your grave." '[28] According to Yeats's mystical thought, a soul that has not fully resolved its conflicts in life has to go through a prolonged period re-enacting its memories – the so-called 'Dreaming Back' phase, followed by the more distant process of 'Return' – before it can move on in the great scheme of things. Yeats frequently returned to this mystical idea in his later work, with particular effect in the play *Purgatory*. It therefore amounts to more than an exclusively esoteric idea, only applicable to life after death. Yeats is also very much concerned on a mundane, day-to-day basis with the desire to rid himself of excess baggage – particularly in terms of memories – that can obstruct the possibility of development and new acts of creativity.[29]

One might be forgiven for suspecting that a repeated recourse to memory need not be the obvious route to leaving behind one's past – and certainly one should not over-simplify what are very complex and multifarious acts of commemoration. Yet Yeats's autobiographies are, from the beginning, partially motivated by a desire to put his ghosts finally to rest by summoning them for one last time. Thus the preface to *Reveries over Childhood and Youth*, pointedly dated 'Christmas Day, 1914' starts off like this: 'Sometimes when I remember a relative that I have been fond of, or a strange incident of the past, I wander here and there till I have somebody to talk to. Presently I notice that my listener is bored; but now that I have written it out, I may even begin to forget it all' (*CW3* 39).[30] Although the tone is a little too ingenuous for one to take Yeats at face value here – for this is surely just as much a defensive forestalling of criticism as an instance of personal confession – his insistence upon his own personal needs should not be dismissed out of hand. The autobiographical writings can, in part, be understood as contributing to a concerted attempt to direct and control his own heritage. Both Yeats and Gregory use their life stories to counteract – in Foster's words – how 'Irish history since 1916 had taken a direction which threatened to marginalize and make redundant their enterprise of creating a common culture that would be pluralist, avant-garde, English-speaking yet distinctively Irish'.[31] Yet Yeats also has other motivations, closer to home, and one of them is a hope that he might even 'begin to forget it all' by fixing his life in writing. Thus after writing *The Trembling of the Veil*, he claims that 'this memoir writing makes me feel clean, as if I had bathed and put on clean linen. It rids me of something and I shall return to poetry with a renewed simplicity' (to Olivia Shakespear, 1 August 1921; *CL Intelex* 3958).

Although Yeatsian autobiography is just as much an exercise in comedy as in tragedy, the notion of catharsis – to be revisited in Chapter 7 – is very apposite here. Yeats writes recollective texts not only in order to monumentalize and appropriate the past, but also as a concerted attempt to leave it behind. Autobiography becomes a movement of both memory and forgetting. It assumes in Yeats's hands a radically different function with regard to commemoration than the one that predominates Foster's biography. Where the former wants to create an imaginative pattern that both preserves and erases the past, the latter is more concerned with presenting as a rich and manifold a narrative of the day-to-day workings of a life as possible. Foster has effectively created something like a chronological archive that gives us unique access to what Yeats did or thought at every phase of his life. This is an archive of retrievable information, which generally functions in a trustworthy and very useful way – especially useful for scholars. It reflects one half of what Jacques Derrida, in a complex and multifarious discussion that I radically abridge here, has called *archive fever*. Foster's endeavour impressively reflects what Derrida describes as our 'compulsive, repetitive and nostalgic desire for the archive' that also entails 'an irrepressible desire to return to the origin'.[32] For Yeats, an archive of this sort is both desired and repulsed. In some ways, his organicism may be said to spell out the fundamentals of the desire for a unified and systematically structured archive, or what Foster – poking fun at literary incursions into the domain of history – has called 'a sort of universal random memory bank'.[33] At the same time, though, the minimal unit of the modern archive troubles Yeats. The original given of embodied fact is, even when valued as part of the rag and bone shop of his heart, consistently transformed at the very moment Yeats embraces it. And this act of transformation also indicates an irrepressible and compulsive desire to leave the archive completely behind. Derrida has identified a similar duality in Freud's writings, arguing that:

> All the texts in the family and of the period of *Beyond the Pleasure Principle* explain in the end why there is archivization and why anarchiving destruction belongs to the process of archivization and produces the very thing it reduces, on occasion to ashes, and beyond.[34]

There is one poetic passage of Yeats's that resonates especially well with this characteristically Derridean conflation of preservation and destruction, namely the famous ending of the elegiac poem 'In Memory of Eva Gore-Booth and Con Markiewicz', which we encountered in the previous chapter by way of Foster's interpretation. Foster reads the 'innocents and the beautiful' of line 24 of the poem as exclusively referring to the Gore-Booth sisters, who have lost their original blessedness to the stony single-mindedness of their fanatic hearts. Yet in the context of our reading of Yeats's biographical drive, and also in light of (to take but one example) the references to Yeats's former 'pretty plumage' and lost innocence in 'Among School Children' (*VP* 444; *CW1* 220) it is hard not to see the speaker himself as being implicated here:

> The innocent and the beautiful
> Have no enemy but time;
> Arise and bid me strike a match
> And strike another till time catch;

Should the conflagration climb
Run till all the sages know.
We the great gazebo built,
They convicted us of guilt;
Bid me strike a match and blow.

(*VP* 476; *CW1* 237–8)

Although the speaker is undoubtedly in the process of settling some of the historical scores informatively sketched out by Foster's interpretation of this poem, he is also doing more than that. He is expressing a desire to leave time behind, cleansing himself of the archives and heritages that bring so much bitterness with them.[35] This desire for demolition is not an isolated instance in Yeats's work. Indeed, it is a characteristic that links up with Yeats's major concerns with the mask. With regard to the latter, too, the need for forgetting is a powerful impetus:

I think all happiness depends on having the energy to assume the mask of some other self, that all joyous or creative life is a rebirth as something not oneself, something created in a moment and perpetually renewed in playing a game like that of child where one loses the infinite pain of self-realization, a grotesque or solemn painted face put on that one may hide from the terrors of judgment, an imaginative Saturnalia that makes one forget reality. (*Mem* 191)

The otherness of the mask bears in it the promise of oblivion, of leaving the constrictions of the present behind. This may not be the most fashionable side of Yeats – and it certainly is not the most amenable to the needs and consolations of the academic industry – but still it is is an important part of his heritage.

Ancient Frames in *A Vision*

A Vision is one of Yeats's strangest texts. This mystical tract combines poetry, history, art history, astrology, psychology and philosophy in a peculiar way, and presents a tough challenge to interpreters also because its second edition – published in 1937 – includes significant departures from the original, 1925 edition. In both its versions, this is a text that self-consciously frames its own argument. In the latter edition, the remarkable prefatory material collected in 'A Packet for Ezra Pound' repeatedly dwells on the issue of geometrical abstraction, and how the text's doctrines may present an overly austere challenge to the reader. Even before any explicit mention, the opening sentence's evocation of the Rapallo landscape anticipates the spatial frameworks of the main doctrine:

> Mountains that shelter the bay from all but the south wind, bare brown branches of low vines and of tall trees blurring their outline as though with a soft mist; houses mirrored in an almost motionless sea: a verandahed gable a couple of miles away bringing to mind some Chinese painting. (*AVB* 3)

The relationship between the gyres and cones at the heart of *A Vision* and the architecture of Yeats's thought may be construed in two different ways, both suggested by this quotation: will the former provide sheltering solidity for the latter, like the mountains surrounding Rapallo, or will the forbidding abstraction of the gyres and related paraphernalia instead envelop and obscure the text's main contents 'as though with a soft mist'? Later in 'A Packet for Ezra Pound' – which itself, as a framing paratext, exemplifies the very paradox at work here – Yeats goes on to write of the intricate articulations of Pound's *Cantos*, expressing a hope for clarity that also is relevant for his own work: 'I may, now that I have recovered leisure, find that the mathematical structure, when taken up into imagination, is more than mathematical, that seemingly irrelevant details fit together into a single theme' (*AVB* 5). But the later pages of the introduction are full of reservations about the 'arbitrary, harsh, difficult symbolism' that lies at the text's heart (*AVB* 23). Yeats wistfully evokes the possibility of leaving behind the rigors of that symbolism once it is mastered: 'We can (those hard symbolic bones under the skin) substitute for a treatise on logic the Divine Comedy, or some little song about a rose, or be content to live our thought' (*AVB* 24). The skeleton of these 'bones under the skin' is indeed sufficiently bare, for Yeats's sources – the mysterious instructors that allegedly communicated the system via his wife's mediumship – to complain: 'if my mind returned too soon to their unmixed abstraction they would say, "We are starved"' (*AVB* 12).

Are the geometrical and symbolical articulations of *A Vision* an essential framework that upholds the whole – like a spine, say – or is it an external generalization, an abstraction, that can be left behind like the 'coat / Covered with embroideries / Out of old mythologies' in his poem 'A Coat' (*VP* 320; *CW1* 127)? Functioning very much like metaphors – indeed, they are embraced as metaphors in Yeats's poetry – are these framing devices merely external ornamentation, or do they contain valuable heuristic or mimetic force? Yeats was not sure, but he was in any case uneasy. This sense of structural vacillation also affects his deployment of classical philosophy as a source used to elucidate the system. Yeats's use of numerous thinkers of the Platonic tradition can both be explained as innate to the very workings of *A Vision*, and as a superficial philosophical coating added to the firm outlines of a canvas provided by his supernatural instructors. This chapter will pursue the related facets of the difficult issue of framing; it will be more engaged in scrutinizing the multiplicity of structural effects that occur in Yeats's use of Plato, Plotinus and other ancient philosophers, than in providing anything close to an exhaustive summary of actual doctrinal overlaps and discrepancies involved. Jonathan Culler has distinguished between frames and contexts in a way that is relevant here:

> the notion of context frequently oversimplifies rather than enriches discussion, since the opposition between an act and its context seems to presume that the context is given and determines the meaning of the act. We know, of course, that things are not so simple: context is not fundamentally different from what it contextualizes; context is not given but produced; what belongs to a context is determined by interpretive strategies; contexts are just as much in need of elucidation as events; and the meaning of a context is determined by events. Yet when we use the term context we slip back into the simple model it proposes. Since the phenomena criticism deals with are signs, forms with socially-constituted meanings, one might try to think not of context but of the framing of signs: how are signs constituted (framed) by various discursive practices, institutional arrangements, systems of value, semiotic mechanisms?[1]

The framing questions guiding this chapter will be: What role does philosophy have in the system presented by *A Vision*? What kind of thought does Yeats want from his classical philosophers, and how does he relate them to the system already largely established by the mystical instructors that communicated with him via his wife's mediumship? How does Yeats relate to the framing question of genre, for instance in terms of classical precedents such as Platonic dialogues and the fragments of the pre-Socratics? And, finally, how does *A Vision*'s intertextual engagement with Plato, Plotinus and other ancient philosophers relate to the more encompassing ideological frames? Received opinion on the role of classical philosophy in *A Vision* emphasizes that this is an influence especially relevant to the second, 1937 version of Yeats's work. The relative paucity of philosophical references in the earliest version reflects Yeats's respectful subservience to the advice of his instructors, who did not want him to mix up the systems and concepts of others with their own: 'they asked me not to read philosophy until their exposition was complete, and this increased my difficulties. Apart from two or three of the principal Platonic Dialogues I knew no philosophy' (*AVB* 12). Yeats typically accepts a distinction between true instructors and so-called 'frustrators' who deliberately give misleading or erroneous knowledge, but in this respect even the former seem to frustrate him. In retrospect, the lifting of the embargo against philosophy is presented as a liberating experience, the effects of which were felt simultaneously with the 1925 publication of the first version: 'When the proof sheets came I felt myself relieved from my promise not to read philosophy' (*AVB* 19). Even if Yeats exaggerates a little here – after all, both the first edition and the automatic script clearly indicate some philosophical reading took place prior to 1925 – there certainly is a large difference in emphasis between the 1925 and 1937 editions of *A Vision*.[2] When Yeats looks back at that first version, it is with deep misgivings:

> The first version of this book, *A Vision*, except the section on the twenty-eight phases, and that called 'Dove or Swan' which I repeat without change, fills me with shame. I had misinterpreted the geometry, and in my ignorance of philosophy failed to understand distinctions upon which the coherence of the whole depended. (*AVB* 19)

Philosophy, then, is largely a supplementary addition coming after 1925, yet still provides more than mere extraneous scaffolding to Yeats's system. For 'the coherence of the whole' only comes about, only becomes understandable, through philosophical treatment. Interestingly, something of the same doubleness is present even earlier in the gestation of *A Vision*. On a surface level, philosophy might seem to be banished from the proceedings that generated the automatic script, as Yeats obeyed the instructors' embargo. On the other hand, a notebook entry of 11 January 1921 arguably presents Plato as a presiding genius for the foundation of the crucial dichotomy between primary and antithetical phases. Yeats states that

> in a recent sleap [sic] communicator said that all communications such as ours were begun by the transference of an image later from another mind. The image is selected by the daimon from telepathic impacts & one is chosen not necessarily a recent one. For instance the script about black & white horses may have been from Horton who wrote it to me years before. (*YVP3* 65)[3]

The mention of the horses appears the first day of preserved automatic script (5 November 1917) as the instructor Thomas of Dorlowicz's reference to 'one white one black both winged both necessary to you' (*YVP1* 56). According to Yeats's explanation, this again refers even further back, to a scrap of paper presented to him by his friend W. T. Horton, and an automatic script stemming from Edith Lyttelton in 1914, both of which ultimately reach back to Plato's *Phaedrus* and Socrates' allegorical account of the soul in terms of 'the composite nature of a pair of winged horses and a charioteer'.[4]

Despite having a seemingly crucial role for Yeats's system, Plato largely drops out of sight in the automatic script: his dichotomy establishes what might be termed the vital germ or seed for the system, but its contents are subsequently modified and husbanded by seemingly external frameworks. Barring an off-hand reference, in the dedication to the first edition, to Horton's living 'through that strange adventure, perhaps the strangest of all adventures – Platonic love' (*CW13* liii), and a few other passing mentions, Yeats conceals the original importance of Plato's understanding of love to the proceedings of the automatic script. In particular it was crucially linked, at the beginning of the automatic script, to his balancing interpretation of his relations to the most important women of his life. Nevertheless, Plato and the entire mainstream of western philosophy are for the most part conspicuously absent during the automatic sessions – and for a reason. In the script of 1 January 1918, Fish expressed scepticism concerning 'Wisdom of thought', claiming, in a rather Nietzschean vein, that 'a metaphysician is a nihilist not a creator' (*YVP1* 184). On this premise, both Kant and Hegel were said to possess no true wisdom. Yet only days later, on January 14, another instructor made a distinction between different philosophies. Responding to Yeats's question, 'When you are giving me a profound philosophy why do you warn me against philosophy,' Thomas responded: 'I warn you against the philosophy that is bred in stagnation – it is a bitter philosophy a philosophy which destroys – I give you one which leads – I give you one which is from outside – a light which you follow not one which will burn you' (*YVP1* 252). An important, but far from water-tight, distinction is established. At one level it might simply be taken as setting down a clear opposition between the rationalism of academic philosophy and the mysteries of esoteric thought, yet the very use of 'philosophy' as a common term indicates both continuity and room for overlap. The 1937 version of *A Vision* explores this common ground with some diligence, and classical thought will play an especially important role as a kind of thought that is, presumably, 'from outside' – even as it is accepted within the institutional framework of mainstream philosophy.

The framing distinction between inside and outside is germane for an understanding of how philosophy intersects with the thought of *A Vision*. As in the automatic script, large parts of western philosophy are effectively sidelined also in the published versions of Yeats's work. Especially in the second version, classical philosophy looms large, but does so to the detriment of most of the philosophical heritage – with minor exceptions in figures such as Berkeley, Croce and Whitehead – coming after Plotinus. As a result, this means that for instance the important critical philosophy of Kant, as well as modern aesthetics, is simply shunted aside. Insofar as Yeats's philosophical recidivism acknowledges these developments, it is only to dismiss them, instead emphasizing a cosmological tradition, speculating on concrete essences behind universal world processes, that was effectively brought to an end as a central philosophical concern with Kant and his more linguistically oriented successors. For Yeats, however, the benefits probably outweighed any possible drawbacks – for not only do the pre-Socratics, for instance, give him access to a kind of thinking which does not clearly distinguish reason from irrationality, or science from magic, but their thought also permits him to aspire to prophetic powers: 'What if there is an arithmetic or geometry that can exactly measure the slope of a balance, the dip of a scale, and so date the coming of that something?' (*AVB* 29). Yeats's chosen classical philosophers were also eminently qualified to deliver and develop the 'metaphors for poetry' (*AVB* 8) that were supposed to issue out of the system. Never far separated from ontic determinations and mythical narratives, thinkers such as Plato and Empedocles could provide a far more full-flavoured diet than the seemingly murderous abstraction of modern philosophy. This is touched upon in the automatic script, where Yeats uses the relative level of concretion of the 'figurative' symbolism of Platonic myth as a point of reference for understanding the status of the images and diagrams passed on to him by his instructors (*YVP1* 126, 141).

If Yeats's privileging of classical philosophy excludes most later philosophical developments, it is also highly selective within the confines of ancient thought. Within the Greek tradition, Yeats's cosmological bias means that important political and ethical issues, for instance, are marginalized. A major figure such as Aristotle is largely ignored, as Yeats squarely focuses on Plato and his pre-Socratic forerunners. Even within Plato's writings, the Socratic *elenchus* – a form of logical refutation of a position through proving an opposite point – is only one of many important dimensions eschewed or overlooked. A broader focus would have been possible: certainly, the run-through of the 28 incarnations is, for instance, rich enough to open up for interesting echoes of Greek and Roman thought on practical philosophy (particularly with regard to the issue of the good life) and epistemology. Yet after 'Plato and Aristotle', Yeats claims in the historical summary of 'Dove or Swan' section of *A Vision*, the mind was 'exhausted' (*AVB* 272). As a result, Roman thought can be largely ignored and the Stoics can be ingenuously disparaged as 'the first benefactors of our modern individuality, sincerity of the trivial face, the mask torn away' (*AVB* 272).

Yeats wanted to use classical philosophy for other purposes: he especially wanted to use it to buttress his own recourse to framing diagrams. The schematic use of gyres and other geometrical symbols constitutes one of the key deployments of ancient thought in *A Vision*. In the 1925 version, Book II is opened with the poem 'Desert Geometry or the Gift of Harun Al-Raschid', which evokes Parmenides as a possible, but actually erroneous, source:

> The signs and shapes;
> All those abstractions that you fancied were
> From the great Treatise of Parmenides;
> All, all those gyres and cubes and midnight things
> Are but a new expression of her body [. . .]

> (*CW13* 102; *VP* 469)

In the 1937 version, the important two first parts of Book I, 'The Great Wheel', are significantly marked by ancient thought. The opening paragraph features a lengthy quotation of Empedocles on the interplay of Discord and Concord in a single vortex, and goes on to claim (in an imprecise rendering of the forty-fourth fragment, as presented by Burnet) that it was 'this Discord or War that Heraclitus called "God of all

and Father of all, some it has made gods and some men, some bond and some free'"
(*AVB* 67). With this opening, Yeats strikes two keynotes of considerable importance
for his system as a whole; he will create a geometrical system in order to grasp the
underlying patterns of existence, but he will also stress aspects of tension and strife in
the process.

Heraclitus and Empedocles are, however, only used as examples – as it does not
take long for Yeats to point out that linking together one vortex for Concord (which
Yeats later identifies with the objectivity of the *primary Tincture*) with another
for Discord (equated with *antithetical Tincture*) gives 'the fundamental symbol of
my instructors' (*AVB* 68). One gains a sense that classical philosophy is here cast
in a secondary, supporting role, somehow buttressing Yeats's system – a sense not
contradicted by the subsequent quick references to Yeats's favourite quotation from
Heraclitus ('Dying each other's life, living each other's death') and the observation
that the 'first gyres clearly described by philosophy are those described in the
Timaeus' (*AVB* 68).

Hazard Adams has perspicaciously noted the peculiar effect this creates:

> There is something oblique about these predecessors as authorities invoked to
> give status to Yeats's endeavor. Not one of them presents a figure quite like Yeats's
> principal symbol. Empedocles' concord and discord are not quite the same as
> Yeats's primary and antithetical (although it will take a little while for this to
> become clear). Neither is Yeats presenting what verges on a physical theory, as in
> *Timaeus*. Same and other have some relation to primary and antithetical, but it is
> oblique.[5]

The same discrepancy between old and new is evident if one inspects the comparable
passage in the first edition (see *CW13* 106–7). Adams's explanation for this effect,
namely that Yeats wants to contrast his own 'tradition of iconic creativity' with one
of 'dogmatic authority', is less than entirely convincing. The identified problem can
however open up a fruitful line of questioning: it is not quite clear what function
Yeats wishes to give his cited, ancient sources. The common opinion, suggested by
Yeats's own prefatory comments to *A Vision*, has been that the thinkers of the Platonic
tradition are there to bring clarification: Yeats is using the lucidity of those minds to
make his own system more transparent. Not incommensurable with this reading is
the idea, sometimes suggested in passing by Yeats himself, that his own supernatural
instructors actually were inspired by these predecessors. Thus the introduction
presents Empedocles as influence rather than example: 'Although the more I read
[after the first edition] the better did I understand what I had been taught, I found
neither the geometrical symbolism nor anything that could have inspired it except the
vortex of Empedocles' (*AVB* 20). But insofar as the ancient models are subtly different
from those provided by Yeats's instructors, there is a risk of merely further muddying
the waters. Hence the interpretative need for other, supporting explanations, such
as the one provided by Adams in passing here: the ancient thinkers may also have
a legitimizing function. Reaching out to a wider, less exclusively esoteric audience
in the second edition of *A Vision*, Yeats thus brought increased respectability to his

own system and its 'unfashionable gyre' ('The Gyres' *VP* 565; *CW1* 299) through classical references and allusions. Claiming that much of his own system was 'as old as philosophy' (*AVB* 71) would ensure that it avoided any accusation of idiosyncrasy – as well as the incomprehension that dogged William Blake's potentially comparable system. It also ensured that Yeats's system was less vulnerable to being interpreted as being in any way a mere reformulation of Blake's.[6]

Alternatively, Yeats can be seen as effectively testing his theory in light of the wisdom of tradition, using the thought of Empedocles and other classical thinkers as the philosophical equivalent of an Arnoldian touchstone. Rather than simply finding fault with the insufficiency of his precursors, Yeats may in fact be engaged in a process of adjusting his own invention in the light of tradition. Here again these words, quoted earlier in this study, are relevant: 'Talk to me of originality and I will turn on you with rage' (*CW5* 213). Indeed, Yeats may be doing several different things at once. Matthew DeForrest, in a close inspection of Yeats's use of some of the sources for *A Vision*, encapsulates this well when stating that Yeats's 'purpose' in using Plotinus is 'twofold'; it is both an attempt to 'validate his system' and to 'illustrate' the instructors' material 'through an examination of comparable material'.[7] Yeats may on occasion be deflating tradition, but he might just as well be submitting to it as an arbiter in what amounts to a complex double bind. Several rhetorical functions tend to be at work in any given passage, so complex are the shifts of tone and so surprising the juxtapositions one finds in *A Vision*.

If such questions of rhetorical function have previously been relatively neglected, the key doctrinal overlaps between Yeats and the parts of the tradition that he finds relevant to his interests have nevertheless been mapped in some detail. There is a general consensus that a Platonic worldview, with a dualism between spirit and matter, and an important mediating role played by the intermediary beings called *Daimons*, is crucial to *A Vision*. Despite his own intentions, James Olney's overly systematic run-through of Yeats's links to Plato and the pre-Socratic quartet of Pythagoras, Parmenides, Heraclitus and Empedocles makes it obvious that Yeats's interest was not evenly divided; although he respected Pythagoras' geometrical impulse (see for instance the mention of his perfect sphere in *CW13* 107) and made colourful use of Parmenides, as mentioned earlier, in 'The Gift of Harun Al-Raschid', neither of these thinkers really made much of an impact on Yeats's thought in *A Vision*. The relevance of Empedocles's overall conception is, however, hard to dispute: 'the system that Yeats's Instructors revealed to him [. . .] was, at least in its basic configuration and its largest outline, an Empedoclean system of continually alternating half-cycles set in a time without beginning and without end.'[8]

Other commentators have avoided Olney's general dismissiveness towards the Neo-Platonist tradition. Rosemary Puglia Ritvo's close reading of the overlap between the 1937 *Vision* and Plotinus's thought, makes it clear that Yeats's praise for Stephen MacKenna's 'incomparable translation' (*AVB* 20) amounted to far more than window-dressing. She especially demonstrates the detailed concordance that exists between Yeats's four *Principles* (*Husk*, *Passionate Body*, *Spirit* and *Celestial Body*) and Plotinus's metaphysical hypostases,[9] but also for instance points out the crucial agreement between the two with regard to 'the notion of Person at the highest levels of existence'.[10] While engaged in opposing Harold Bloom's gnostic reading of Yeats's thought, Brian Arkins basically affirms Ritvo's central thesis: 'Yeats subscribes to Plotinus's hierarchical world-view, founded on, but by no means identical with, the dualism of Plato'.[11] However, Arkins goes further in highlighting Yeats's small, but important differences from Plotinus – differences which become very important indeed in a poem such as 'News for the Delphic Oracle' (*VP* 611–12; *CW1* 345–6). Where Ritvo asserts in passing that Yeats's *Daimon* is more closely drawn to the sensory world than Plotinus's guiding spirits, Arkins points towards a more general tendency in Yeats to contradict Plotinus's privileging of the spiritual over the material world. In general, Plotinus's stress on unity is counteracted by Yeats's insistence upon the dynamic and conflictual aspects of the pre-Socratics, even using Heraclitus as a stick with which to beat Marxism: 'It is the old saying of Heraclitus, "War is God of all, and Father of all, some it has made Gods and some men, some bond and some free," and the converse of Marxian Socialism' (*AVB* 82n).

Matthew Gibson's recent article on Yeats and classical philosophy shows that Yeats misreads Plotinus, collapsing the individual into the universal, but also points out that this is a creative misreading that is understandable given Yeats's aims.[12] Gibson further provides valuable spade-work on Yeats's use of the ancient idea of the Great Year: he demonstrates how a close reading of Pierre Duhem's modern account of ancient thinkers, such as Proclus and Simplicius, in *Le Système du Monde* informed Yeats's historical scheme, whereby the Great Year was understood to span 26,000 years, involving lesser units of two millennia. This unearthing of the formative importance of a secondary source is in line with Gibson's tendency to stress the mediated nature of Yeats's Platonism, mentioning not only contemporary sources such as Pater and MacGregor Mathers, but also the Cambridge Platonists and Plutarch. This can be taken further, however, as the main focus for Gibson, Arkins, Ritvo and Olney – the existence of similarities and differences between Yeatsian and classical thought – only gains significance from several more encompassing frameworks. These commentators have frequently pointed out that, even while there is general concordance in his prose, Yeats's poetry is less than simply affirmative of the Platonic tradition. Arguably, though, such a neat division presupposes that one reads *A Vision* as a straightforward positing of doctrine, devoid of any of the irony and ambivalence found in Yeats's literary work. Even the central chapters would seem to be informed with a gentle sense of irony, as Yeats – more than once misspelling John Burnet's name, misquoting various sources, and even mixing up Heraclitus and Empedocles on one occasion – engages in an obtuse parody of scholarly prose. It would make more sense to read these metatextual parts of *A Vision* as partially anticipating, say, a work such as Nabokov's *Pale Fire* than simply as a poet's bungling attempt to pull off an alien, academic genre.[13] In 1915, in 'The Scholars' (*VP* 337; *CW1* 141), Yeats had poked fun at the 'Old, learned, respectable bald heads' engaged in literary philology, and that irreverent distance from the scholarly community did not desert him overnight.

The overlap here is not only with the style of contemporary academics, but also with that of the ancient philosophical commentators on Plato and Plotinus that Yeats had studied. Further, the generic diversity of the primary sources also has an effect on *A Vision*. The fragmentary nature of the pre-Socratics' writings can be linked to the elliptical way in which Yeats's system appears to its readers. In the first edition, Owen Aherne writes that the whole philosophy was originally 'expounded in a series of fragments which only displayed their meaning, like one of those child's pictures which are made up out of separate cubes, when all were put together' (*CW13* 11). Of course, the writings of figures such as Heraclitus and Empedocles are fragmentary for a reason; they are handed down to us via the more complete manuscripts of thinkers such as Theophrastus, a student of Aristotle. According to Walter Pater, the rephrasing rearticulation of other thinkers was in fact characteristic of Plato, whom he presents very much as an anticipation of the postmodern *bricoleur*:

> in truth the world Plato had entered into was already almost weary of philosophical debate, bewildered by the oppositions of sects, the claims of rival schools. [. . .] In the *Timaeus*, dealing with the origin of the universe he figures less as the author of a new theory, than as already an eclectic critic of older ones, himself somewhat perplexed by theory and counter-theory.[14]

A view of Plato as more of a mediator of others' ideas than an original purveyor of doctrine may go against the grain for many, but it is actually in line with more recent, postmodern treatments of his *oeuvre*.[15] When Yeats provides extensive prefatory material before the central argument of *A Vision*, hedging his bets and expressing serious reservations about the truth-value of his system, is he really closer to this variant of what he called 'Platonic tolerance' ('Two Songs from a Play', *VP* 438; *CW1* 217) than he would have been if he merely had presented his thoughts in a doctrinal tract in the manner of the *Enneads*? Olney seems to suggest as much:

> Hence, the myth of Aherne, Robartes, the Judwalis, and the Speculum (not to mention the Instructors) that Yeats wraps around his Vision, though he could scarcely be said to keep a very straight face in narrating it, has a kind of daimonic logic of its own, as do all the myths in Plato, and is neither trivial nor outrageous, as might at first seem to be the case.[16]

Thus when Thomas Parkinson puts 'A Packet for Ezra Pound' down as a collection of 'numerous droll and evasive preambles', he is missing an important point.[17] Doubtless Gérard Genette's claim that paratexts can equally well function as 'impediments' as helpful conduits to the main business at hand is amply borne out by the prefatory material of *A Vision*.[18] Yet something more than mere digressive idiosyncrasy is going on here. Whether or not we believe Yeats when he claims, at the end of the 'Introduction to "A Vision"', that the whole system provides no more than 'stylistic arrangement of experience comparable to the cubes in the drawing of Wyndham Lewis and to the ovoids in the sculpture of Brancusi' (*AVB* 25), this expression of suspended disbelief has an illustrious predecessor. If *A Vision* gives him merely a flexible frame through which to perceive the world, it functions rather like mythology did for Socrates. In a passage from the *Phaedrus*, which Yeats himself quoted at the end of an introduction early in his career, Socrates defends his own use of mythology, claiming that he has 'not time for such enquiries' as those made by sceptics who want to explain away the myths.[19] He has use for those latter myths, without worrying about their lack of verifiable truth-value. Something comparable also occurs in Yeats's 1937 discussion of the Great Year. Coming across a number of different interpretations of this concept, Yeats returns to the conception presented in the *Timaeus*: 'Plato may have brought such an ideal year into the story, its periods all of exactly the same length, to remind us that he dealt in myth' (*AVB* 212–13). Yeats's section on 'The Completed Symbol' constantly worries about the discrepancy between symbol and reality, and it is Plato's obviously playful stance that leads the Irishman to a point of crisis: 'Will some mathematician some day question and understand, as I cannot, and confirm all, or have I also dealt in myth?' (*AVB* 213).

The open-ended form of the Platonic dialogue plays a significant role in Yeats's later poetic output, finding a modern analogue in the dialogue between Owen Aherne and Michael Robartes that appears at the beginning of *A Vision*. Margaret Mills Harper has emphasized what she calls the 'dialogic method' of the automatic script that preceded the writing of *A Vision*, but it is possible to see the tentative and exploratory nature of this genre as infecting the final product of the latter work, too.[20] Initially, of course, the ideas on which it built were meant to be presented (as Yeats stated in a letter to John Quinn) in 'a dialogue in the manner of Landor' (29 November 1917; *CL Intelex* 3367). There may have been more than a trace of anxiety of influence to explain Landor's dislike of Plato – but in any case Yeats was, in his own fashion, adapting both of their examples in toying with the genre.

In a reading of how frames operate in Kant's aesthetics, Jacques Derrida claims that 'what has produced and manipulated the frame puts everything to work in order to efface the frame effect'.[21] The self-conscious bravado with which Yeats framed his use of the ancient philosophers makes sure we never lose sight of the fact that his access to them was never immediate. He may at times have believed he was engaged in an *anamnesis* of timeless truths, of a kind sketched by Pater: 'Pythagoreanism too, like all the graver utterances of primitive Greek philosophy, is an instinct of the human mind itself, and therefore also a constant tradition in its history, which will recur.'[22] Yet Yeats's understanding was embedded in concrete horizons of understanding, and even his intentions in, say, quoting a pre-Socratic fragment were to some degree building on established conventions. As a member of the Golden Dawn and a long-time student of theosophy, for instance, Yeats would have had the precedent of other recent esoteric literature at the back of his mind while writing *A Vision*. In Madame Blavatsky's *The Secret Doctrine*, for instance, we read:

> It was not Zeno alone, the founder of the Stoics, who taught that the Universe evolves, when its primary substance is transformed from the state of fire into that of air, then into water, etc. Heracleitus of Ephesus maintained that the one principle that underlies all phenomena in Nature is fire. The intelligence that moves the Universe is fire, and fire is intelligence. And while Anaximenes said the same of air, and Thales of Miletus (600 years BC) of water, the Esoteric Doctrine reconciles all those philosophers by showing that though each was right the system of none was complete.[23]

Yeats's former spiritual teacher also quotes figures such as Plato and Pythagoras quite copiously. Another important esoteric forerunner, MacGregor Mathers's *The Kabbalah Unveiled*, similarly appropriates Pythagoras to his cabalistic purposes.[24] While one should not underestimate important differences in both purpose and detail – Madame Blavatsky does not, for instance, refer to Plotinus at all, having no Stephen MacKenna to inspire her – there is something of a generic precedent for Yeats's work here. Graham Hough's insistence on how Yeats's thought takes place within an occult heritage is still valid, and *A Vision* must be read as a text that at least partially places itself within an existing literary tradition of that particular heritage.[25]

As a result of that ancestry, Yeats's use of classical philosophy places itself in the very outer margins of British Hellenism – an ideological framework of considerable importance and scope in the context of the imperial ideology of Victorianism and its aftermath. At one stage in 'The Soul in Judgment' (Book III of the 1937 *A Vision*) Yeats denounces as illusory 'the pure benevolence our exhausted Platonism and Christianity attribute to an angelical being' (*AVB* 230); this is characteristic of an important distance between his own appropriation of ancient thought and that of many others. While figures such as Benjamin Jowett and George Grote expended much energy on reconciling Plato with modern Christianity and morality, for instance finding parallels between the Athenian *polis* and modern British politics, Yeats could approach the Greeks from a rather different perspective.[26] Historically, his stress on Heraclitean flux and strife, as well as Empedoclean circularity, rather than the ideal state of Plato, is indicative of the postwar disillusionment with Victorian ideals that looms so large in a poem such as 'Nineteen Hundred and Nineteen' (*VP* 428–33; *CW1* 210–14). In this respect, Nietzsche – who listed Heraclitus and Empedocles as two of his own most important inspirations – is a significant forerunner.[27] Yeats also situated himself at some remove from the homosexual aestheticism that played such a large role for writers such as Pater, Symonds and Forster,[28] although that movement's cult of beauty – also important for aestheticism during the latter stages of the Victorian era – is closely related to the beautiful bodies and 'immovable trance' (*CW13* 59; *AVB* 136) characteristic of Yeats's Phase Fifteen in *A Vision*.

More unexpectedly, perhaps, the esoteric context of *A Vision* places this work at an oblique angle to one of Yeats's major uses of the classical heritage; it in no way replicates the blatantly nationalist use Yeats made of ancient Greece earlier in his career. At a surface level, and despite the fact that Yeats's attraction to Plotinus was partly motivated by the fact that this philosopher's most eminent modern translator was an Irishman (MacKenna), there is no strong Irish dimension to Yeats's use of the classical past at this stage. Claire Nally has recently argued for a presence of nationalist discourse and themes in *A Vision*, yet this is largely a subterranean affair.[29] Concomitantly with a vastly expanded knowledge of the traditions of western metaphysical thought, this apparent distance to local matters enabled Yeats to reinvent himself as a wide-ranging, philosophical poet of considerable speculative verve, with the kind of international relevance that would merit a Noble Prize, during the later stages of his career. Ultimately, though, he could not withstand the temptation of using this philosophical power as an explicit tool in the ideological struggles within Ireland. In 'The Statues', for instance, the concluding stanza belligerently declares the ancient ancestry of the Irish, using the Easter Rising's upsurge of national identity to contrast the Irish identity's classical roots to the deracinated decadence of the 'filthy modern tide' ('The Statues', *VP* 611; *CW1* 345). For better or for worse, without scrutinizing Plotinus and his Greek predecessors, Yeats might never have had the bravery to confront the particular dogmas he belligerently opposed in his late writings. As he puts it in 'The Need for Audacity of Thought':

> We must consider anew the foundations of existence, bring to the discussion – diplomacies and prudences put away – all relevant thought. Christianity must meet to-day the criticism, not, as its ecclesiastics seem to imagine, of the school of Voltaire, but of that out of which Christianity itself in part arose, the School of Plato [. . .]. (*CW10* 201)[30]

Those philosophical gains are perhaps the most indisputable ones of Yeats's use of classical thought in *A Vision*. Although selective and at times misleading, the philosophical formulation of Yeats's esoteric system is in any case a complex and fascinating phenomenon. It never represents a simple mirroring, or taking over, of timeless truths, but should rather be conceived of as a complex and many-faceted act of mediation. Like Walter Pater before him, Yeats had too much respect for the sensual side of life to not be suspicious of 'the ascetic pride which lurks under all Platonism, resultant from its opposition of the seen to the unseen, as falsehood to truth.'[31] While embracing the dualism and much of the idealism of Plato and Plotinus, he tempered it with the stress on temporal flux and conflict found in the pre-Socratics. Yet classical philosophy did more than supply Yeats with warring dogmas; it also provided him with the precedent of a mode of thinking flexible enough to question its own verities through generic multiplicity, scepticism and sheer ludic energy. Although his approach to them was inevitably subject to numerous conventional and mediational contingencies, Yeats's ancient philosophical sources provided the basis for an invigorating reframing of the concerns endemic to *A Vision*.

Disputing *The Resurrection*

One of the major challenges for someone interpreting Yeats's work consists in figuring out what to do with his self-interpretations. When, as we saw in Chapter 3, R. F. Foster both wants to imitate and to debunk Yeats at one and the same time, it is a confusing but quite understandable response to this quandary. Those metatextual passages and introductions where Yeats comments upon his own work are powerful and enticing. They are also very much part of the Yeatsian *oeuvre*: a rigid distinction between the literary work and more contextual material (such as Yeats's letters, essays and *A Vision*) – whereby one becomes no more than a passive background for the other – is impossible to uphold, as the texts in question overlap and repeat one another. The paratexts impinge upon, indeed sometimes are continuous with, the texts. At the same time, however, the attentive critic will soon become dissatisfied with mere replication of Yeats's explications of his own work. Not only does such a practice smack too much of a mechanical exercise, but it must also quite frequently tie itself into knots in order to avoid remarking evident inconsistencies. Despite their audacious and polemical splendour, Yeats's self-interpretations quite frequently either contradict both themselves and the texts they comment upon, or provide overly simplified accounts of what are actually very complicated textual landscapes.

In this chapter, framing devices concerning architextuality (in the form of genre), paratextuality (in terms of introductory or framing material) and historical context will be shown to complicate any simple account of Yeats's play *The Resurrection*. This dramatic text spends a lot of time depicting religious disputation, and this chapter will show that the very form of the play contributes in no small way to the conflict of interpretations at hand. More generally, Yeats never shied away from conflict in his theatrical work: as a dramatist, he was a fundamentally combative writer. He was concertedly trying to construct a kind of drama that was essentially different from the most accepted modes of his day. The pervasiveness and popularity of the modes he was trying to counter meant that this was a very difficult, indeed some would even say quixotic, endeavour. Hence it is not uncommon to find critics dismissing both Yeats's plays and his ideals, and often this happens with more than a touch of *Schadenfreude*: here was a practice and theory completely out of touch with reality – it is either implied or stated outright – particularly the reality of the Irish audiences Yeats was trying so ineffectually to engage. Thankfully, however, such simplistic notions about the given reality of Yeats's day, and how his drama might relate to it, are not always allowed to remain uncontested. Critics such as Katharine Worth and Michael McAteer have shown – by casting their net widely, and adopting a European rather than strictly Irish context – that if Yeats was out of touch with his own age, it was due to an avant-garde bent that was in fact ahead of its own time.[1]

The radicality of Yeats's challenge to the drama of his time is captured by the outspoken opening of his 1903 Samhain address: 'I think the theatre must be reformed in its plays, its speaking, its acting, and its scenery. That is to say, I think there is nothing good about it at present' (*CW8* 26). There is no doubt that this is a comprehensive challenge to the institutions involved in the business of theatre. In the sense of utter disillusionment with the commercial theatre of his day that is expressed here, it becomes evident that Yeats was in many respects an inheritor of Romanticism. Alienated by the spectacle and melodrama that dominated the popular theatre of their age, romantics such as Blake, Wordsworth, Shelley and Byron turned their back to the stage and constructed instead a 'mental theatre' where artistic questions, rather than pecuniary concerns, were crucial. As Alan Richardson has demonstrated, this turn toward a more internalized and self-conscious form of theatre gave birth to major works – including *The Borderers*, *Manfred* and *Prometheus Unbound* – that remain crucial to our understanding of Romanticism.[2] Although Yeats is more often thought of as an inheritor of the romantics in his poetic rather than his theatrical work,[3] he alluded to this dramatic kinship when writing of his desire for 'a mode of drama Shelley and Keats could have used without ceasing to be themselves, and for which even Blake in the mood of *The Book of Thel* might not have been too obscure' (*Ex* 255).

This general agreement with the romantic turn away from conventional drama has tended to be overshadowed by a more exotic cultural link. Famously, Yeats's embrace of a more radically internalized form of theatre in the second half of his career is irrevocably associated with his fascination with Japanese Noh drama: the latter would provide him with a separate means of access to the 'deep of the mind' sought by the romantics (*CW4* 165). Working with Ezra Pound in the country seclusion of Stone Cottage at Ashdown Forest, Yeats became enthralled by the American's work on Ernest Fenollosa's unpublished notes on the Japanese theatre form.[4] This provided a key impetus for a turning point in Yeats's career as a dramatist, the Noh influence being particularly evident in the plays brought together in *Four Plays for Dancers* (1921): *At the Hawk's Well*, *The Only Jealousy of Emer*, *The Dreaming of the Bones* and *Calvary*. But also other works in his later oeuvre have been linked – both by Yeats and his critics – to the technical innovations gleaned from the Noh.

The influence of Noh theatre on Yeats goes against the grain of one of the most powerful articulations of generic innovation in twentieth-century literary theory. He arguably found common cause with Pound, who in 'A Station at the Metro' and the Chinese translations included in *Cathay* revivified western poetry by immersing himself in eastern conventions. Neither quite fits in with the template provided by the Russian Formalists, who claimed that the most important generic innovations came about through the adoption of popular genres in high-brow literature: the insertion of conventional traits from the crime fiction, for instance, led to a defamiliarization of the serious novel. Another Russian Formalist argument, provided by Yuri Tynyanov, looks outside of literature for the source of generic innovation: 'Art finds the phenomena it needs in the field of everyday *life*.'[5] As we saw in Chapter 2, though, Yeats's writings include no straightforward embrace of everyday life. His turn to Noh theatre is a complex manoeuvre – and might be said to fit in with another Formalist notion, which roots generic innovation in the vivification of elements that are marginalized in a tradition[6] – but it cannot be said to provide change through the adoption of popular art or everyday life.

Noh is a traditional Japanese theatre genre, distinctive from both modern forms and other traditional forms such as Bunraku and Kabuki. As an inherently conservative genre, it is not an obvious source of radical modernist experimentation. But then there is agreement among critics that Yeats did not seek, let alone achieve, a simple copying of Noh convention. He adapted the form for his own purposes, choosing – in a kind of generic *bricolage* – particular features in order to arrive at his own template. In the words of Augustine Martin:

> He had a radical vision of theatrical possibility and the Noh was his inspiration. From it he took all the elements he needed for his new genre – the sense of religion and ritual, the sacredness of place, the omnipresence of the supernatural, custom and ceremony, the eloquence of gesture, mime, dance, the dramatic power of silence and stillness; above all, perhaps, an impersonality which would replace the modern naturalistic preoccupation with character and personal idiosyncrasy.[7]

Andrew Parkin – who argues persuasively that Yeats's enthusiasm for Noh drama was prepared by preceding exposure to related Japanese influences – makes a similar point when he comments that Yeats 'was not merely trying to replicate original Noh plays in English', and that the result was a 'new genre' where eastern and western impulses engaged with one another.[8]

Once one tries to more fully elucidate the transfers and combinations involved in this meeting of East and West, a complex generic make-up comes into focus. In his important introduction to *Certain Noble Plays of Japan: From the Manuscripts of Ernest Fenollosa, Chosen and Finished by Ezra Pound, With an Introduction by William Butler Yeats* (published by Cuala Press in September 1916), Yeats is less than completely consistent on precisely how trailblazing his own form is. At the very end of the introduction, he states that he is 'adapting for European purposes' a foreign form (*CW4* 173). At the beginning of the same text, however, he swaggeringly claims that 'with the help of Japanese plays "translated by Ernest Fenollosa and finished by Ezra Pound", I have invented a form of drama' (*CW4* 163). It is interesting that Yeats here singles out the individual plays of Noh drama, rather than the conventions of the form, as providing the impetus behind his own work: subsequent scholarship has revealed that even if Yeats's knowledge of the extensive repertoire of Noh plays was relatively limited, specific plays such as *Nishikigi* and *Aiono-ue* played a formative role as exemplars for his own works.[9] Equally notable, though, is Yeats's claim that he 'invented' an individual form on the basis of Noh. This is a strong statement, accentuating the poet's imaginative powers and the autonomy of his creation. The same introduction casts that autonomy in a more modest light, though, expressing Yeats's desire to 'record all discoveries of method and [then subsequently] turn to something else. It is an advantage of this noble form that it need absorb no one's life, that its few properties can be packed up in a box or hung upon the walls where they will be fine ornaments' (*CW4* 163–4).

The insistence upon the simplicity of staging reflects Yeats's disillusionment with the overly lavish and complicated staging of contemporary plays: one of the reasons why he had been attracted to Edward Gordon Craig's screens lay in the flexible simplicity they provided on this score. Implicitly, there is also a suggestion here that Yeats felt that adopting a specific genre would make the process of composition a less complicated business. He had already spent many years writing and rewriting plays such as *The Shadowy Waters* and *The Player Queen*. Yeats's attention to detail is well-known, and the claim in 'Adam's Curse' that 'A line will take us hours maybe' was no idle boast (*VP* 204; *CW1* 78). Such verbal perfectionism was time-consuming enough on its own; when it was coupled with an uncertainty about the general generic framework of his plays the result was a great drain of time and energy. Inevitably, there was a sense of liberation when 'the conventions used in *At the Hawk's Well* gave him a new genre with a format that greatly helped to speed up his writing process.'[10] But the claim that 'this noble form [...] need absorb no one's life' adds another dimension: Yeats is suggesting, at a very early stage of his engagement with Noh drama, that this new genre is easily left behind. Rather like Beckett's sense of writing in French as an exercise that provided him with a freer, more distant relation to language than writing in English, it would seem that Yeats is here relishing a sense of aesthetic detachment. Unlike other forms with which he is more at home, the dance play constructed with the help of Noh comes without too much native baggage; in adapting a traditional Japanese form to his own purposes, then, Yeats is allowed to be both a traditionalist and a more unfettered and fancy-free poet in the modernist mould.

The introduction to *Certain Noble Plays of Japan* casts Yeats's new genre as a fusing of western and eastern impulses. A significant instance of overlap between West and East occurs when the economy of the Japanese form is interpreted along lines provided by Pound's Imagism. Here Yeats is circumspect, asking whether he is being 'fanciful in discovering in the plays themselves (few examples have as yet been translated and I may be misled by accident or the idiosyncrasy of some poet) a playing upon a single metaphor, as deliberate as the echoing rhythm of line in Chinese and Japanese painting' (*CW4* 171). Classical Greek drama also enters the equation, but in a more complex fashion: on the one hand, Yeats follows Fenollosa – who described Noh as a 'form of drama, as primitive, as intense, and almost as beautiful as the ancient Greek drama at Athens'[11] – in using parallels between Noh and Greek tragedy as a means of legitimizing the former. At the same time, though, there is a latent tendency to allow the Greek precedent to usurp the position of both Noh and Yeats's own invention. Yeats refers to the 'half-Asiatic Greece' of Kallimachos, thus implicitly showing that ancient Greece anticipated his own blending of West and East. The opening of the introduction also interprets the Irish mythological hero Cuchulain, as he is bodied forth in *At the Hawk's Well* (Yeats's first use of the new form), as someone who 'will appear perhaps like an image seen in reverie by some Orphic worshipper' (*CW4* 163). Furthermore, specific features of Yeats's new form – such as his use of masks and chorus, his proximity to religious rite and evocation of the sacredness of place – are almost equally reminiscent of Greek drama as of Japanese Noh. The tragic tenor and plot structure of his plays – which will be addressed in greater depth in the next chapter – hearkens more exclusively to the Greek tradition. In the latter respect, as Masaru Sekine and Christopher Murray have pointed out, 'he ignored or refused to take up, the harmonious blend of Shinto and Buddhism which permeated the Noh plays that he took as models: religious optimism was omitted.'[12]

Japanese and Greek influences overlap with others. Although the high point of Yeats's use of a decidedly Shakespearean idiom was reached with the blank verse *On Baile's Strand* in 1904, discoveries made in that play – as well as Elizabethan theatre conventions in general – remained reference points later on.[13] Cooperation with Craig had led Yeats to adopt European avant-garde stage practices, involving a various weave of realist, symbolist and expressionist impulses.[14] Part of this avant-garde tendency was informed by a desire to let medieval commedia dell'arte practices move theatre into a more non-mimetic direction. Furthermore, as will be demonstrated later in this chapter, Yeats also never completely left behind the heritage of 1890s *fin de siècle*, showing (among other things) a long-term sensitivity to the example of Oscar Wilde's plays. Generically the result of all these influences working at the same time is a rare complexity and over-determination. Noh may be the most important new influence on Yeats's mid-career drama, but the plays themselves are irreducibly plural in their generic make-up.

The very act of mixing genres is often considered a heritage of Romanticism, and it is one of the many virtues of David Duff's *Romanticism and the Uses of Genre* that it provides a nuanced way of talking about the combination or co-existence of several genres in one literary work. Building upon the romantic theories of Friedrich Schlegel, Duff suggests a distinction between what he calls 'rough-mixing' and 'smooth-mixing'. Whereas smooth-mixing provides an organic blend, where the constituent genres lose their individuality in forging a new entity, the rough kind of combination is more explicitly hybrid: in the latter, 'the joins are visible' and the individual parts are experienced as juxtaposed rather than fused.[15] In the case of Yeats's drama, the mixing at work is perhaps too complex to be fully comprehended by this opposition. In one sense the result is a 'smooth' mix, since the plays – apart, perhaps from the combination of tragic and comic elements that will be addressed in the next chapter – usually can be experienced as highly concentrated, unified works of art. At the same time, the *effects* of the mixing may as it were be 'rough'. If several genres overlap in a particular passage or technique, the result of that instance may vary depending upon which genre is identified. Thus, to take an example provided above, the 'innerness' of Yeats's dance plays is liable to be interpreted in rather different ways, depending upon whether one reads it as resulting from the spiritual ideals of Noh theatre (which are largely Buddhist) or as a heritage of romantic subjectivity. The frame may be innocuous and smooth to the point where it blends in with its environment, while nevertheless issuing in a sharp 'roughness' at a crucial interpretative juncture.

The roughness of diverging frames – both generic and paratextual – will be at the heart of the following reading of *The Resurrection,* a play written in the aftermath of Yeats's most intense engagement with Noh. For after *Four Plays for Dancers,* Yeats's relation to Noh certainly became more distant. Notwithstanding the particular exception of *The Cat and the Moon* (which is related to the comic Noh form called *Kyogen*), none of his later plays fit quite as comfortably into the template established by *At the Hawk's Well*. Liam Miller describes this as the end of 'his apprenticeship to the Nō theatre', remarking that Yeats 'never again approached his classical model in the mood of reverent imitation in which he had conceived his earlier works in the form.'[16] Yeats did not, however, make a radical turn away from tradition *tout court*. If anything, the formative influences of later plays such as *The Resurrection* are even more complex, more multifarious, than what is the case with *Four Plays for Dancers*.

A crucial issue for the following reading of *The Resurrection* will be how content signifies by formal means. The content in question is of a religious nature: where the previous chapter asked how Greek a text *A Vision* really was, the crucial question here will be: How Christian is *The Resurrection*? In a discussion of this play, Harold Bloom has suggested that 'In some sense that Yeats would not altogether acknowledge, the play hesitates upon the threshold of becoming Christian drama.'[17] Yeats is known to have devoted much of his adult life to esoteric forms of occult mysticism and eastern forms of thought distant from conventional Christianity, so the idea that he might, in this play, have been of the Saviour's party without knowing it is an arresting one. The suggestion gains added heft if one takes into account that it contradicts Bloom's overarching reading of Yeats as a gnostic, as well as – more tangentially – the gist of his claim that the title of 'The Second Coming' is 'not only a misnomer, but a misleading and illegitimate device for conferring upon the poem a range of reference and imaginative power that it does not possess, and cannot sustain.'[18] Since Bloom tends to stress the distance separating Yeats from conventional Christianity, then, it becomes particularly interesting when he suggests a sense of doctrinal proximity. In approaching the alleged Christianity of *The Resurrection*, special emphasis will be given here to the notion of a 'threshold' referred to by Bloom in passing. In line with the interpretative strategy used in Chapter 5, particular attention will be given to the way in which various frameworks – involving Yeats's compositional process, genres, historical contexts and spatial articulation – serve to complicate our understanding of the play. Throughout, connections will be made with Oscar Wilde's *Salomé*, highlighting both similarities and differences between Yeats and this classic expression of late Victorian decadence.

Yeats's relationship to Christianity went through several phases, and is seldom completely extricable from the varying political situation in Ireland. In his autobiographies, he writes of his sorrow for how his artist father deprived him of his childhood faith. As a young writer in the 1890s, Yeats shared a fascination with Catholicism with other Decadent figures and friends from the London-based Rhymers' Club. In his case, this was politically tinged by the baggage that came with his own Protestant background: seeking to unearth a collective cultural identity in the Irish Revival involved attempting to transcend one's own specific horizons in order to achieve a common perspective (in some ways analogous to the religiously inclusive perspective of Wolfe Tone and the United Irishmen of the 1798 rising).[19] Later, Catholic reaction against *The Countess Cathleen* and the values of other early plays of the new Abbey Theatre, led Yeats to a stronger sense of alienation from particularly the organized forms of Catholicism. By this time, Nietzsche's influence had pushed Yeats towards a view that coupled Christianity and middle-class mediocrity as symptoms of the decay of modern society. At the same time, though, Yeats's life-long distaste for rationalism and materialism meant that Christianity and other religions – being enemies of his enemies, so to speak – were always prone to be drawn in as fellow interlocutors in an on-going internal dialogue on the nature of spiritual reality. This is perhaps most openly acknowledged in the eighth section of the poem 'Vacillation' (1932), where an opening question signals his affinity with the modern Catholic theologian Baron Friedrich von Hügel: 'Must we part, Von Hügel, though much alike for we / Accept the miracles of the saints and honour sanctity?' (*VP* 503; *CW1* 256).

Yeats's most significant treatments of Biblical narratives concerning the life of Christ are to be found in *The Resurrection* and *Calvary*. First published in 1920, the latter play adopts an uncompromisingly oppositional stance towards the Biblical message. Rather than instantiating a process of purgational suffering, Jesus's travails on Calvary are interpreted as a series of collisions with facets of existence alien to Christian doctrine. The opening song declares that 'God has not died for the white heron' (*VPl* 780; *CW2* 329). During the rest of the play, Lazarus, Judas and three gambling Roman soldiers follow suit with the heron, all denying, in one way or another, Christ's relevance for their lives. The conflict of the play corresponds with Yeats's division, in *A Vision*, of existence into two opposing spheres – the primary and the antithetical: as Christ belongs exclusively to the selfless and objective primary side of existence, his example and message is without consequence for the self-expressive and subjective side that makes up the other half. Yeats openly acknowledged that he found the germ of *Calvary* in Oscar Wilde's prose poem 'The Doer of Good'. Wilde's drama is also of vital importance for Yeats, as is the entire context provided by how 'the theatre of the late-1880s and 1890s made a decisive break with its earlier Victorian character.'[20] The specific case for the influence of Wilde's play *Salomé* on Yeats's later dramatic output has been convincingly made in an article by Noreen Doody.[21] Doody makes no reference to *The Resurrection*, however, even if there are notable similarities between the play and *Salomé*. *The Resurrection* is certainly different from *Calvary*: where the earlier play depicts the sufferings of an ineffectual Christ (blamed even by Lazarus), the later play turns the perspective around, making him the powerful vehicle of a bewildering and paradigm-altering epiphany for others. The difference does not entail that Yeats simply has left the system of *A Vision* behind – while working on the first draft, he in fact described the play as 'a sort of overflow' from *A Vision* (to Lady Gregory, 11 May 1925; *CL Intelex* 4725) – but there is a change in emphasis that poses compositional and interpretative challenges. Whereas *Calvary* presents the limitations of Christianity internally in the plot, as a difference in purpose between Christ and other characters of the play, in *The Resurrection* the acts of delimitation tend to be subtler and more marginal – mainly by means of textual hints that the Christian dispensation is only valid for a certain historical era.

How does *The Resurrection* display its Wildean lineage? The play shares with *Salomé* the use of Biblical narrative as its basis. As was the case with Wilde's play, which was banned from the English stage soon before its planned premiere in 1892, this placed obstacles in the way of early performance. In the introduction to the 1931 version, Yeats admits that he early on saw 'that its subject-matter might make it unsuited for the public stage in England or in Ireland' (*VPl* 901) – and British censorship laws did not, in fact, allow any representation of Christ on stage. Yeats had previously been pleased by the fact that the lack of official censorship in Ireland had made it possible to plan staging *King Oedipus* there even while it was impossible in England, but the introduction of a censorship bill to Ireland in 1928 rendered much of *The Resurrection* potentially too controversial for performance.[22] Uncertainty about the staging of the play affected Yeats's writing of it, as he remained in doubt whether it could be performed 'at the Peacock Theatre before a specially chosen audience' or would have to be enacted 'in a studio or a drawing-room' (*VPl* 901). In other words, the very subject-matter of the play made it difficult to envisage a suitable context for its performance.

Both *Salomé* and *The Resurrection* were liable to – and were indeed intended to – shock the average theatre-goer of the time. These plays aestheticize the Biblical text, downplaying the morality that was a mainstay of Victorian Christianity. In Wilde's play this is primarily evident in Salomé's complete obliviousness to Jokanaan's prophecies and admonitions: her only interest in him is as an aesthetic object of desire. As a forbidden sexual object Jokanaan is also terrible, and to present this the play makes use a gothically inflected version of the sublime. Arguably, Wilde was inspired by Renan's *Life of Jesus* – which he appreciatively described as the fifth gospel[23] – and other instances of Higher Criticism in his attempt to reimagine Biblical events.[24] *The Resurrection* comes out of a similar desire to reimagine history, reframing the events of the past from another perspective: 'Yes, that must have happened,' Yeats writes of his central vision in an early draft of the introduction to the play.[25] His version of reimagined history shares with Wilde an emphasis on terror. The 1927 version has the Egyptian reflecting on those who 'come from the mountain to tell what they have seen': these witnesses 'know, but they do not know how terrible it is' (*VPl* 930). The climax of the play has the Greek screaming in horror after he has passed his hand over Christ's body, having felt the Saviour's heart beating. This is not merely explicable in term of romantic or gothic aesthetics; in his note to the play, Yeats concludes: 'It has seemed to me of late that the sense of spiritual reality comes whether to the individual or to crowds from some violent shock, and that idea has the support of tradition' (*VPl* 935). A link is evident here to the modernist notion – proposed by Ezra Pound – of art as a conveyor of the 'shock of the new'. The violent shock of Christ's appearance is indeed not just a sudden irruption of what Yeats calls 'spiritual reality', but also (according to Yeats's historical scheme) the violent epiphany of historical change. A whole civilization is giving way – 'The Roman Empire stood appalled', as the opening song of the play has it (*VPl* 903; *CW2* 482) – to a new Christian era. In this historical sense, Christ himself is the privileged vehicle of the modern 'shock of the new' in *The Resurrection*.

Another notable similarity with *Salomé* is established by the manner in which Yeats's play distinguishes between characters on the basis of their cultural extraction, and then uses that identity as the basis for their contribution to religious disputation.[26] Where Wilde's play includes a Syrian, a Cappadocian, a Nubian and Jews, Yeats has just three characters apart from Christ and (in the later version) a group of musicians. In the first printed version of the play – published in 1927 in *The Adelphi* – these three followers of Christ are identified as a Hebrew, an Egyptian and a Syrian. In the revised, 1931 version, the Egyptian is replaced by a Greek (recalling that the first draft identified him as a Greek from Alexandria). These three characters are responsible for the guarding of the remaining apostles, soon after the Crucifixion. The play charts their changing views and responses to the Resurrection, with the appearance of a silent, masked Christ figure miraculously drifting through a wall providing the climax towards the end. The Hebrew is an empiricist who believes that events have shown that Christ is a man and no God. His scepticism echoes that shown in *Salomé* by Herodias, who – when she is told that Jokanaan is drunk with the wine of God – irreverently asks: 'What wine is that, the wine of God? From what vineyards is it gathered? In what wine-press may one find it?'[27] In Yeats's play the Greek follower, to the contrary, believes that Christ has been divine all along – and that all divine instantiation in human body is a mere matter of appearances. In one of the passages of *The Resurrection* that would have been calculated to shock members of a contemporary audience, he exclaims that 'To say that a god can be born of a woman, carried in her womb, fed upon her breast, washed as children are washed, is the most terrible blasphemy' (*VPl* 911; *CW2* 485). The Syrian comes bearing testimony from the women who have found the tomb empty and met the resurrected Christ. His position transcends the other two, ultimately accepting the paradoxical fusion of the human and the divine.

Wilde's play is set in King Herod's palace, above a banqueting hall. An old cistern used as a prison for Jokanaan is just out of sight, providing a key spatial embodiment of all the forbidden impulses hovering close to the surface of the play. In *The Resurrection*, space is inflected in a more complex – though equally concentrated – way. The action takes place in an upper chamber in a building in Jerusalem. The apostles are in an inner room to the right, while another door leads to stairs down to the street. Poised between the unruly energies of the street and the fragile waiting post for the sacred represented by the disciples, this is very much a liminal space. The consistent use of such a space is reminiscent of Yeats's earlier play *The King's Threshold* (1904). Michael McAteer has claimed that the latter play's positioning of 'Seanchan on the steps between the entrance to the court and the space in which his students are gathered' gives it a meaning that is 'entirely spatial'.[28] Similarly, the placing of the action in *The Resurrection* nicely embodies the pervading sense of a lurking dislocation of rational schemas: the terrible is just around the corner, harrying a cornered rationality. In his introduction to the play, Yeats evokes a long-time sense of having 'always at my left side just out of the range of the sight, a brazen winged beast that I associated with laughing, ecstatic destruction?' (*VPl* 932). Yeats's note to this passage claims that this was an impetus for the poem 'The Second Coming'. A related, spatial figuration of the threat of destruction is given in the play by the Syrian. When the Greek identifies human knowledge as something 'that keeps the road from here to Persia free from robbers, that has built the beautiful humane cities,' the Syrian counters that there may always be 'something that lies outside knowledge, outside order' (*VPl* 925; *CW2* 490). This 'something' he goes on to identify as 'the irrational' (*VPl* 925; *CW2* 490).

Twenty years later E. R. Dodds would influentially link irrationality with Greek culture.[29] The same connection is implicit in Yeats's play, as the rituals of the Dionysian revellers in the street are denounced by their own countryman. There is copulation in the street, the roughly insistent music of 'barbaric gong and rattle',[30] and a theatrical enactment of Dionysius's death and rebirth. The Greek character cannot accept that

'all that self-surrender and self-abasement is Greek, despite the Greek name of its god'
(*VPl* 917; *CW2* 487). In draft versions of the play he identified the revellers as the
dregs of the population, coming from the 'foreign quarter' of Jerusalem (*RMM* 323,
325, 409). Just as Jerusalem is being taken over by an outside influence, the Roman
empire is being overturned by a combination of political and religious forces coming
from its margins. In *The Resurrection*, that conquering force is embodied by both
Dionysius and Jesus. The negotiation between these two embodiments of the sacred is
one of the trickiest aspects of the play. Here both the historical and performative frames
of Yeats's drama play a role. A Christian interpretation of the play of the kind hinted
at by Harold Bloom would involve seeing the Dionysiac rites as mere prefigurations
or anticipations of the Christian resurrection. The Syrian's interpretation of the
resurrection, in the 1927 Adelphi version, is broadly in line with such a comparative
view:

> Suddenly it came into my head [. . .] that all over Greece, all over Asia Minor and
> Magna Grecia, from generation to generation, men have celebrated the death and
> Resurrection of Attis, or Adonis, or Dionysus, of God under some name or other,
> and now God Himself, that He might, as it were, sanctify man's tragedy, has turned
> all those songs and dances into prophesy. (*VPl* 924)

This passage was excised from Yeats's later versions of this play – and as such this is
only one of several alterations that push the meaning of *The Resurrection* in another
direction. For against the comparative interpretation, and despite the influence on Yeats
by the schemas of Frazer's *Golden Bough,* it is possible to argue that the play's argument
is more pluralistic, seeking (in Terence Brown's words) 'to enforce an awareness of all
religion as ritual which gives direct, sensuous experience of an eroticized divinity.'[31] In
line with this, Yeats's own systematic philosophy would seem to argue for a circular
rather than progressive version of history, where Greek and Jewish religions are
essentially of equal weight. According to Richard Ellmann, this is the explanation of
the opening song's imagining of God's death 'as if it were but a play' (*VPl* 903; *CW2*
482); the fact that God's resurrection is a repeated event that takes many guises, rids
it of any absolute status or pure sense of presence.[32] The compositional history of the
play suggests that Yeats was forced to make some changes in order to ensure that the
circular version of history was not overshadowed by the intense focus on Christianity.
Here he may have been stung into action by fact that the play's 'Dionysian heresy
seems to have passed its [original] audience by.'[33] The two most significant steps in this
direction are of a paratextual nature: (a) the addition of an introduction to the 1934
printing of the text in the *Wheels and Butterflies* collection, and (b) the alteration of the
concluding song for the 1931 version of the play. In the 1934 introduction, Yeats hardly
mentions Christianity, identifying instead an episode in Sir William Crookes's *Studies
in Psychical Research* as the surprising inspiration behind the climactic episode of the
Greek feeling Christ's heart beating. Christian revelation becomes a mere objective
correlative, as it were, for the spiritual reality of the occult. There is no need to dispute
the resurrection, one may infer, if it is merely a symbol for a very different event. Yeats's
wife would later express her concern, when this introduction – together with those of

two other plays from the same period – was omitted from a planned deluxe edition of his works.[34]

Equally important is the framing gesture provided by the addition of a second stanza to the song that concludes the 1931 version. Even while working on the first draft, Yeats had observed that the framing lyrics had 'without any intention of mine become much less Christian than the play' (to Lady Gregory, 22 May 1925; *CL Intelex* 4735). As these songs are accompanied by the ritual folding and unfolding of cloth that *The Resurrection* inherits from Yeats's Noh plays, their function as a framing device is made explicit; their semi-autonomous status is also underlined by their publication as 'Two Songs from a Play' in *The Tower* volume of poems. Originally, the tensions between the songs and the central Christian focus of the play they frame were not overly pronounced. In the 1927 version, the concluding song ended with an evocation of how 'Odour of blood when Christ was slain / Made Plato's tolerance in vain, / And vain the Doric discipline' (*VPl* 930). Four years later, this affirmation of how the Christian sacrifice supersedes the values of classical antiquity is supplemented by a more relativistic stanza that affirms the finitude of all endeavour: 'Everything that man esteems / Endures a moment or a day' (*VPl* 931; *CW2* 492). Helen Vendler has expressed her approval of this alteration. In her view, it emphasizes the fact that the play is not a 'theological piece about historical Christianity', but rather 'a play about the waning of one source of imaginative strength and the revivifying appearance of a new creative force.'[35] By adding the last stanza, then, Yeats clarifies what might be supposed to be the true meaning of *The Resurrection*. Yeats, one might say, makes a compositional gesture of control, making sure that the play's immersion in a Christian world-view remains measured. As such, he is like the Greek's ideal man, who 'remains separate. He does not surrender his soul. He keeps privacy' (*VPl* 919; *CW2* 487). The Greek is also a rationalist and a believer in order. The similarity between Yeats the playwright and this character is ironic: Vendler, for instance, is keen to distinguish the two, as she finds the Greek a 'dispassionate intellectual' out of sync with the religious mystery that unfolds before his eyes.[36]

If Yeats similarly remains at a distance from Christian doctrine, then this might have something to do with the generic framing of the play. This becomes evident if one views *The Resurrection* in terms of the generic conventions belonging to the form of dance play Yeats created through adaptation of the Japanese Noh form.[37] In his preface to *Certain Noble Plays of Japan*, Yeats claimed that all 'imaginative art remains at a distance and this distance once chosen must be firmly held against a pushing world' (*CW4* 165). The ritualized medium of Noh helps in keeping the world at a certain remove: 'Verse, ritual, music, and dance in association with action require that gesture, costume, facial expression, stage arrangement must help in keeping the door' (*CW4* 165). Interestingly, Yeats's metaphors here anticipate the action of *The Resurrection*: where his metatextual comments on anti-mimetic theatre imply that the conjoined artistic resources made use of in Noh theatre are successful in 'keeping the door' so as to shut out 'a pushing world', the protagonists of his later play keep vigil on a threshold, so as to hold off the outside masses. Of course, the followers' attempt to keep the mob outside is impotent: they cannot ward off the miraculous entry of Christ. Can the same be said of the generic features of Yeats's play? Are they equally powerless to prevent

The Resurrection from becoming a Christian play? Or should *The Resurrection* rather be interpreted in terms of a constant process of 'conceptual reframing', whereby the audience can respond with some freedom to the 'polygeneric' strategy of the play at hand?[38]

The perhaps most eye-catching and idiosyncratic generic feature of Yeats's dance plays is related to the framing songs. As has been mentioned, the songs are accompanied by the folding and unfolding of a cloth, undertaken by the musicians at both the beginning and end of the plays. Even if the latter feature is characteristic of Yeats's Noh-inspired plays, it has no place in their eastern predecessors; Augustine Martin has remarked on how amazed he was, when he attended a performance of an original Noh play and realized that this generic feature was invented by Yeats, without there being any equivalent in the Japanese genre.[39] Andrew Parkin has suggested that Yeats's source for this might have been the Indian theatre form of Kathakali.[40] Although cloths play important roles in both *Nishikigi* (where the narrow *Hosonunu* cloth represents the female lead's unattainability) and *Aiono-ue* (where at one stage a folded cloth represents the title character, sick in her bed), they do not have a similar framing role in Noh drama. One might also refer to the important role played by costumes and cloths in Yeats's own oeuvre – 'He Wishes for the Cloths of Heaven' (*VP* 176; *CW1* 70) is a notable instance – although there, too, the function is radically different. In that respect, a conventional stage feature of western theatre provides a better parallel: Liam Miller thus suggests that the folding and unfolding of cloth 'might perhaps be considered as a link or "bridge" between the Nō technique as adapted by him and the European conventional stage with its front or "tableau" curtain.'[41] Why, one might ask, would such a 'bridge' be necessary? According to Miller, the device is Yeats's 'primary concession in adapting the Nō theatre to his own purpose',[42] and he suggests that some kind of formal framing device was needed in order to prepare western audiences for the alien form of ritual theatre they were about to experience. It is almost as if Yeats needed to add invisible scare-quotes to his own text, in order to force his audience to suspend their disbelief of an unfamiliarly unrealistic dramatic form.[43] This is in line with Rick Altman's stress on the pragmatic aspect of genres, whereby audience's expectations not only are created in reaction to genre identification but also have a shaping influence on genre.[44] In itself, though, the folding and unfolding of the cloth is an empty ritual, a framing device that is quintessentially formal. Devoid of any determinate content, it would appear to be an outstanding example of just how far Yeats could move in the direction of abstract Modernism. There is an analogy here to the 1937 version of *A Vision*: at the end of the introduction to the latter text, Yeats describes his schematic phases of the moon as 'stylistic arrangements of experience'. He acknowledges that even if 'sometimes, overwhelmed by miracle as all men must be when in the midst of it, I have taken such periods literally', nevertheless this is followed by a more distant phase of comprehension when 'my reason has soon recovered' (*AVB* 25).

Does genre then protect Yeats also against the Christian miracle, providing a formal stay against any actual immersion in doctrine? Does it, as it were, assist him in acting 'As though God's death were but a play' (*VPl* 903; *CW2* 482)? If *The Resurrection* were straightforwardly non-referential, devoid of any intrinsic formal connections with

Christian tradition, then this might be the case. Yet the formal palimpsest of Yeats's drama is more complex than that. As has been pointed out earlier, his adaptation of Noh is overlaid with traces of Greek tragedy, the European avant-garde and other generic strands – providing a polygeneric equivalent to the 'adaptive complexes' Chapman has identified with regard to Yeats's allusions. *The Resurrection* is also linked to a distinctive form of Christian drama. Just like *Calvary*, *The Resurrection* has a title that is reminiscent of one of the pageants or mini-plays that formed part of the repertoire of the English mystery play cycles.[45] At first sight, the medieval mystery plays might appear to be far removed from Yeatsian theatre. Where the former presented an accessible spectacle in the streets, which was largely in conformity with the Christian doctrine of its time, Yeats's later drama is apparently more elitist and iconoclastic in its emphasis. However, Yeats showed an early interest in the mystery plays, and under his aegis the Abbey Theatre presented in November 1911 'The Second Shepherd's Play', from the Chester mystery cycle.[46] Although other important influences exist, Yeats's concerted attempt to shape his Cuchulain plays into a series is reminiscent of the way in which this medieval genre strung several plays together into one coherent cycle. The non-naturalistic nature of the mystery plays, whereby each pageant is centred on 'a striking episode which has a powerful visual impact',[47] seems anticipatory of his practice – as is the use of speeches of some metrical sophistication. More specific to *The Resurrection*, the mystery plays tend to use masks for divine and diabolical personages, in order to differentiate them from other characters: in *The Resurrection,* Christ is the only character on stage wearing a mask. In the York cycle, the resurrection pageant involves Christ departing from the tomb in silence; similarly, Yeats's Christ does not speak during his miraculous movement from window to inner room. The Greek's silent prostration before Christ in *The Resurrection* also mirrors the response of the soldiers in the mystery plays: 'We were so rad everilkone [i.e., we were all so frightened], / When that he put beside the stone, / We were so stonied we durst stir none, / And so abashed.'[48] More broadly, there is an interesting proximity with regard to how these plays situate their audience. On the basis of ideas developed in *A Vision*, *The Resurrection* is one of the more didactic of Yeats's plays – and thus is closer than usual to the kind of doctrinal footing in evidence in the medieval mystery plays. According to Helen Vendler's reading, Yeats's play uses the contrasting perspectives of the Greek, the Hebrew and the Syrian to give the audience different role models for how to deal with epochal change. The correct response, she believes, is demonstrated by the Syrian's progressive attitude.[49] Although the theology is different, the way in which the mystery plays positioned their audience is roughly similar:

> One of the principal effects of the cycle as a whole in performance was to place the audience in a position of God-like omniscience as regards the continuing history and nature of their spiritual predicament on earth. Out of this arose a need for them to examine their consciences and to decide where their allegiance lay in the conflict between good and evil for possession of the souls of the human race.[50]

Although Yeats no doubt has twisted Scripture into an idiosyncratic form in *The Resurrection*, he may ultimately be laying a similar burden upon his audience.

Is such a parallel, and the other evidence adduced here, sufficient to demonstrate that *The Resurrection* is Christian? That would be too simplistic an answer to a difficult question. Hopefully, however, it has been demonstrated that generic and paratextual features of *The Resurrection* pull in different directions with regard to the issue of religious doctrine. The play is generically plural in a way which echoes the cultural plurality of the Jerusalem it depicts. The reach of univocal readings of *The Resurrection* in light of Noh conventions or Yeats's own esoteric thought are disputed by romantic 'roughness' and the ghostly voice of the mystery plays. Harold Bloom's claim, that the play 'hesitates upon the threshold of becoming Christian drama', has some validity. It is precisely by crossing the threshold, and adding contextualizing frameworks, that Yeats tries to banish what might be termed the Christian temptation at work in this text. The result is a play that cleaves to the Decadent heritage of the provocative and ironically displacing treatment of Christianity exemplified by Oscar Wilde's *Salomé*. At the same time, though, Yeats's text involves a more thorough exploration of the Christian narrative, and the medieval mystery plays provide an underlying basis for comprehension that should not be ignored in favour of more explicitly formulated influences. Further, every performance will necessarily involve a detachment from the very framing devices that make irony and distance possible. Experienced on stage, without the textual paraphernalia of critical editions and supplementary works by Yeats, the play should prove a peculiarly bewildering experience for the theatre-goer. Unsettlingly akin to Christian drama, it is shocking in its complex negotiations with history, politics and the sacred.

This chapter has focused on two separate stages of Yeats's engagement with dramatic genre. First, it was shown how his adaptation of Noh conventions is a complex affair. Yeats himself gives mixed signals with regard to the question whether he is merely adapting the Japanese form or inventing a new genre of his own. In any case, an adaptive process takes place that certainly cannot be said to result in a simple replication of the Japanese form: Yeats's so-called dance plays are not identical to Noh. Yeats seeks both the endorsement of tradition and the freedom more characteristic of Modernism. Matters are complicated by the fact that so many of the generic features that he takes over from the Noh overlap with generic characteristics of other forms, including that of Greek tragedy. The reading given of *The Resurrection* effectively focused on a later stage, where the Noh conventions are present in a more residual form. Here a polygeneric strategy becomes even more noticeable, with the conventions of the dance plays being overlaid with content from *A Vision*, modernist abstraction and features characteristic of medieval mystery plays. This chapter, then, has shown how a small group of plays engage in a complex diversity of genres. In the next chapter, we will follow how one genre – tragedy – goes through a complex process of change, in how it is used by Yeats, in writings spanning almost the last 30 years of his career.

Tragic Modulations

'The Gyres' is the opening poem of the last volume of poetry Yeats published during his lifetime, the 1938 *New Poems*. It begins as follows:

> The gyres! The gyres! Old Rocky Face look forth;
> Things thought too long can be no longer thought
> For beauty dies of beauty, worth of worth,
> And ancient lineaments are blotted out.
> Irrational streams of blood are staining earth;
> Empedocles has thrown all things about;
> Hector is dead and there's a light in Troy;
> We that look on but laugh in tragic joy.
>
> What matter though numb nightmare ride on top
> And blood and mire the sensitive body stain?
> What matter? Heave no sigh, let no tear drop[. . .].

> (*VP* 564; *CW1* 299)

Some details that may seem unclear at the first reading of these lines can be filled in relatively easily.[1] The entity addressed as 'Old Rocky Face' at the beginning of the poem has been identified as a personification of the oracle at Delphi. The references to Empedocles and Troy similarly concern philosophical and legendary matters of classical Greece. And the initial, excited mention of the gyres can be contextualized in terms of Yeats's system in *A Vision*, where succeeding historical eras are compared to spinning cones. But what is one to make of the central injunction to laugh – rather than sigh or cry – in the face of vast destruction? Is what Yeats here calls 'tragic joy' a fitting or even believable response to a situation where, in the words of line five, 'Irrational streams of blood are staining earth'? Surely a humane response to destruction and bloodshed involves a more measured and compassionate engagement than what seems to be projected in these lines?

This chapter will not try to defend, or render credible, the notion of 'tragic joy' that features centrally in 'The Gyres' and other noteworthy texts by Yeats. Instead, it will seek to explicate how tragedy and comedy acquire an important place in his drama, poetry and poetics – as well as impinge upon his politics and general view upon life. Particularly tragedy plays a major role, and late in his career Yeats indeed described himself as 'a tragic poet' (to Ethel Mannin, 2 June 1935; *CL Intelex* 6243). An itinerary will be traced from the important early articulation of ideas in the 1910 essay 'The Tragic Theatre' to a more transitional phase involving the play *The Player Queen*. Yeats's work with the latter text from 1907 to its first production in 1922 involved a complex negotiation with, and development of, central positions regarding the tragic and the comic. Its composition process – and some of the different versions of the play – will be scrutinized in order to show how Yeats prepares the ground for his later experiments in verse and on stage. After looking at how tragedy and comedy are related to Yeats's 1920s responses to historical phenomena such as the Easter Rising and his own Victorian past, I will return to 'The Gyres' and its companion poem, 'Lapis Lazuli'. The concluding interpretation of the latter two poems will explore some of the paradoxes of Yeats's conception of 'tragic joy'.

The concepts of tragedy and comedy provide excellent means for linking together Yeats's poetry and drama: they provide central vehicles, one might say, for the mediation between his eminently dramatic poetry and outspokenly poetical drama. The contents of these concepts do however change, and often function in ambiguous fashion. One of the central ambiguities concerns how tragedy and comedy can be deployed both as generic and modal categories. As genres, they function as kinds of dramatic texts, providing conventional elements that not only assist Yeats in the process of composition, and readers in their acts of interpretation, but also situate the plays in question in a larger context of literary history. Thus when the noble Cuchulain, in the play *On Baile's Strand*, is led to kill his own son – and ends up fighting the waves in a bewildered state – we recognize him as a tragic hero made in the same mould as such figures as Oedipus and Lear. Tragedy can however transcend the merely generic. Thus we speak of the 'tragic' and the 'comic' – just as we speak of the 'elegiac' or the 'pastoral' – as involving themes and values that transcend a particular genre. Alastair Fowler has shown how such modulation of generic terms involves the construction of adjectival forms that may be somewhat vague, and always include only a selection of features from the original genre, but which precisely therefore have a wide range.[2] As such, these concepts denote traits that appear in other kinds of texts, and perhaps can even be used justifiably to denote experiences and events that we encounter outside of literature, under exceptional or unexceptional circumstances in our own lives.

Yeats starts thinking consistently, and in depth, about the concepts of tragedy and comedy in the first few years of the twentieth century. The key text here is the essay 'The Tragic Theatre', first published in the quarterly journal *The Mask* in October 1910, and later appearing in Yeats's essay collection *The Cutting of an Agate* in 1912. The importance this essay had for Yeats at the time is indicated by the fact that a revised version of it functioned as the preface for the 1912 collection *Plays for an Irish Theatre*, a collection of his entire dramatic output up to that point. 'The Tragic Theatre' shares a feature common to many of Yeats's writings of this time, in that it is decisively marked by the example and recent death of Synge. Nicholas Grene has observed that Synge's death was an event around which Yeats 'gathered a more pervasive sense of alienation and loss of purpose'. It also 'brought home to Yeats the feeling of mortality', due to his intense identification with Synge.[3]

Tragedy frequently involves an attempt to make some sense of death, or to confront it in some way, and it is notable that Yeats also uses Synge's drama as an aid to help him articulate the nature of the tragic for himself: this is particularly evident in how Yeats's personal response to Synge's final, unfinished play *Deirdre of the Sorrows*, produced at the Abbey Theatre earlier that year, is used to open the essay. Yeats focuses on Deirdre's state of mind at the end of the play, where – moments before taking her own life – she overcomes her grief for the loss of Naisi and his brothers to Conchubar's forces. Deirdre claims to have 'put away sorrow like a shoe that is worn out and muddy' and describes her experience as 'a joy and triumph'.[4] Yeats finds in her limit experience at this point 'a reverie of passion that mounts and mounts till grief itself has carried her beyond grief into pure contemplation' (*CW4* 174). It will remain important for Yeats's conception of tragedy that it involves transcendence, in the sense of achieving a higher level of existence: grief outdoes itself in a controlled process where the dreamy, wandering trance of reverie arrives at what he calls 'pure contemplation'. Typically, there is a moment of insight at the heart of this conception of tragedy, whereby 'passion [. . .] becomes wisdom' (*CW4* 175). This alerts us to the fact that Yeats is working with what might be termed a concentrated extract of the tragic plot as it has been conceived of by Aristotle and later theorists. Aristotle stipulated that protagonists of tragic plays would have a moment of insight or recognition, of *anagnorisis*, after circumstances or fate had conspired against their plans – but also had room for much more.[5] Yeats extrapolates and emphasizes this moment of revelation. In addition, he gives it his own psychological elaboration, describing it very much as a mood or state of mind.[6] In this respect, one can see the concept already being pushed in a direction that will make it amenable to application, in a modulated form, to lyric poetry; if tragedy essentially is a matter of mood and state of mind, then it is well-fitted to the modern understanding of lyric form as 'a concentrated expression of individual emotion'.[7]

Yet even while Yeats reveals his modernity – by homing in on the subjective, psychological lineaments of the protagonist's changing experience – he also seeks to tap into what is most permanent and unchanging. When Deirdre, 'in the paroxysm before she took her life, touched with compassionate fingers him that had killed her lover', the audience is 'carried beyond time and persons' (*CW4* 175). This is a distinctively tragic process in Yeats's eyes, and it is diametrically opposed to the workings of comedy. Where one deals with human individuals, the other allows us access to a more profound experience. This opposition is clearly formulated in the 1909 diary notes that Yeats would publish by the title of *Estrangement* in 1926. 'Tragedy is passion alone', Yeats writes there, 'and rejecting character, it gets form from motives, from the wandering of passion; while comedy is the clash of character' (*CW3* 348). Yeats believes tragic passion enables a limit experience, referring in the process to what he calls 'that tragic ecstasy which is the best that art – perhaps that life – can give' (*CW4 175*).[8] Later on in his career, this notion – renamed 'tragic joy' – will take on central importance.

Otto Bohlmann and other critics have accurately identified the Nietzschean tenor of Yeats's thought in this essay, especially evident when he claims that 'tragedy must always be a drowning and breaking of the dykes that separate man from man, and [. . .]

it is upon these dykes comedy keeps house' (*CW4* 176).[9] Nietzsche, too, saw tragedy as transcending human individuality. He, however, identified the interplay between individuality and transcendence as interior to tragedy – as part of its Apollonian and Dionysian constituents – whereas Yeats, by banishing the kind of individuality he identifies by the term 'character', is here seeking a purer, more rarefied form of tragedy.

Following upon Nietzsche's call for a revival of the ancient Greek tragedy, writers such as Yeats and T. S. Eliot sought to restore this genre from its modern neglect by returning it to its ancient roots in verse and ritual. The way forward lay in a return to the more primitive and pure roots of the past. Although Jeffrey Perl has written forcefully about this trend,[10] there are many factors complicating Yeats's particular place in the resulting narrative. One concerns the fast and loose way in which the Irishman treats the concept of tragedy. In his prose writings, he seems relatively uninterested in many of the more detailed mechanics of the genre. 'The Tragic Theatre', for instance, begins by deriding appreciations of Synge's play on Deirdre that neglected 'the qualities that made certain moments seem to me the noblest tragedy', even while they fastened on to 'what seemed to me but wheels and pulleys necessary to the effect' (*CW4* 174). Here one suspects Yeats is referring, by elision, to fundamental constituents of the genre – and it is noticeable that central elements of tragic drama such as the tragic reversal (*peripeteia*) and catharsis (*katharsis*) are sidestepped or only implicitly present in his writings on tragedy. Further, Yeats is very happy to unmoor the central experience of tragedy from its generic underpinnings. In 'The Tragic Theatre', this is evident in how he links the opposition between tragedy and comedy to a related one between poetry and other art forms. Poetry is an 'art of the flood' that transcends the merely literary, let alone the merely poetical, since it can be seen both in 'the art of Titian when his *Ariosto*, and his *Bacchus and Ariadne*, give new images to the dreams of youth' and in 'Shakespeare when he shows us Hamlet broken away from life by the passionate hesitations of his reverie' (*CW4* 177). By implying that the concept of the tragic is a modal phenomenon that can transcend its generic roots in drama, Yeats is already in 1910 laying the foundation of a more encompassing understanding that would later allow him to conceive of himself as a tragic poet.

While 'The Tragic Theatre' strenuously insists upon a clear dichotomy between the transcendent visions of tragedy and the everyday characters of comedy, there is much in the essay that militates against too pure an opposition. For instance, Yeats describes Shakespeare as a writer of tragi-comedy and grants that one 'may not find either mood in its purity' (*CW4* 177). The evocative ending of the essay seems also to grant that pure tragedy involves a very inconstant and precariously achieved experience: 'We feel our minds expand convulsively', Yeats writes, 'or spread out slowly like some moon-brightened image-crowded sea. That which is before our eyes perpetually vanishes and returns again in the midst of the excitement it creates, and the more enthralling it is, the more do we forget it' (*CW4* 178–9). One may seek to define and circumscribe the tragic experience, Yeats seems to be telling us, but in its essence it is something peculiarly elusive.

The composition process of *The Player Queen*, one of Yeats's most troublesome texts, certainly backs this up. In this play, a flamboyant and untrustworthy actress saves an unspecified kingdom from violent insurrection by taking the place of its reluctant and ill-suited queen. Yeats started writing *The Player Queen* in 1907, three years prior to his programmatic essay on 'The Tragic Theatre'. By March 1909, however, it had become clear that the compositional process was going to be anything but plain sailing. In a letter to Lady Gregory, Yeats complained: 'Every day up to this I have worked at "Player Queen" in the greatest gloom & this morning half the time was the worst yet – all done against the grain' (6 March 1909; *CL Intelex* 1104). After much toil and trouble, he set it aside in 1911 or 1912. Only after returning to it a few years later, and reworking it, was Yeats able to bring this play to a shape with which he was happy: the first productions of *The Player Queen* were in 1919. Yet further revisions were made later on, effectively making this play a bridge between different stages of Yeats's career.

The Player Queen* caused Yeats particular problems due to its generic impurity. In both his 1922 note to the play, and in comments made in *Wheels and Butterflies* in 1934, he describes a complete revamping of its generic foundations: what had begun as a tragedy, ended in a farce. Thanks to the meticulous transcriptions and analyses made by Curtis Bradford, we now know that this scenario should not be taken completely at face value. There is no simple transition point in Yeats's work with the play, and from the very first drafts it did not simply adhere to the tenets of a tragic play as presented by either Yeats or others. But the manuscripts of *The Player Queen* show Yeats struggling to uphold the purity of his critical categories in his literary work: the text refuses to submit, one might say, to metatextual discipline. Presumably it was work with this play that early in 1909 led him to admit to his father: 'I am coming to the conclusion that I am really essentially a writer of comedy, but very personal comedy' (to J. B. Yeats, 17 January 1909; *CL Intelex* 1053). Certainly the play seems to veer between genres, never quite settling down into any single groove. At a later stage in the composition process, Yeats would describe it to his father as 'a wild comedy, almost a farce, with a tragic background – a study of a fantastic woman' (to J. B. Yeats, 12 September 1915; *CL Intelex* 2761).

This generic open-endedness is mirrored by thematic ambiguity. A central tenet of the play concerns the plasticity of the actor's soul. In the longest of the unpublished versions – a full three-act draft – this is reflected in the servants' discussion while they wait for a masque about Noah and the flood – starring Septimus and Decima (who will later become queen) as Noah and his wife – to get underway. The servants describe the actors as 'slippery as the eels in the river', and compare them to 'mortar that never hardens' (*MTPQ* 218). Seen in the light of the player queen's role-switch from actress to queen, there are two important aspects involved here. First, the player queen shows how the capability for self-reinvention is one that crosses the border between art and life. On the basis of nothing more than the example of Septimus's play about ancient royalty, she is able to take on the role of real-life queen. In an anticipation of how Yeats subsequently nimbly connected artistic plot structures and life narratives, she is able to project the attitude of a tragic heroine beyond the confines of her art. The plastic soul of the actor also has consequences for interpretation. When the player queen sings a song concealed in a vat in the queen's castle, the ambiguous nature of her song is made manifest by the variety of ways in which it is understood: one soldier believes it is an insurrectionary song, crying for vengeance from the overtaxed populace. Another soldier takes it to be 'a love song or some sort of vanity' (*MTPQ* 196). The queen offers a different opinion, interpreting the song as coming from a ghost 'sent to warn me that I was doing wrong' in 'not staying at my prayers' (*MTPQ* 197). This diversity of response is instructive; in what amounts to an allegory of the arbitrariness of reception, we are being warned that the same expressive gesture may be read either as political or personal, as vain or ominously prescriptive, as high or low.

The fluidity of genre in *The Player Queen* confirms this open-endedness. The key generic doubleness of the play lies in how it straddles farce and tragedy. The example of Oscar Wilde – whose *Salomé* was shown to be a significant influence on *The Resurrection* in the previous chapter – may arguably be of some importance also here. Wilde was a crucial source of Yeats's early development of the idea that one should seek active 'virtue as distinguished from the passive acceptance of a current code' through a process that is 'theatrical, consciously dramatic, the wearing of a mask' (*CW3* 347). Dramatically, Wildean farce did not provide a template Yeats publicly acknowledged as relevant to himself. Especially in its ending, though, where much befuddlement concerning the queen and player queen's assumed identities is intended to cause some merriment among the audience, *The Player Queen* would seem to be closer to *The Importance of Being Earnest* than any classical tragedy. The misprision of identity that plays such a predictable role in farce is of obvious utility for Yeats's play, even if his original intention apparently was for a nobler and more elevated tone. In a somewhat different vein, there are also notable instances of self-parody in parts of the play. It is as if Yeats has already tired of some of the positions adopted in 'The Tragic Theatre', and wants to free himself from them through recourse to an outside, ironical vantage point. This is particularly evident in the character of Septimus, who seems to be a parody of the purity and straightforward earnestness characteristic of some of Yeats's early work. Like the author of *The Player Queen*, Septimus is a merciless critic of realism and indulges in a love affair that seems to be based on a particularly cruel variant of courtly love. This overall tendency is reflected in Yeats's comment, in *Per Amica Silentia Lunae*, that after his 'imagination became sterile for nearly five years', he could only 'escape at last when I had mocked in a comedy my own thought' (*CW5* 10).

Yeats's own poetics was pushing him in the same direction. For even while he distinguished clearly between farce and tragedy, he also identified common ground between the two genres. In his writings on dramatic form around the time of *The Player Queen*, Yeats establishes a hierarchy of three basic forms: tragedy is the most elevated form, followed by comedy, and then finally by the lowly genre of farce. The lowest and the highest, however, share one basic characteristic: both reject plot-lines exclusively driven by individual character. Thus his diary notes that 'Tragedy is passion alone, and rejecting character, it gets form from motives, from the wandering of passion; while comedy is the clash of character. Eliminate character from comedy and you get farce' (*CW3* 348). Construct a play where characters are never set, but rather hastily embraced and divested in a process that embraces both passion and incident, and you get a case where extremes meet. *The Player Queen* thus approaches the status of tragi-farce, without being unique in this respect: the peculiar combination of the burlesque and the solemn in Yeats's later plays – such as *The Words on the Window Pane*, *The Great Herne* and *The Death of Cuchulain* – is rehearsed in this underestimated and importantly transitional play.[11]

At one stage in his biography of Yeats, R. F. Foster describes *The Player Queen* as a play of Yeats's that 'continued to mean more to him than it ever would to his audience'.[12] Despite its frequently overlooked riches, *The Player Queen* is certainly not without its problems, and it would be hard to claim that Yeats was simply mistaken in his resolve to rework some of the material discussed here. Curtis Bradford suggests with some justification, for instance, that draft 16 – which is the appellation he gives the last full manuscript version of the play extant from the period prior to Yeats's leaving it aside – has too many ideas.[13] He is however on flimsier ground when he identifies another key problem of the early conception of the play to be its combination of a tragic plot with a use of an early version of Yeats's doctrine of the mask: 'the idea that choosing a mask might have tragic consequences simply did not work out dramatically – serious consequences, yes, but not tragic' (*MTPQ* 27–8). This contradicts the key role the mask plays for Yeats's conception of the tragic at this period. In the diary notes of 1909, Yeats notes that tragedy entails a choice of masks that 'contain neither character nor personal energy. They are allied to decoration and to the abstract figures of Egyptian temples. Before the mind can look out of their eyes the active will perishes, hence their sorrowful calm' (*CW3* 348). The player queen chooses the self-sacrificing mask of a political leader – a queen – who is willing to die for her country. In draft 16, the heroic nature of the player queen's choice is shown by the tragic joy she embraces in her desire to 'die laughing' (*MTPQ* 237). In some of the earlier scenarios for the play, she goes through with this plan. Scenario six, for instance, ends abruptly with her suicide from the castle battlements: 'She has thrown herself from the top' (*MTPQ* 29).

It is true that this tragic ending does not survive into the later draft versions of the play. Nor does Yeats include another possible fulcrum for a tragic finale, Nona's rape or death, in the final version. But rather than focusing on the individual psychologies of these characters in order to explain the play's swerve away from a tragic endings, it might be more instructive to look at the larger social context projected in *The Player Queen*. In *Modern Tragedy*, Raymond Williams questions the modern tendency to isolate the tragic hero from his surroundings. Against this, Williams calls for readings that take the entirety of the tragic plots into consideration, approaching tragedy as 'a response to social disorder'.[14] It is often overlooked that *The Player Queen* – like *The Resurrection* – is a play about social disorder: when the former play's story starts the town is in a volatile state where rebels threaten to bring down the government and the withdrawn, ascetic queen. The resolution of the plot comes through an act that placates the people – installing a new leadership – but effectively preserves the status quo. This is in fact one of the most steadfastly comic dimensions of the play – if one defines a comic plot as restoring a sense of final harmony after dissension – through all of its many versions from Yeats's first scenarios to the revised version that appeared in the *Collected Plays* of 1934. In all of these, the rebels are presented as a relatively hapless mob, and in the published text they are dominated by oafish and ignorant countrymen. The rebels are obviously not fit to rule, and the insistence upon a static political situation is heightened by the exotic, medieval setting.[15] This can be linked to Yeats's lack of faith in any radical political alternative to Home Rule in Ireland around 1910, a view that soon enough would be left behind in the dust-heap of history after the 1916 Easter Rising. Moving on to take a look at the latter, and Yeats's response to it, we can gain a sense of how Yeats's notion of the tragic developed after the most intense period of work on *The Player Queen*.

The Rising was a shattering and shocking experience for the Irish people, and as with all public events of any magnitude, there was a struggle to make some kind of sense of what had happened. From the very first, Yeats saw the events as an instance of real-life politics following the mould of literary form. A letter to Lady Gregory on April 27 described it as 'a tragic business' (*CL Intelex* 2934), while another on May 9 referred to 'this tragic heroic lunacy of Shinn Feinn [sic]' (*CL Intelex* 2945). A subsequent letter referred to Maud Gonne's thought that 'tragic dignity has returned to Ireland' (to Lady Gregory, 11 May 1916; *CL Intelex* 2950). Yeats's ensuing literary treatment of the Rising basically adheres to this mould, insofar as a tragic interpretation is consistently upheld, even if the interpretation of the motives and values of the rebels veers from the satirical to the heroic. Most famously, the poem 'Easter, 1916' (*VP* 391–4; *CW1* 182–4) balances disquietude about the stony hearts that drove Griffiths, Connolly and the other rebels to the ultimate self-sacrifice with respectful reverence before their status as inaugurators of a new chapter in the national narrative. Yeats depicts them as comical figures who have become transfigured into tragic heroes through a combination of their deeds and external circumstances. Yeats's speaker places himself in the same comical context at the end of the first stanza; both he and the rebels appeared like fools, both 'they and I / But lived where motley is worn' (ll. 13–14). Being finished with their parts 'In the casual comedy' (l. 37), the rebels have assumed a tragic role – rather like the player queen – while Yeats himself seems to aspire to the role of witness or chronicler of their drama. As in tragedy, a specific turning point – what the Greeks called the *peripeteia* – changes all: after the events in Dublin, we are told in the repeated refrain, all is 'changed utterly' (l. 15). The poem's reference to the birth of a 'terrible beauty' can be interpreted as a paradoxical fusing of the sublime and the beautiful, but Yeats's poetics of drama is also relevant here. Terror is, according to classical Aristotelian poetics, an emotion resulting from the tragic experience.[16] For Yeats, also beauty is a facet of tragedy. In 1909 he writes: 'I think the motives of tragedy are not related to action but to changes of state. [. . .] is not ecstasy some fulfilment of the soul in itself, some slow or sudden expansion of it like an overflowing well? Is not this what is meant by beauty?' (*CW3* 348–9). The rebels relate less clearly, however, to Yeats's poetics of tragedy in terms of how they are positioned with regard to wisdom. Has their experience given birth to a tragic insight, allowing them to put on knowledge with their power? Yeats grants that they have had the dream of the tragic hero – 'We know their dream', he writes in line 70 – but it seems that in this historical tragedy whatever insight is possible must come to survivors and heirs in the aftermath of the event. In recent years, Edna Longley and other commentators have noted the open-ended and deliberating nature of the end of the poem: one way of reading this is that Yeats sees it as his own duty to begin the process of understanding of this particular crisis, even while admitting its obscure or even noumenal nature.[17] He will continue this process in the 1919 play *The Dreaming of the Bones*, as well as several other poems included in *Michael Robartes and the Dancer*.

These works break with Yeats's frequently expressed determination to keep politics out of his poetry. One reason why he nevertheless is able to combine these – as well as the public and the private – in 'Easter, 1916', is the thorough practice he has had in his autobiographical prose. Beginning writing *Reveries over Childhood and Youth* in 1914, and following that effort with several money-making excursions into reminiscence, Yeats becomes increasingly adept in roaming freely across borders of which he had previously been more wary. Such freedom cannot, however, be indulged without any plan or template. One of the most privileged templates for Yeats is that of tragedy: 'We begin to live when we have conceived life as tragedy', he writes at one point (*CW3* 163). In the section of *The Trembling of the Veil* (1922) entitled 'The Tragic Generation', Yeats seems almost embarrassed by his own effort to bring the past into some sort of manageable shape: 'as I have set out to describe nature as I see it', he writes, 'I must not only describe events but those patterns into which they fall, when I am the looker-on' (*CW3* 253). In 'The Tragic Generation' a tragic framework underlies the presentation of the diverse fates of his friends and colleagues from the 1890s, ranging from Oscar Wilde and Aubrey Beardsley to fellow-members of the London literary society that went by the name of the Rhymers' Club. Yeats's memories of these writers have proved extremely influential, providing an interpretation of the Nineties and the Decadent writers of the period that has been difficult to circumvent. Daniel O'Hara has claimed that Yeats's autobiographical writings use both friends and relatives as 'metaphors of possible selves',[18] and there is reason to be careful in interpreting such descriptions in too literal fashion. In 1935, a few years after his most influential writings on the Decadents, Yeats criticizes those who 'have built up an impression of a decadent period' – in the sense of one bereft of vigour – 'by remembering only when they speak of the Nineties, a few writers who had tragic careers.' Against this tendency he insists that the final decade of the nineteenth century was 'in reality a period of great vigour, thought and passion were breaking free from tradition' (to Maurice Bowra, 31 May 1935, *CL Intelex* 6239).

Yeats himself created the stereotype he is repudiating here. Still, one of the more interesting features of 'The Tragic Generation' is that while Yeats uses tragic plot as a kind of skeletal framework for his narrative, he simultaneously abstains from giving a too unequivocal or unreserved verdict on its significance. Where some later commentators have been happy simply to dismiss the period for an effeminate aestheticism, Yeats balances this dimension against obvious admiration for the heroism with which artists such as Beardsley, Lionel Johnson and Ernest Dowson rebelled against the conventional norms of Victorian society: 'We knew that we must face an infuriated Press and public', he writes at one stage of the artists associated with the magazine the *Savoy*, 'but being all young we delighted in enemies and in everything that had an heroic air' (*CW3* 249). Like conventional tragic or romantic heroes, many of these figures either died young or failed to live up to their early promise, but Yeats is surprisingly circumspect in how he avoids providing any simple explanation. Some came to a bad end because of an overly ambitious desire to combine perfect thought with perfect form. Yet Yeats also suggests that the timing might simply not have been right. The 'tragic generation' failed not because they pursued tragedy – since this, Yeats insists frequently enough, is a timeless ideal – but because they did so in a transitional age where tragedy itself was quickly becoming impossible. This relates to the large-scale, phasal history that plays such an important part in *A Vision*, 'The

Second Coming', and other key late texts by Yeats. The artists of 1890s were living on the verge of a major sea-change, whereby tragic ideals were being replaced by a comedic insistence upon realism and personality. When the Rhymers' Club was active in the early 1890s, Yeats writes, 'that sense of comedy which was soon to mould the very fashion-plates, and, in the eyes of men of my generation, to destroy at last the sense of beauty itself, had scarce begun to show here and there, in slight and subordinate touches, among the designs of great painters and craftsmen' (*CW3* 234). Literary Modernism is also fitted into this narrative. Rhymers such as Yeats, Dowson and Arthur Symons were the last of a tragic school who 'claimed the whole past of literature' as their heritage, and in this they were unlike those whom Yeats calls 'the young men in the age of comedy that followed us' – the latter group sought instead to legitimize their ideals 'in some new, and so still unrefuted authority' (*CW3* 235).

The idea of tragic and comic eras relieving one another appears in one of Yeats's later poems, 'Parnell's Funeral' (*VP* 541–3; *CW1* 285–6). There, recent Irish political history is cast as a cyclical series of periods, with tragic and comic eras alternating. The key figure of Catholic Emancipation, Daniel O'Connell (1775–1847), is called 'the Great Comedian' (l. 1) while Charles Stewart Parnell (1846–91) – the nationalist leader who came to grief over his affair with Kitty O'Shea – is cast as a tragic hero whom later Irish political leaders such as Eamon de Valera (1882–1975) and Eoin O'Duffy (1892–1944) have been unable to emulate. Ultimately, though, 'Parnell's Funeral' seems to question the value of tragedy as an apt figure for a working body politic. A more primitive cultural form – a sacrificial ritual – is called for, whereby succeeding rulers have to devour the heart of the preceding hero. Only such ritual, it is implied, can banish the element of distance and insincerity that the poem finds to be endemic in Irish history. Thus tragedy falls short, as for instance in the 1798 uprising when, the speaker of 'Parnell's Funeral' tells us, the general public 'lived like men that watch a painted stage. / What matter for the scene, the scene once gone: / It had not touched our lives' (ll. 18–20). In this poem Yeats seems to be anticipating Antonin Artaud's calling for a more savage form of theatrical practice, breaking down the barriers between audience and actor. In a more measured form, the promise of such ritual transcendence was also part of the attraction of Noh. Theatre had to become more immediate, more direct, even if one had to aim for smaller audiences and import stylized conventions to bring this about. In the introductory essay to *Certain Noble Plays of Japan*, which we dwelt upon in the previous chapter, Yeats states that 'the measure of all arts' greatness can be but in their intimacy' (*CW4* 165). This dimension is precisely what has been lost in the modern realism espoused by Ibsen, Shaw and their ilk: 'The stage-opening, the powerful light and shade, the number of feet between myself and the players have destroyed intimacy' (*CW4* 164). In Yeats's writings of the 1930s, clashes in form and increasingly striking use of colloquial idioms are meant to shock the audience out of complacency, bringing back an immediacy that has become gradually less accessible, thanks to modernity.

This can be read as corroborating the views of others – such as George Steiner and Arthur Miller – who have questioned whether tragedy has a place in modern society. In Steiner's view, 'Tragic drama tells us that the spheres of reason, order, and justice are terribly limited and that no progress in our science or technical resources will enlarge their relevance.'[19] In modern times, such a view has become increasingly untenable and as a result, Steiner claims, 'the tragic voice in drama is blurred or still.'[20] For Yeats the problem is that his contemporaries lack what he calls 'the Vision of Evil'. As he puts it in 'The Tragic Generation': 'who will thirst for the metaphysical, who have a parched tongue, if we cannot recover the Vision of Evil?' (*CW3* 251). Yeats's final play, *The Death of Cuchulain*, addresses this problem. At the end of his heroic life, the legendary Irish hero Cuchulain would seem to have several worthy adversaries. He spurns his former lover Eithne, who believes he lacks 'the passion necessary to life' (*VPl* 1055; *CW2* 549). He once had a son with his enemy Aoife, but killed him in the fight that concluded an earlier play in the same heroic cycle on Cuchulain, *On Baile's Strand*. Also Aoife, Cuchulain grants, has 'a right to kill me' (*VPl* 1057; *CW2* 550). Instead, however, of losing his life at the hands of these illustrious opponents, or anyone else he has crossed in his conflict-ridden life, Cuchulain finally meets his demise at the hands of a blind old beggar, for the price of 12 pennies. He is killed by a random stranger, for mercenary motives, rather than for a worthy cause – and this reflects an age that is out of joint. The prologue of *The Death of Cuchulain* is spoken by a cantankerous old man who has nothing but contempt for what he calls 'this vile age' (*VPl* 1051; *CW2* 546). The play itself appears to be a lament for an illustrious past and a noble genre that are in the process of passing away. Even while tragedy is becoming impossible, or nearly impossible, Yeats nevertheless insists upon tragic form.

This survival can in part be explained by an ambiguity at the heart of Yeats's thought, linking his mature doctrine on the mask with his understanding of the situation of the tragic hero. In *Per Amica Silentia Lunae*, Yeats claims that the poet 'finds and makes his mask in disappointment, the hero in defeat. The desire that is satisfied is not a great desire, nor has the shoulder used all its might that an unbreakable gate has never strained' (*CW5* 12). This stress on the excessive nature of the hero's desire finds a counter-thrust in a belief that the heroic quest is just within the limits of the possible. Thus in 'The Phases of the Moon', for instance, antithetical man is said to follow 'whatever whim's most difficult / Among whims not impossible' (*VP* 374; *CW2* 165). Yeats's vacillation on this point obeys and reflects an overall ambiguity between a stress on human freedom and fateful determinism – between conceiving the tragic protagonist as primarily a hero, or casting him or her predominantly as a victim. Such ambiguity fits in with much western thought on tragedy. If one adds to this dualism the alternative of tragedy being caused by an unforeseen and ignoble event (akin to the intervention of the beggar in *The Death of Cuchulain*), then one basically has Terry Eagleton's three alternative causes for tragedy: 'Either tragedy results from accident, which is undignified; or from destiny, which is unjust; or from the hero's own actions, which makes him unpalatable.'[21] The challenge is to find a state, or *modus operandi*, where these tendencies are kept in balance or a state of vacillation. Thus even while external circumstance and the externalities of form appear to militate against the use of tragedy as a viable formal template in later Yeats, there is a counter-movement: tragic form is reborn out of its own ashes. Perhaps the most significant way in which this occurs is in the late lyrics where Yeats celebrates tragic joy.

In the final two decades of his career, the themes of ageing and mortality are closely linked with tragedy in Yeats's poetry. In the title poem of *The Tower*, vigour of imagination is shown to not only combat, but even be drawn forth by, personal loss. Having enumerated some choice examples of figures where this is true, the speaker states that 'the tragedy began / With Homer that was a blind man' (*VP* 411; *CW1* 199–200). This confirms a classical link between tragedy and blindness also present in Sophocles's two plays about Oedipus, translated by Yeats in 1928 and 1934. But key performances in *The Tower* are hesitant and searching when faced with personal and political upheaval, and tend to build on elegiac rather than tragic patterns. Michael Wood has shown how the speaker of 'Nineteen Hundred and Nineteen' has few constructive ways to respond to a time of disillusionment and loss both at home and abroad.[22] The poem starts off by emphasizing the ephemerality of what seemed like ultimate expressions of cultural accomplishment:

> Many ingenious lovely things are gone
> That seemed sheer miracle to the multitude,
> Protected from the circle of the moon
> That pitches common things about.

(VP 428; CW1 210)

The poem cited at the beginning of this chapter, 'The Gyres', includes a thematically similar lament for 'ancient lineaments' and 'A greater, more gracious time' (*VP* 564; *CW1* 299). However in 'The Gyres' the speaker engages in neither self-mockery nor self-questioning, affirming instead a Nietzschean return of the same. Current destruction can be borne, since history repeats itself. The speaker embraces what Michael Valdez Moses has called a 'superhuman transhistorical perspective'.[23] In 'The Gyres' this perspective is given a distinctively classical ring through references to the oracle of Delphi, Empedocles, and the Trojan war. The first stanza's concluding couplet – 'Hector is dead and there's a light in Troy; / We that look on but laugh in tragic joy' (*VP* 564; *CW1* 299) – assimilates the stance taken to grief as part of this Greek heritage. Yeats is reaching back to the era where the historical roots of tragedy are located.

As mentioned earlier in this chapter, the concept of 'tragic joy' showed up fairly early in Yeats. However, in the two opening texts of *New Poems* – 'The Gyres' and 'Lapis Lazuli' – it acquires an unprecedented importance. In a valuable discussion of the tragic in Yeats, Edward Engelberg has argued that 'tragedy again touches comic gusto' in Yeats's concept of tragic joy.[24] In this radical experience extremes meet: tragedy and comedy are one, as laughter and sorrow come together in peculiar fashion. This appears to be a seamless blend, very unlike the disconcertingly heterogeneous mixture of laughter and seriousness found in *A Player Queen*: to use David Duff's concepts (as referred to in the previous chapter) 'smooth' rather than 'rough' mixing is at work in this fusion. 'The Gyres' and 'Lapis Lazuli' are not only paradoxical in their combinations of joy and sorrow: they also share a tendency to audaciously affirm a destruction of the past and present even while they insist upon striking a self-consciously traditional pose. In 'The Gyres', the rocky face of the Delphic oracle exhorts the speaker to rejoice in change, indeed even to 'laugh in tragic joy' (l. 8). The situation is more complex in 'Lapis Lazuli', where a catalogue of theatrical responses to tragedy is combined with a poetic interpretation of a Chinese stone-carving. The latter poem also places itself more solidly in a particular historical moment, as the opening stanza clearly evokes public concern in the time preceding the onset of World War I:

> I have heard that hysterical women say
> They are sick of the palette and fiddle-bow,
> Of poets that are always gay,
> For everybody knows or else should know
> That if nothing drastic is done
> Aeroplane and Zeppelin will come out,
> Pitch like King Billy bomb-balls in
> Until the town lie beaten flat.

(*VP* 565; *CW2* 300)

Referring to 'poets that are always gay', Yeats deploys a key adjective that will replace the 'joy' referred to in 'The Gyres'. Why has tragedy here become 'gay'? Read in the context of Yeats's fascination with the supernatural, the word may reflect the fact that Yeats's poet aspires to an elevated state of being. In the early poem 'The Man who Dreamed of Faeryland' (*VP* 126–8; *CW1* 39–41), for instance, a man troubled by 'money cares and fears', wandering on Lissadell strand, finds an alternative to his own unrest in the faeries: 'a gay, exulting, gentle race'. Similarly, the faeries rushing out of Ben Bulben at night are described as a 'gay rabble' in *The Celtic Twilight* (*Myth* 70). As with many Yeatsian words and turns of phrase, though, 'gay' comes with diverse baggage. In his explication of the drafts to this poem, Jon Stallworthy claims the same word is in fact an echo of Ernest Dowson's 'Villanelle of the Poet's Road', a poem that speaks of poets as 'bitter and gay'.[25] As Yeats in 'The Tragic Generation' underlined how the Nineties poets actively combated conventional Victorian opinion, an allusion to Dowson here would be particularly apposite.

The word 'gay' occurs in an end-rhyming position on no less than four occasions in 'Lapis Lazuli'. After the initial contrast between what 'hysterical women say' with 'poets that are always gay', it still has three more important appearances to make. An inspection of these instances can clarify the significance of tragic joy – and by extension both tragedy and comedy – at this juncture of Yeats's career. In the second stanza, ordinary people caught up in tragedy are said to prove themselves 'worthy their prominent part in the play' (l. 14) only if they 'Do not break up their lines to weep. / They know that Hamlet and Lear are gay; / Gaiety transfiguring all that dread' (ll. 15–17). Gaiety transfigures here, in a movement comparable to how Baile and Aillinn are 'Transfigured to pure substance' and 'purified by tragedy' in Yeats's supernatural version of catharsis in the 1934 poem 'Ribh at the Tomb of Baile and Aillinn' (*VP* 554–5; *CW1* 289–90). But gaiety is also of value to the poet for the simple reason that 'gay' rhymes with 'play'. The theatrical theme of the poem, the stress on a tragic joy that is imbricated with

Shakespeare's drama, comes to the fore. In a roll-call of Shakespearean heroes such as Hamlet, Lear, Ophelia and Cordelia, the tragedy of Yeats's poem is thus rooted in the stage. The modal, expanded use of 'tragic' in a foreign genre – the lyric – thus bears an overt trace of its more specific foundation in the genre of dramatic tragedy. This is akin to Yeats's use of excerpted songs from his plays as individual poems in his later poetry collections, but functions in an even more self-conscious manner.

The third stanza comes up with another rhyme on the same key word. Stressing that the Greek artist Callimachus created wonderful, but ultimately ephemeral objects, Yeats writes that they 'stood but a day; / All things fall and are built again / And those that build them are gay' (ll. 34–6). Since tragic gaiety demands that one must affirm both change and destruction, the rhyme is an apt one. Indeed, Yeats is so appreciative of it that it reappears soon after in the *New Poems* volume, in the fifth stanza of 'The Three Bushes,' where 'gay' and 'day' keep rhyming company with 'say' (*VP* 570; *CW1* 303–4). 'Play' returns to rhyme with 'gay' once more, in the final flourish of 'Lapis Lazuli'. In his allegorical description of the Chinese men stopping on the mountain of their life, they look down from a halfway house on 'all the tragic scene' (l. 52) of what they have lost. This is the time for music:

> One asks for mournful melodies;
> Accomplished fingers begin to play,
> Their eyes mid many wrinkles, their eyes,
> Their ancient, glittering eyes, are gay.

> (ll. 53–6)

Here the play to which Yeats refers is not of a specifically theatrical nature, but rather evokes another aesthetic activity: Yeats imagines that the musical instrument, earlier in the poem said to be carried by a man who is 'doubtless a serving-man' (l. 40), is used to play a tune. And although the tune is 'mournful', it nonetheless is borne forth in vivacity and joy.

The poem ends with the *act* of playing: this is an activity, rather than a final product. As with music, no specific discursive content is at hand here, and the acting thus also functions as a quasi-autonomous phenomenon that does not refer beyond itself. Yet when we look back at the rest of the poem, we are reminded that music does not rule the roost alone: the repetition of the 'play' / 'gay' rhyme in two different contexts alerts us to the fact that this is also a general form of artistic activity. In this light it is misleading to read 'Lapis Lazuli' straightforwardly as either representing a work of art or as embracing an expanded sense of play-acting or drama. It does both, and through doing both it engages in a form of play itself. On these grounds, it becomes justified to see Yeats's poem as also engaging with philosophical aesthetics: via Matthew Arnold, he inherits the German idealist understanding of art as something that engages multiple possibilities, in an open-ended form of activity that engages with thought but never can be pinned down to any single conceptual determination. The disengaged nature of the Chinamen's glance down the mountainside becomes understandable, in this light, as a particular instance of the aesthetic indifference that is a hallmark of the same philosophical understanding of art. Surprisingly, perhaps, in light of Yeats's previous temptation to set aside tragedy for the immediacy of ritual, it is precisely the ability to forge a distanced response to a given spectacle that is essential here. Thus we are returned to the 'distance [. . .] firmly held against a pushing world' that the previous chapter identified as central to Yeats's attraction to the highly conventional practice of Noh drama (*CW4* 165). Aesthetic distance is also opposed to the devouring and distracted position of someone enjoying their breakfast, as we encountered it in Chapter 2.

By interpreting 'Lapis Lazuli' in this fashion, it would seem that we are in danger of losing sight of the specifically tragic or comic nature of the text. Reading the poem as an aesthetic manifesto, we understand the actors and the Chinese wanderers to be 'gay' not because they engage in a specifically tragic form of insight or experience, but because they are artists. Tragic joy or gaiety becomes merely a species of artistic play, and contrary to Edward Engelberg's position (mentioned earlier) there is not a meeting of tragedy and comedy but a transcendence of both modes. Modulating the tragedy of the stage into tragic poetry, Yeats has ultimately left behind any substantial relation to both comedy and tragedy. Such a reading can find some support in Yeats's prose. The 1907 essay 'Poetry and Tradition', for instance, identifies a typically Yeatsian understanding of tragic joy when it localizes a 'self-delighting happiness' in Shakespeare's characters when they are faced with death (*CW4* 185). The essay goes on, though, to grant that this 'freedom of self-delight' is also present in comedy, where it becomes something particularly conscious and personal. The reason why it is present in both tragedy and comedy is that it is in fact, according to the argument of the same essay, a matter of style: it is an experience of 'joy', which, 'because it must be always making and mastering, remains in the hands and in the tongue of the artist' (*CW4* 186). Style subsumes genre. Thirty years on, the same year he writes 'Lapis Lazuli', we find Yeats making a similar point in the preface to his collected poems: 'A poet writes always of his personal life, in his finest work out of its tragedies, whatever it be, remorse, lost love or mere loneliness; he never speaks directly as to someone at the breakfast table, there is always a phantasmagoria' (*CW5* 204). We dwelt at length on one dimension of this statement in Chapter 2. In light of the present discussion, we see that the preface grants the tragic a constitutive place for poetic composition, but – as in the case of Wordsworth's frequently misunderstood dictum regarding the spontaneous overflow of powerful feelings – it is firmly located at the origins of the poetic process, and not in its final product. This seems to be confirmed later on in the introduction, when Yeats insists: 'There may be in this or that detail painful tragedy, but in the whole work none' (*CW5* 213).

From this vantage point tragic joy or gaiety is in fact neither tragedy nor comedy, but something more fundamental than both. Where Yeats pretends to be tapping into particular genres and traditions of western literature, he is in fact affirming his own, poet-centred understanding of the aesthetic creativity that is the bedrock of much of modern aesthetics. There are reasons, however, for not endorsing this position without reservation. For even if such an interpretation of tragic joy is perhaps not entirely unwarranted, it risks eradicating the lineage and detail of Yeats's modulation of tragedy in both his literary and critical works. The Scribner introduction goes on to show that Yeats is, in fact, also making a more specific point: 'I have heard Lady Gregory say', he writes,

> rejecting some play in the modern manner sent to the Abbey Theatre, 'Tragedy must be a joy to the man that dies.' Nor is it any different with lyrics, songs, narrative poems; neither scholars nor the populace have sung or read anything generation after generation because of its pain. (*CW5* 213)

Here Yeats is entering into the same territory covered by his introduction to the 1936 *Oxford Book of Modern Verse*, where he defends his controversial exclusion of the World War I poetry on the grounds that 'passive suffering is not a theme for poetry' (*CW5* 199). Thus when the Scribner introduction discusses 'pain' and 'tragedy', its argument is in part circumscribed to the particular motif of suffering – and only tangentially relates to the wider, modal understanding of tragedy which, Yeats arrives at in his late poetry. He does not dismiss tragedy per se, but only the dominance of what he either calls 'painful tragedy' or 'passive suffering'. This effectively builds – at least in part – upon classical theory: Aristotle famously stipulated that the tragic hero had to be of a certain stature in order for the audience to be willing to identify with him or her.

Still, poems such as 'The Gyres' and 'Lapis Lazuli' can be read in different ways. They can be represented as particular Yeatsian performances that embrace a superhuman affirmation of joy in extreme loss. As such I think they are fascinating and vigorous utterances, but ultimately represent untenable positions. Who would wish to, let alone would be able to, banish sighs and tears when (in the words of 'The Gyres') 'Irrational streams of blood are staining earth'? Yeats seems to be intimating as much in his 1938 poem 'Man and the Echo' (*VP* 632–3; *CW1* 353–4), which can be read as a critique of the stoicism of 'The Gyres' and its affirmation of tragic joy. In 'Man and the Echo', the poet is situated at the Alt cleft at the foot of Knocknarea, in dialogue with his own echo. What was a clear statement of position in the earlier poem is now reduced to a tremulous question: 'O rocky voice / Shall we in that great night rejoice?' (ll. 37–8) The embrace of a superhuman wisdom is, at the end of the poem, lost:

> But hush, for I have lost the theme,
> Its joy or night seem but a dream;
> Up there some hawk or owl has struck
> Dropping out of sky or rock,
> A stricken rabbit is crying out
> And its cry distracts my thought.
>
> (ll. 41–6)

This is a moment of compassionate concern for another living being that replaces ecstatic joy with a more solicitous and humane position.

As in earlier stages of his career – such as in the writing of *The Player Queen* – we find Yeats unwilling to settle into or accept any single version of the poet's tragic vocation. Although this chapter has been very selective, hopefully something of the breadth and suppleness of Yeats's dealings with both comedy and tragedy have come across. Both these categories are of importance to him to the very last, but with changing emphases and in varying senses. Ultimately, the depth and flexibility of Yeats's dealings with these modal and generic concerns amounts to an inclusive practice, evocative of the wisdom he presents himself as imparting in the poem 'All Soul's Night':

> [. . .] I have a marvellous thing to say,
> A certain marvellous thing
> None but the living mock,
> Though not for sober ear;
> It may be all that hear
> Should laugh and weep an hour upon the clock.
>
> (*VP* 471; *CW1* 232)

Yeats is indeed such a gifted writer that he can make us 'laugh and weep' more profoundly than most. This is also why he is a poet who can help us engage both with the heaviest and most light-hearted moments of our lives, and this doubleness touches upon the essence of the 'marvellous thing' he has to say.

Vox Populi

As a tragic poet and dramatist, Yeats was preoccupied with establishing exactly what kind of knowledge his texts could give access to. If the tragic hero has a moment of insight (*anagnorisis*) according to the traditional theory of tragedy, then this insight should be communicable to readers. Early on in his career, Yeats struggled to bring this to the fore, observing a tendency in his own writings to embrace the realm of dreams rather than more cognitive dimensions. Writing to Katharine Tynan on 14 March 1888, the young Yeats found fault with the poem 'The Stolen Child' for only expressing 'longing and complaint – the cry of the heart against necessity. I hope some day to alter that and write poetry of insight and knowledge' (*CL1* 54–5). To a certain extent this aspiration anticipates Yeats's later attempt to turn from what he conceived of as the feminine, Apollonian dreaminess of his early symbolist verse to a harder and more defined style in the early 1900s. In 1900, in the essay 'The Symbolism of Poetry', he was embracing the use of 'intellectual symbols': these symbols evoke ideas and allow the poet to become 'a part of pure intellect' (*CW4* 118–19).[1] Later, with the aid of the system elaborated in *A Vision*, Yeats conceived of himself as a philosophical poet with privileged access to a form of esoteric knowledge. With esotericism and mysticism, however, come strictures on exactly how clearly and indiscriminately the poet's 'mysterious wisdom won by toil' can be conveyed to others (*VP* 373; *CW1* 165). Yeats was adamant that the wisdom of his poetry was not identical to the knowledge communicated by modern science, and he would never return to anything approaching the 'irrelevant descriptions of nature, the scientific and moral discursiveness of *In Memoriam*' (*CW5* 183), against which he and his late-Victorian associates had rebelled.

If poetry provides knowledge then the question arises whether this knowledge can be communicated. Insofar as it can be shared, it establishes a sense of community between the poet and his audience. As we saw in Chapter 6, Yeats did not have an easy rapport with, or a simple faith in, the audience of his plays. Poetry he understood as more straightforwardly intimate, and therefore as less prey to the temptation of the market-place. This does not mean, however, that poetry could simply eschew the populace and the popular. In an early essay on the concept of 'popular poetry' – titled, quite simply, 'What is "popular poetry?"' – Yeats spends considerable time establishing the complexity and variety of content such a concept might embody. This conceptual instability is implicitly linked with the vicissitudes of his career, and he claims that it is ultimately derived from the crooked essence of nature itself: 'though we dig the canal beds as straight as we can, the rivers run hither and thither in their wildness' (*CW4* 6–7). This metaphor provides an apt rejoinder to the common tendency to cast Yeats as an irredeemably elitist artist; the flexibility and waywardness of his career is simply too loaded with paradox and tension to bear out such a simplistic claim.

To some extent this issue returns us to concerns addressed in Chapter 2, where the tension between quotidian and hieratic notions of art in Yeats was addressed. Here, though, that tension will be articulated in a particular way: I will examine how Yeats, in his poetry, allows alien words to impinge upon his own. This might be framed as simply a matter of how allusion can lead to a state of stylistic heterogeneity, but as Mikhail Bakhtin has pointed out: 'Where there is style there is genre.'[2] If style is a recurrent or pervasive mode of writing, affecting a text beyond the micro-level of words and sentences, then it also is affected by conventional forms of address that do not find their origin in the particular speaking subject. In concurrence with this view, Genette aligns genres and modes of discourse as examples of the more general category of architextuality. Typically, we think of genre in literature as a distinctively intra-literary affair, and this is also the main way in which genre has been approached in this book. Bakhtin alerts us, however, to the fact that literary genres are affected by non-literary ones. In fact, he claims that important changes in the history of literature can come about by means of this influence:

> In each epoch certain speech genres set the tone for the development of literary language. And these speech genres are not only secondary (literary, commentarial, and scientific), but also primary (certain types of oral dialogue – of the salon, of one's own circle, and other types as well, such as familiar, family-everyday, socio-political, philosophical, and so on).[3]

This chapter will investigate two instances of Yeats allowing his literary language to be significantly affected by what Bakthin calls 'primary' speech genres. First, I will return to 'Easter, 1916' (which was briefly addressed in the previous chapter), demonstrating how a popular dimension – most importantly embodied in the ballad genre, and popular orality as opposed to the supposedly civilized virtues of writing – is at work in this celebrated poem. The second reading will argue for the hidden presence of a surprisingly populist allusion in 'Among School Children'.

The idea that the words we use are somehow not fully our own, tends to produce either incredulity or anxiety, and it can also result in a fundamental distrust in language per se – such as is found in much of Samuel Beckett's writings. As we saw in Chapter 2, Yeats's need to distance himself from the extra-literary context associated with breakfast tacitly implied a distrust of everyday conversation and journalistic discourse. 'For words alone are certain good': this credo of sorts, uttered in 'The Song of the Happy Shepherd' in Yeats's very first volume of poetry (*VP* 66; *CW1* 6), is open to all sorts of questions and qualifications. Does Yeats mean written words, spoken words, or simply words in general? Contemporary accounts typically portray him as creating his poetry by murmuring lines to himself while walking, and Yeats also aimed for effects that could only be realized through his poetry being read aloud. The reader reception theorist Wolfgang Iser has stressed how literary texts demand a transformative 'actualisation' by the reader, whereby the initially merely latent structures of the text are fulfilled.[4] In Yeats's case, that concretion has an irreducibly oral element. Indeed, the over-determined nature of that oral concretion is such, that typical reader response theories – which merely focus on the performance and understanding of the text – seem insufficient. Yeatsian orality, for example, not only has effects that relate to musicality and meaning, but it also aims to activate the memory in ways which are less immediately approachable in terms of reception theory than cognitive accounts of the workings of auditive memory.[5] The sound of Yeats's poetry not only makes it meaningful – it makes it memorable.

Remembering Yeats's poetry in all of its complexity involves, however, an acknowledgement that orality does not exist in splendid isolation. Even a cursory reading reveals poetry extraordinarily self-conscious of its own inscription: Yeats not only frequently refers to the fact that his work is written down, but also meditates on the fact that his poetry is printed in books. The ensuing stress on the written word, and the desire for a written work of absolute status, is to a large degree one he inherits from Stéphane Mallarmé and the Symbolists. Especially in the early poetry, a tendency towards a highly wrought and convoluted style evolves out of a desire to cultivate the specific characteristics of the written medium. At the same time, though, Yeats is always conscious of a long tradition whereby poetry draws upon the resources of song.[6] Certainly this Irish context is of particular importance to Yeats, interacting with a patriotic ballad tradition he was exposed to via John O'Leary[7] – as well as his early fieldwork collecting folklore handed down orally through the generations. Yeats writes of Lady Gregory that she 'formed her style upon the Anglo-Irish dialect of her neighbourhood, an old vivid speech with a partly Tudor vocabulary, a syntax partly moulded by men who still thought in Gaelic' (*CW5* 207). Though Yeats eschews dialect for a style built on elements from the mainstream of the tradition, he nevertheless insists that 'folk song' exists just below the surface as of his poetry as 'a ghostly voice, an unvariable possibility, an unconscious norm' (*CW5* 214).

Orality is not just a public inheritance for Yeats; it is also a personal one. For the struggle, or complex interrelation, between orality and writing has a deep, psychological resonance in his biography. A comparison with Seamus Heaney is perhaps instructive here. While Heaney's poem 'Digging' presents an oedipal struggle where the son counters the father's prowess with the spade with his own skill with a pen,[8] Yeats's poetry to a certain degree countered the talent his father, John Butler Yeats, had for talk with his own accomplishments as a writer.[9] And, as with Heaney, there is a kind of reconciliation or counter-movement, where the son endlessly returns to pay homage to, and to subsume, the father's particular gift: in Heaney's poetry this is evident in how the poet constantly takes agricultural work as a template for his own artistic activity, while in Yeats a similar gesture is sketched by how the son repeatedly returned to the idea that great poetry should approach the status of impassioned speech. Elizabeth Cullingford has pointed out that Yeats associated his mother 'with Ireland and with the oral tradition, emphasizing her fondness for exchanging stories about fairies and supernatural events with the fishermen's wives at Howth.'[10] Yet the recorded references to this link are few and far between; the more frequently made identification of the father with orality is a singular twist to Yeats's parental relations that skews the typical psychoanalytical identification of the mother with bodily relations and the father with the symbolic order.

If we return to the poem 'Easter, 1916' (*VP* 391–4, *CW1* 182–4), we find that this tragic poem both covertly and overtly negotiates with various modes of communication. It begins with an evocation of what really is a lack of communication:

> I have met them at the close of day
> Coming with vivid faces
> From counter or desk among grey
> Eighteenth-century houses.
> I have passed with a nod of the head
> Or polite meaningless words.
> Or have lingered awhile and said
> Polite meaningless words,
> And thought before I had done
> Of a mocking tale or a gibe
> To please a companion
> Around the fire at the club.
>
> (ll. 1–12)

A lack of closeness and intimacy is registered here: Yeats and the soon-to-be rebels were familiar with one another in Dublin, but did not have any significant contact. There are more things happening in these lines, however. For one thing, it is significant how concretely Yeats describes central Dublin; the result is that oral speech is specifically rooted in time and place, in a way which his concluding written inscription of the rebellion (at the very end of the poem) will not be. Equally striking is the repetition of the phrase 'polite meaningless words': it is suggested that urban life is, to a large degree, characterized by a form of verbal intercourse that is conventional and superficial. We are not too far removed from Wordsworth's strong denigration of city life, and its lack of face-to-face encounters, in the seventh book of *The Prelude*. Even further back, eighteenth-century philosophers and critics, basing themselves on Rousseau and Herder, contrasted the atrophied and degenerate language of civilization's prose with the more original and emotional cry of poetry.[11] One can find traces of such an opposition in Yeats's writings – most clearly perhaps in the poem 'Paudeen', where the 'fumbling wits' of the urban mercantile class are pitted against more transcendental values in a revelatory meeting with curlews (*VP* 291, l. 1; *CW1* 108–9). By contrasting the sound made by the curlews with the 'confusion of our speech' (l. 7), Yeats momentarily identifies himself with the shopkeepers, but his real sympathies are with the 'sweet crystalline cry' (l. 8) of the birds. In 'God's eye' (l. 6), he claims, no soul can be said to lack the transcendent cry.

One of Yeats's typically romantic twists on the eighteenth-century motif of the originary and primitive lyrical cry, is to make it animalistic. This takes a burlesque form in 'Solomon and the Witch' (*VP* 387–9; *CW1* 179–80), where the 'Arab lady' (l. 1) lets out a cry which is described as being 'said, sighed, sung / Howled, miau-d, barked, brayed, bellied, yelled, cried, crowed' (ll. 7–8). This combination of primitive cry and animal is not apparent on the surface of 'Easter, 1916', but impinges upon the margins of the text. At the beginning of the second stanza, the potential sweetness of Countess Markiewicz's voice is contrasted with the shrillness of her argumentation:

> That woman's days were spent
> In ignorant good-will,
> Her nights in argument
> Until her voice grew shrill.
> What voice more sweet than hers
> When, young and beautiful,
> She rode to harriers?
>
> (ll. 17–23)

The relation between the shrillness of oppositional speech and a more original sweetness is brought out in a bird metaphor of another poem included in the collection *Michael Robartes and the Dancer*. In this poem, 'On a Political Prisoner' (*VP* 397; *CW1* 186), the youthful Markiewicz is said to 'have grown clean and sweet / Like any rock-bred, sea-borne bird' (ll. 17–18) – a bird that ends the poem crying 'out the hollows of the sea' (l. 24).

One key difference between Yeats and the eighteenth-century cult of the primitive cry lies in that the former never cultivates any purely natural ideal. The claim proffered in 'A Prayer for My Daughter', that 'in custom and in ceremony / Are innocence and beauty born' (*VP* 406, ll. 77–8; *CW1* 192), is fairly far removed from the position of someone like Rousseau (even with due allowance for the fact that the Frenchman was less primitivist than what is often inferred to be the case). Nevertheless, if we return to 'Easter, 1916', we encounter an opposition between natural life and unnatural distortion in the third stanza. The rebels are implicitly cast as being single-minded, with fanatical hearts of stone:

> Heats with one purpose alone
> Through summer and winter seem
> Enchanted to a stone
> To trouble the living stream.
>
> (ll. 41–4)

R. F. Foster has linked these evocative lines with a letter where Yeats derided '"Dublin talkers" who "value anything which they call a principle more than any possible achievement".'[12] The combative nature of their speech acts is tied to the general concept of 'opinion', which makes frequent appearances in Yeats's writings and thought of the time. 'Opinion' is a kind of speech and thought that he diagnoses as not only dominating the public life of Ireland, but also having roots in himself. Yeats's struggle to protect his own poetical gift from ephemeral controversy, as well as his rather inconsistent ponderings on the force of hatred and bitterness, show that this is not simply a handy abstraction with which he can pigeonhole his opponents, but very much the cause of inner struggle.

These categories are related in complex fashion to the different modes of speech that claim his attention. Edna Longley has linked the fanaticism of the stone with the 'mechanical refrains' and 'rhetorical repetition' that she claims characterized Young Ireland Ballads.[13] At the same time, however, the ballad form's oral roots make it very amenable to oral recitation and performance – a quality that should create an affinity with the more flexible and vital 'living stream', which Yeats contrasts to the stone. The oral tradition is also implicitly present at the beginning of the fourth and final stanza, when Yeats writes that it is

> our part
> To murmur name upon name,
> As a mother names her child
> When sleep at last has come
> On limbs that had run wild.

(ll. 60–4)

Here art is absorbing the practice of a more everyday form of speech. According to Mikhail Bakhtin, literature consists of genres that are in fact dependent upon such exposure to what he identifies as the 'primary' genres of everyday life:

> Secondary (complex) speech genres – novels, dramas, all kinds of scientific research, major genres of commentary, and so forth – arise in more complex and comparatively highly developed and organized cultural communication (primarily written) that is artistic, scientific, socio-political, and so on. During the process of their formation, they absorb and digest various primary (simple) genres that have taken form in unmediated speech communion. These primary genres are altered and assume a special character when they enter into complex ones.[14]

What does the written poem – articulating a lyrical version of tragedy characteristic of Yeats – garner from the mother's words here? And what sort of 'special character' is lent to those words by the context of Yeats's poetry? In his *Autobiographies*, Yeats claims that his own murmuring of names was inspired by hearing an Irish Member of Parliament recite a ballad that involved a similar list (see *CW3* 233). Thus this could be construed as a completely intra-literary affair, and not a crossing of a 'primary' (everyday) genre with a 'secondary' (artistic) one. Yet the use of a mother figure at this juncture also has other resonances. Jahan Ramazani has described this as 'a momentary shift in gender, when the poet leaves behind the stern and judgmental voice of the paternal Minos for the loving murmur of the elegiac mother.'[15] Arguably, the identification with the mother figure in 'Easter, 1916' marks a stage in a development where the poetry's relation to the voice of femininity is far from stable. Yeats's early poetry may have cultivated a rather aestheticized idea of youthful, feminine beauty, but even then he not only adopted feminized positions himself, but also gave voice to different roles for women. For instance, some critics have claimed that 'The Song of the Old Mother', in *The Wind among the Reeds*, is an ironic poem that does not really identify with the practical anxieties expressed by its speaker, but by *Responsibilities* (published in 1914), Yeats's persona is unequivocally adopting a similar stance. The speaker of the poem 'A Memory of Youth' claims that he has his 'share of mother-wit' (*VP* 313; *CW1* 122), and an identification with old females – often mother-figures – is underway, which will later include not only 'Easter, 1916' but also the vigorous rebelliousness of Crazy Jane.

Despite evidence of such a 'feminisation' of Yeats's persona, the poet seems at his most self-assertively masculine towards the end of the poem:

> I write it out in a verse –
> MacDonagh and MacBride
> And Connolly and Pearce
> Now and in time to be;
> Wherever green is worn,
> Are changed, changed utterly:
> A terrible beauty is born.

(ll. 74–80)

The strong link made here between writing and history is not accidental, if we are to believe Michel de Certeau. He claims that 'in the West, for the last four centuries, "the making of history" has referred to writing.'[16] This traditional notion of history he understands as one of subjection, whereby the body and the materials of the narrative are controlled in an act of will-to-power. Yeats's act of history writing does not, however, fully belong to the mainstream of this tradition. As was remarked in Chapter 7, the change undergone by the rebels in 'Easter, 1916' involves a transition from a comic to a tragic paradigm. At the same time, the very issue of sudden and complete transformation is borrowed from mythology – evoking not only Ovidian metamorphoses, but also the alterations described in the popular legends of an oral Irish tradition collected by Yeats early on in his career. Thus only two years before the Easter Rising, Yeats writes an essay titled 'Witches and Wizards and Irish Folk-Lore', where he describes the 'transformation or projection of the sidereal body of witch or wizard. Once the soul escapes from the natural body, though but for a moment, it passes into the body of air and can transform itself as it please or even dream itself into some shape it has not willed' (*CW5* 76). This supernatural metamorphosis finds an echo towards the end of 'Easter, 1916', when Yeats says of the rebels: 'We know their dream; enough / To know they dreamed and are dead' (ll. 70–1). Owing to the unpredictability of national politics, the result of their dream may to some degree have caused them to be transformed – like the witches and wizards of folklore – into 'some shape [they had] not willed', but the completeness of the change is in any case similar in both cases.

The striking alteration of the rebels derives something of its mysteriousness from a seeming discrepancy between cause and effect. One can trace a similar incoherence in the narratives of the actual historical event; there was a gap between what was publicly known of the rebels and organizations such as the Irish Volunteers and Irish

Civil Army, and their sudden and, in some ways, rather haphazard actions on Easter Monday. The failed rising and its transformation in light of public opinion and national history are also separated by a lacuna. In both cases, the interstices between present and unpredictable future were filled with a plethora of rumours. First there were the various accounts and messages circulated among the rebels, due to the internal divisions and secrecy among them, and the confusion caused by Eoin MacNeill's countermanding order. Then there was the lack of information during the actual rising. According to Charles Townshend, there 'was "absolutely no authentic news" to be had; just rumours of German invasion, rumours of provincial Volunteers flocking to Dublin, rumours of annihilation, "each rumour more fantastic than the last".'[17] Finally, there was the dearth of news after the rebellion, when English censorship meant that all information about the events that contradicted the official view was suppressed. Particularly the last of these factors had an impact on Yeats, since he was in England at the time. In general the Rebellion comes across as an elliptical event, where accounts and opinions were created through the unpredictable mediation by word-of-mouth. Thus the discrepancy in Yeats's poem, between the 'polite meaningless words' (l. 6) and the final, assertive 'write it out in a verse' (l. 74), to a certain degree stems from the force of event itself, and not just Yeats's own poetics.

Raymond Williams has differentiated between how revolutions are considered in their own time, on the one hand, and how they are understood with the benefit of tranquil hindsight on the other. The first of these is 'so evidently a time of violence, dislocation and extended suffering that it is natural to feel it as tragedy, in the everyday sense.'[18] Later, however, the revolution (if it succeeds) 'becomes no tragedy but epic: it is the origin of a people, and of its valued way of life.'[19] One of the strengths of Yeats's poem is that it manages to embrace aspects of both these perspectives: 'Easter, 1916' captures the sense of bewilderment and waste characteristic of a contemporary response, even as it accepts the inaugural force of the event. Between these two, however, there is a lacuna: knowledge of what exactly happened during the Rising is unsure, and the suddenness of the Rising causes it to come across as something akin to a revelation. Still, despite the force of the event, and Yeats's earlier immersion into the role of motherhood in the poem, the ending of 'Easter, 1916' can be read as an aggrandizement of the poetical voice. This would involve ultimately subsuming the voices of mother and revolutionary heroes from a position of elevated and lyrical solitude: what Bakhtin terms the 'secondary' speech genre of the literary text expands its dominion through the appropriation of the 'primary' genre of the mother's speech. The aesthetic distance we encountered in the previous two chapters recurs in a slightly different guise, pitched closer to the raw, changeable matter of history.[20] We would not, by such a reading, be that far removed from a poem such as 'To be Carved on a Stone at Thoor Ballylee', which asks: 'may these characters remain / When all is ruin once again' (*VP* 406, ll. 5–6; *CW1* 193). At the very end of his introduction to Scribner's planned edition of his collected works, Yeats claimed that 'State and the Nation are [. . .] not worth the blade of grass God gives for the nest of the linnet' (*CW5* 216), and it is possible to see the poet as merely using the events of the Easter Rising to feather his own poetical nest. As prose sublates poetry in the teleology of Hegel's thought, the written word would transcend and yet incorporate the riches of orality in the final, transformative apocalypse of Yeats's poem: that which would change everything utterly would in fact be the beautiful but terrible ruthlessness of the poet's own writing. Such a reading could gain support from Paul de Man's claim that Yeats's mature style 'accentuate[s] the distinction between spoken and written language',[21] thereby assuming a certain autonomy for itself.

Yet theorists such as Bakhtin and Paul Ricoeur have reminded us that writing works, not as an isolated force, but as a mode of communication that interacts with the more localized effects of living speech. Subjected to closer examination, the self-reflective utterance 'I write it out in a verse' (l. 74), may not be quite the isolated *fiat* that it seems to be at first glance. There is for instance the coupling of personal agency with the act of inscription, which goes against the grain of the impersonality often stressed in post-structuralist and symbolist accounts of writing. In addition, one might consider Yeats's many concrete references to the act of writing stemming from this period. As Lucy McDiarmid has pointed out, these references just as often denigrate or point to problems concerning the act of writing, as they exalt it.[22] One particularly striking example is Michael Robartes's chiding remarks in 'The Phases of the Moon', where the poet who 'seeks in book or manuscript / What he will never find' is compared unfavourably to Owen Aherne – whose 'thought is clear' precisely because he 'never wrote a book' (*VP* 372–7; *CW1* 164–8). Here it is possible to envisage the poet's position as a tragic one; due to the impediment of writing, he will never gain the position of immediate knowledge attained by Owen Aherne. The best possible insight, in this respect, would be a paradoxical knowledge of non-knowledge.

Edna Longley claims that the pronouncement made at the end of poem may, perhaps, 'not be quite straightforward: does the self-evident statement intend a monument or a plain record?'[23] The tensions, evident in the poet's stance earlier in the poem, survive in the ending. This is also true of his mode of speech: for what the poet spells out in verse is written according to the dictates of a style that he has admitted is at least partially derived from an oral tradition. Here we once more come across the problem of Yeats's relation to everyday speech, previously addressed in Chapter 2. The late Yeats claims that he has 'tried to make the language of poetry coincide with that of passionate, normal speech' (*CW5* 212). Does this mean that poetry appropriates passionate speech, or does it – on the contrary – subject and return itself to the living flow of that speech? Rather than presenting some facile solution to this conundrum, it might be best to leave it open. Yeats's poetry alerts us to the fact that there is a dizzying force that distinctively belongs to words existing, as it were, in a disconnected state. On the other hand, his verse also bears witness to the obvious truth that no words can do any good in complete isolation. This poetry's glory begins and ends, one might say, in its alliance with living speech.

Despite being fascinated by the fixity and quasi-autonomous power of the written word, Yeats had little time for those who saw poetry as something created autonomously out of the subjectivity of the poet. He understood himself as working within and through tradition, rather than as an isolated artist. This position is occasionally taken to be anti-modernist, but chimes at least broadly with the modernist aesthetic Yeats's younger contemporary T. S. Eliot presented in 'Tradition and the Individual Talent'. Eliot's essay famously includes the following *gnomon:* 'Some one said: "The dead writers are remote from us because we *know* so much more than they did." Precisely, and they are that which we know.'[24] Another poem of Yeats's – 'Among School Children' (*VP* 443–6; *CW1* 219–21) – approaches the problem of knowledge by borrowing the words of tradition. 'Among School Children' turns from the tragedy of wasted lives – the lives of the speaker, his beloved, and the school children he observes as a visitor – to a vision of fulfilled being. The narrow ken of the knowledge attained by the school children and a number of named philosophers is contrasted with a state of being where 'body is not bruised to pleasure soul' (l. 58). The poem is a complicated affair, however, involving eight numbered stanzas that do not progress in a straightforwardly ordered fashion. The concept of knowledge – and a small tradition of earlier poems about learning – will provide a means here to argue for a sense of cohesion between elements of the poem usually not brought into intimate contact with one another.

Ulysses may constitute a significant exemplar for 'Among School Children'. We know that Yeats read the novel in 1922,[25] and that debates about free speech provoked him to consistently champion Joyce over the next few years. Declan Kiberd has argued that 'Joyce's entire work is a sustained meditation on true and false pedagogy',[26] and the Yeats who set about writing a poem on ideals of teaching and learning would have found much of interest in *Ulysses*. Book two, 'Nestor', is of particular relevance: Stephen's discussion with his pupil, Cyril Sargent, after class at a private school in Dalkey, anticipates 'Among School Children' in more ways than one. Sargent's unprepossessing exterior provokes Stephen to speculate about the pupil's mother:

> Ugly and futile: lean neck and tangled hair and a stain of ink, a snail's head. Yet someone had loved him, borne him in her arms and in her heart. But for her the race of the world would have trampled him under foot, a squashed boneless snail. She had loved his weak watery blood drained from her own. Was that then real?[27]

Here Joyce anticipates a key feature of Yeats's poem, namely its stress on the fragility of human existence as reflected in the barely started lives of school children. Yeats's notes have revealed that the original germ of his text was a prose stub on 'School Children & the thought that life will waste them [:] perhaps that no possible life can fulfill their own dreams or even their teacher s [sic] hope' (*TMM* 361).[28]

Although Yeats's poem begins by stressing the distance between the dutiful children and the 'sixty-year-old smiling public man' (l. 8) who visits them, the third stanza quickly breaks down this sense of alienation, as one of the children reminds the speaker of his beloved. In 'Nestor', there is a similar, revelatory point of identification as Stephen sees an earlier version of himself in Cyril Sargent: 'Like him was I, these sloping shoulders, this gracelessness. My childhood bends beside me.'[29] Later on in the same book, Stephen's discussion with the schoolmaster Mr Deasy politicizes the context for this educational encounter. There is no direct parallel in Yeats, yet there is a slight hint of a surprising, submerged convergence between Yeats's poem and Stephen's famous claim, in this passage, that 'History [. . .] is a nightmare from which I am trying to awake.'[30] In

Yeats's poem, the generational impulse of life itself is briefly cast in similar terms in the fifth stanza, as the poem's 'youthful mother' (l. 33) is 'betrayed' (l. 34) into childbirth, and 'must sleep, shriek, struggle to escape / As recollection or the drug decide' (ll. 35–6). This perspectival shift from male speaker to female character is representative of the different stances of the two texts; not only does Yeats's poem take place in a school room of girls rather than boys, but the speaker is also far more willing to identify with female figures than what is the case with Stephen's more misogynist stance.

'Nestor' is full of quotidian detail, ranging from the school books and a game of hockey, to the portrait of Prince Edward hanging on Mr Deasy's wall. The opening stanza of Yeats's poem is also characterized by a degree of empirical specificity that is rare for this poet:

> I walk through the long schoolroom questioning;
> A kind old nun in a white hood replies:
> The children learn to cipher and to sing,
> To study reading-books and history,
> To cut and sew, be neat in everything
> In the best modern way – the children's eyes
> In momentary wonder stare upon
> A sixty-year-old smiling public man.
>
> (ll. 1–8)

These lines have been subject to differing responses from some of Yeats's most astute readers. Frank Kermode claims there is a sense of dissonance, as the poet 'sees himself as amusingly humiliated, not too seriously betrayed, putting up with the shapelessness and commonness that life has visited upon him.' Kermode interprets the reference to an education conveyed 'in the best modern way' as a 'hint of unambitious irony'.[31] The humdrum activities undertaken at the school decisively distinguish the young girls from Maud Gonne and the self-presence of the dancer, even as the same pupils prepare the entrance of the latter heroic figures. Superficial school learning is no match for the deeper knowledge embodied in the unity of dancer and dance.

Kermode's reading is flatly contradicted by Donald Torchiana. In the essay '"Among School Children" and the Education of the Irish Spirit' – an important basis for both Roy Foster's biographical reading and Elizabeth Cullingford's feminist historicizing of the poem – Torchiana identifies the inspiration of Yeats's poem as primarily stemming from a visit to St Otteran's, a Montessori school in Waterford, in February 1926. For Torchiana, the first stanza is 'not at all ironical in its context', and he finds no 'immediate mockery' in Yeats's use of the phrase 'the best modern way'.[32] Torchiana's interpretation is primarily based upon an inspection of Yeats's senatorial speeches from this period, which show evidence of the poet being very much impressed by both the practice and the principles of the Montessori method. Torchiana ignores, however, the fact that the term 'modern' is seldom used in a straightforwardly positive sense by Yeats – including the famous, derisory reference to 'this filthy modern tide' in 'The Statues' (*VP* 611; *CW1* 345).

Bakhtin claims that 'any utterance, when it is studied in greater depth under the concrete conditions of speech communication, reveals to us many half-concealed or completely concealed words of others with varying degrees of foreignness.'[33] There is indeed a 'foreignness' at work in the passage discussed here that might lead one to wonder whether these words are fully Yeats's own. One reason for Kermode's believing that there is an ironic undertone to the beginning of 'Among School Children' is, presumably, the style of much of the opening stanza. The catalogue of school activities is particularly pedestrian by Yeats's typical standards:

> The children learn to cipher and to sing,
> To study reading-books and history,
> To cut and sew, be neat in everything
> In the best modern way.
>
> (ll. 3–6)

The repeated use of the simple connective 'and' (which is a distinctively light-weight carrier of stress in line 3), as well as the rhythmical simplicity of the three first lines and the descriptive vagueness of 'neat', 'everything' and 'best modern way', all seem to suggest that the poet may be intentionally lowering his tone. Perhaps one could even go so far as to say that poetic utterance is being invaded, or at least subtly deformed by, the force of a bathetically everyday speech? This suspicion is largely confirmed when one brings a possible inspiration for Yeats's lines into the equation. W. S. Gilbert and Arthur Sullivan's 1884 comic opera *Princess Ida* shares with Yeats's poem a focus on learning, as it satirically depicts the establishment of separate educational institutions for women in late Victorian society. In the second act of the opera, the drunken 'kissing song' performed by the character Cyril begins as follows:

> Would you know the kind of maid
>   Sets my heart aflame-a?
> Eyes must be downcast and staid,
>   Cheeks must flush for shame-a!
>   She may neither dance nor sing,
>   But, demure in everything,
>   Hang her head in modest way,
>   With pouting lips that seem to say,
>   'Oh, kiss me, kiss me, kiss me, kiss me,
>   Though I die of shame-a!'
> Please you, that's the kind of maid
>   Sets my heart aflame-a![34]

There is a striking overlap with Yeats in three lines here: 'She may neither dance nor sing, / But, demure in everything, / Hang her head in modest way.' The 'sing'/ 'everything' rhyme is the same, while 'best modern way' is echoed in 'modest way'. Similarly to the opening of Yeats's poem, Cyril's song is presenting an ideal of femininity that exists in a relation of tension with the values that are presented elsewhere in the opera. Cyril's overly conservative and submissive ideal is at the opposite extreme of the amazon independence pursued by Princess Ida and her associates at the castle Adamant, just as the school children's modern submissiveness, in Yeats, is opposed to the heroic autonomy of Maud Gonne and the dancer. Interestingly, dancing is explicitly dismissed in the passage in *Princess Ida*, which thus constitutes a kind of negative foreshadowing of the celebrated embodiment of this ideal at the end of Yeats's poem.

Genette describes 'Serious transformation, or *transposition*' as 'without any doubt the most important of all hypertextual practices.'[35] More perhaps through the highly different context into which they are transported than the modification to which Yeats submits them, the words from *Princess Ida* suffer a sea-change in how they are to be interpreted. Here Genette's definition of 'transvaluation' seems relevant: 'the hypertext takes the opposite side of its hypotext, giving value to what was devalued and vice versa.'[36] To be sure, it is no surprise that one of Yeats's most celebrated poems takes a different tack than a work of comic opera: one may indeed ask whether it is at all credible to present Yeats as being inspired by the populist comedy of Arthur Sullivan's lyrics. The former is of course typically seen as a stalwart defender of elitism in art – as someone who avoided simple solutions and any dabbling in easy appeal. In a recent essay on Yeats and popular culture, Geraldine Higgins takes what might seem to be the safest option: she never even asks what popular culture might have meant for Yeats in his own time, instead investigating how the popular culture of our own time makes use of 'the quotable Yeats'.[37] There is, it appears, only one-way traffic between Yeats and the popular. Yet we know Yeats was exposed to a far wider range of cultural phenomena than some of his pronouncements on the arts might lead one to anticipate. He did not shun Gilbert and Sullivan's operas altogether,[38] and during the period broadly in question – the mid-1920s – one of his long-term collaborators, the artist Charles Ricketts, was busy designing sets and costumes for *The Mikado*.[39] Also, Yeats's curiosity might conceivably have been piqued by the fact that Gilbert and Sullivan's play is fairly closely based on Tennyson's poem *The Princess* (1847–51), via the intermediate link of Sullivan's own *The Princess* (a 1870 burlesque of Tennyson's text). There are several thematic links between Sullivan's libretto and 'Among School Children'. Like Joyce's 'Nestor', *Princess Ida* has a scene that seems to anticipate Yeats's discovery of Maud Gonne in the features of one of the school children. In the first act of the play, the male protagonist Hilarion claims that he can conjure up an inner vision of what Princess Ida now looks like, constructing this image on the basis of a childhood picture. Yeats's attention would have been sharpened by the use of an allusion to *Hamlet* at this point:

HILARION:	She *is* my wife – has been for twenty years!
	(*Holding glass*). I think I see her now.
HILDEBRAND:	Ha! let me look!
HILARION:	In my mind's eye, I mean – a blushing bride,
	All bib and tucker, frill and furbelow!
	How exquisite she looked as she was borne,
	Recumbent, in her foster-mother's arms![40]

Like Yeats's play, Sullivan's libretto has a strong focus on relations between parents and children. The texts also share an interest in classical literature. At the beginning of the second act of *Princess Ida*, Melissa asks 'Pray, what authors should she read / Who in Classics would succeed?'[41] Psyche's response expresses conservative anxiety concerning the exposure of young women to the more challenging parts of the canon:

> If you'd climb the Helicon,
> You should read Anacreon,
> Ovid's *Metamorphoses*,
> Likewise Aristophanes,
> And the works of Juvenal:
> These are worth attention, all;
> But, if you will be advised,
> You will get them Bowdlerized![42]

Such doggerel is a far cry even from Yeats's most relaxed verse, yet the underlying tenor is not all that far removed from the flippantly sceptical account given of Plato, Aristotle and Pythagoras as 'Old clothes upon old sticks to scare a bird' in the sixth stanza of 'Among School Children' (l. 48). In a broader perspective, Sullivan is here positioning himself within the broader ambit of the nineteenth-century debate concerning the use of classical literature for educational purposes. Although the classics then had a prestige and pivotal educational role far removed from what is the case today, many voices questioned that centrality. This is evident in several literary works, including the depiction of Tom Tulliver's ineffectual and wasted efforts to master the classics in *The Mill on the Floss*. Seen in this perspective, our understanding of Yeats's poem gains a new dimension when we are alerted to its allusive play on *Princess Ida*. Typically, critics tend to keep the quotidian detail of the opening rather separate from both the subsequent stanzas on Maud Gonne and the more principled and transcendental discussions of images that conclude the poem. But perhaps the text as a whole sticks closer to its starting point than what is commonly believed? The playful dismissal of the Greek philosophers in the sixth stanza is more clearly motivated, if one sees Yeats as basically continuing a Victorian debate about the value of a classical education.[43]

What is true knowledge and what can it do for us? Not only Victorian education, but also the didactic challenges faced by the new Irish state of the 1920s provide part of the contextual ambit for the poem's response to these questions. As Sean Farren has shown, Ireland was in the 1920s characterized by a situation in which 'the new regime [. . .] decided to "Gaelicise" education'.[44] While modern dancing and the cinema were cultural pursuits that were anathema to the more conservative segments of the new regime, more progressive voices embraced Irish dancing and music as cultural activities that should naturally fulfil an integral part of the new educational dispensation. Elizabeth Butler Cullingford is perhaps bit too quick, in an otherwise impressive reading, to conclude that 'Yeats's dancer, body sensuously "swayed to music", is certainly not performing a "healthy" Irish reel.'[45] One of the most central figures forming the new educational policy on Irish dance and music was in fact an associate of Yeats's, by virtue of being the leader of the Abbey Theatre orchestra. In a letter to Edmund Dulac, dated 21 March 1924, Yeats refers to him as 'a really distinguished man, Dr Larchet, [who] has I believe arranged the whole teaching of music for the Irish schools under our new education act' (*CL Intelex* 4499). In light of this connection, and the poet's own divided loyalties and affinities, Yeats's concluding vision in 'Among School Children' is open to a variety of interpretations. As the one of his fictional speakers puts it in Yeats's article on 'Compulsory Gaelic': 'I am so uncertain about everything, and there is so much to be said upon every side' (*CW10* 176). While the concluding vision of a dancer may have its context partially provided by symbolist aesthetics, as has been generally assumed,[46] it may however also invoke the more historically specific issue of the role of dance in Irish pedagogical thought of the 1920s.

One does not always have to choose between diverging interpretations of Yeats's poems, since they tend to present a flexible blend of – or vacillation between – heterogeneous positions and voices. The complexity of 'Among School Children' may be interpreted as a generic remnant of Tennyson's *The Princess*. As mentioned before, *Princess Ida* is a light-hearted rewriting of Tennyson's text. Gilbert and Sullivan have taken over something of the polyphonic multiplicity of the Victorian Poet Laureate's poem. *The Princess* presents itself as a medley, constructing one tale out of the interwoven speeches of seven different male characters – speeches which are interspersed with songs performed by female members of the same party. The poem's conclusion emphasizes how this leads to some uncertainty about its tone: is the poem to be read as 'mock-heroic' or 'true-heroic'? As a whole, it is neither, staging 'a little feud betwixt the two, / Betwixt the mockers and the realists'.[47] 'Among School Children' continues this feud, choosing neither downright scepticism nor straightforward affirmation in its dealing with the interwoven questions of education and femininity. Carolyn Williams has pointed out how Gilbert and Sullivan's '*Princess Ida* ridicules, from the very beginning, the utopian vision of the women's university, which in Tennyson's poem is vividly and sympathetically portrayed (until it is abolished)'.[48] If the comic opera parodies the benevolent (if limited) account of female education presented by Tennyson's poetry, Yeats is to some degree performing a restorative action. He is, however, not only doing this through a second-level parody of the content of Gilbert and Sullivan's parody, but also through formal means. Sequence poems by Yeats such as 'Vacillation', 'The Tower' and 'Among School Children', where individual sections are given Roman numerals and a modicum of autonomy, present special problems for interpretation – formally challenging the reader's ability to identify and weigh a variety of possibilities up against each other. In this respect, we are not that far removed from Tennyson, whose use of the medley form in *The Princess* provoked considerable consternation among Victorian critics. Like the medley, the sequence poem opens for disconnected and open-ended relations. Both Tennyson and Yeats, then, are involved in a poetical pedagogy of their own, teaching their audience to engage in a more plural and inclusive form of interpretative activity – teaching us, in short, to read in the best modern way.

This chapter has shown how Yeats accommodates more popular voices in two poems. In 'Easter, 1916', the nationally urgent gesture of commemoration comes about through a *rapprochement* with the ballad and orality, while 'Among School Children' engages with the issue of women's education by both appropriating and combating the populist art of Gilbert and Sullivan. Mikhail Bakhtin's notion of 'speech genres' – an inclusive term that includes both literary and non-literary modes – has been deployed in order to articulate how Yeats opens up his writing for more popular forms of communication. The result is an inclusive and wide-ranging form of poetry. Still, the mixture of speech genres takes place in a highly localized and (in the main) controlled way. The question of authorial control will come to the fore in the next chapter, when Yeats's dealings with the visual arts and the genre of ekphrasis are given central stage.

Ekphrasis and Excess

The image has a special place in Yeats's poetics. For him, the images of poetry and those of the visual arts are not isolated from one another. Yeats was the son of a portrait painter (John Butler Yeats), the brother of Ireland's most famous artist (Jack Butler Yeats) and had two sisters (Lily and Lolly Yeats) engaged in the arts and crafts movement.[1] Furthermore, his highest education stems from the Metropolitan School of Art in Dublin. So Yeats has close contact with the visual arts for much of his life, and there is an immediate, biographical context for his willingness to see affinities between literature and art. Throughout his career, Yeats also drew upon the precedents of William Blake's and the Pre-Raphaelites' frequent practice of linking poetry with artistic images. The Symbolist Movement was another key impetus, as Yeats's complementary early essays on 'Symbolism in Painting' (*CW4* 108–12) and 'The Symbolism of Poetry' (*CW4* 113–21) make clear. His continued insistence upon the image's relevance to different forms of art can be seen as untypical of the Modernism that came to the fore in the first decades of the twentieth century. As Jacques Rancière has noted, modernity has been linked with how the individual arts are able to

> assert the pure potential of art by exploring the capabilities of its specific medium. Poetic or literary modernity would explore the capabilities of a language diverted from its communicational uses. Pictorial modernity would bring painting back to its distinctive feature: coloured pigment and a two-dimensional surface. Musical modernism would be identified with the language of twelve sounds, set free from any analogy with expressive language, etc.[2]

But this parting of ways is only part of the story. As Rancière himself is keen to stress, there is an equally significant tendency – evident for instance in Dadaism – to abolish the autonomy of the individual arts 'in favour of a great chaotic juxtaposition, a great indifferent melange of significations and materialities.'[3] As has often been the case in this study, an apparently clear opposition between Yeats and Modernism does not hold water at closer inspection.

In what follows, Yeats's dealings with the literary genre of ekphrasis will provide an opportunity to ponder whether words such as 'chaotic' and 'melange' are apt to describe the imbrication of art and literature in his poetry. Ekphrasis has been defined by James Heffernan as 'the verbal representation of visual representation'.[4] Typically, an ekphrastic poem will respond verbally to a particular painting or visual work of art. This can involve a kind of painting in words where the physical features of the original are copied part-by-part through verbal description. Usually, though, ekphrastic poetry will eschew going too far in such an objective direction by embracing more subjective facets of experience. Increasingly, the museum has come into focus as an institutional site where ekphrastic encounters can take place.[5] The central study on Yeats and ekphrasis, Elizabeth Bergmann Loizeaux's *Yeats and the Visual Arts*, demonstrates that the Irish poet is not an atypical case here. Certainly, his close relationship to the visual arts does not lead Yeats to simply equate the business of poetry with that of painting or sculpture.[6] Early on in his career, he makes some rather straightforward attempts at mimetically ekphrastic poetry, drawing upon artworks by J. T. Nettleship and his own father, but these efforts soon leave him disillusioned. In 1892, we find him deriding the work by Katherine Harris Bradley and Edith Emma Cooper (publishing together under the pseudonym of Michael Field) in this genre, dismissing their intention to 'set to work to observe and interpret a number of pictures, instead of singing out of their own hearts and setting to music their own souls. They have poetic feeling and imagination in abundance', Yeats writes, 'and yet they have preferred to work with the studious and interpretative side of the mind and write a guidebook to the picture galleries of Europe, instead of giving us a book full of the emotions and fancies which must be crowding in upon their minds perpetually' (*CW9* 167–8).

Can ekphrastic poetry with any validity deal with the excess represented here by the 'crowding in upon' minds of a multiplicity of impressions? Such poetry would, presumably, be marked by a chaotic 'melange' of the kind evoked by Rancière. It seems, however, to contradict the ideals of later Yeats, as these have been elucidated by Loizeaux. For her, Yeats's later ekphrastic practice is built upon sculptural principles: 'As his use of Michelangelo in the later poems and his preoccupation with monuments suggest, Yeats came to think of his craft as violently active, of his material as hard and sometimes resistant, and of his product as solid and permanent.'[7] A rather different understanding of images comes to light if we turn to *The Trembling of the Veil*, published in 1922. In the latter, which was among the autobiographical writings addressed in Chapter 4, Yeats depicts his own early struggle to find direction and unity in life, buffeted as he was by warring political, esoteric and aesthetic impulses. The section of this autobiography titled *Hodos Chameliontos* – which Yeats translated as 'the path of the chameleon' – describes his early state of disarray as follows:

> To that multiplicity of interest and opinion, of arts and sciences, which had driven me to conceive a Unity of Culture defined and evoked by Unity of Image, I had but added a multiplicity of images [. . .] now image called up image in an endless procession, and I could not always choose among them with any confidence; and when I did choose, the image lost its intensity, or changed into some other image. I had but exchanged the temptation of Flaubert's *Bouvard et Pécuchet* for that of his *Saint Anthony*, and I was lost in that region a cabbalistic manuscript, shown me by

MacGregor Mathers, had warned me of; astray upon the Path of the Chameleon, upon Hodos Chameliontos. (*CW2* 215)

This passage vividly portrays the problems facing a sensibility overly exposed, or responsive, to images. Yeats here seems to anticipate the kind of image overload associated with Postmodernism, but the thought also represents a far from unnatural consequence of post-romantic aesthetics; if the poet is primarily characterized by his imagination, and that faculty is not ruled by the will, what can he do but follow the beck and call of the images delivered by his primary faculty? Later on Yeats developed a systematic philosophy of his own in order to rein in and control his picture-making proclivities, and he generally shows a tendency to portray his own career as providing a rather straightforward progression from immature bewilderment to assured mastery. The endless 'procession of images' of his early career, we are asked to believe, is replaced by a much more settled and centred state of affairs.

Thus the kind of magisterial force Loizeaux locates at the heart of Yeats's ekphrastic poems is in line with the poet's ideals. But does it accurately reflect the content and effect of ekphrasis in Yeats? Does his actual textual work obediently follow his metatextual self-analyses? The poem that I want to circle around in the first part of this chapter, 'Leda and the Swan' (*VP* 441; *CW1* 218), is among other things about the meeting of the two positions sketched above: an intersection between a vulnerable form of extreme receptivity and an overwhelming, indeed quasi-divine, position of power. In 14 concise lines, making an extremely compact and controlled utterance, Yeats memorably retells one of the many mythological accounts of divine annunciation handed down to us from Greek mythology. It is a highly graphic poem, as the bodily encounter between Zeus (taking the form of a swan) and his rape victim Leda is described in devoted, almost finicky, detail. This physicality threatens to entirely overshadow the mythological context of the encounter, though the concluding sestet does manage to throw in some pointed references to its result: the conception of Helen, and the ensuing Trojan war.

Yeats's rendering of the myth has been credited with reintroducing a focus on the sheer brutality of the rape, which had long been underplayed in artistic and poetic versions of it. The beginning of the poem could hardly be more violent: 'A sudden blow' strikes the reader before he or she knows what is happening (l. 1). This spectacular violence reflects the poem's own dealings with its imagery. This is not only due to the way the poem swiftly presents a curtailed version of the mythological story, dwelling upon physical detail, but also how Yeats draws upon – forcefully selecting and contracting – a variety of visual sources. Furthermore, the poem's afterlife – through its explication by Yeats and various other interpreters – would seem to echo that violence on a metatextual level. If 'Leda and the Swan' is born from violence, it would also seem to engender a certain kind of violence. As such, it does not so much present an example of the poet controlling images, as a process of image calling up image in a potentially endless series. The monstrous issue of the mingling of mortal and swan will, in effect, prove to cast us back onto the path of the chameleon.

'Leda and the Swan' was written in September 1923, only three years after Yeats made a return to the ekphrastic genre with 'Michael Robartes and the Dancer'.[8] By that time

Yeats was certainly in no danger of making his poetry a subservient vehicle for others' images, of the kind he had derided early on in his career. As Ian Fletcher has shown, 'Leda and the Swan' is ekphrastic only in a covert and idiosyncratic way. The poem draws upon a rich tradition of classical, renaissance and more modern visualizations of mythological material. In Fletcher's analysis, the paintings of Michelangelo and Moreau come across as the most significant forebears for Yeats's poem. Giorgio Melchiori anticipated him in pointing to the influence of Michelangelo;[9] the orgasmic intertwining of bird and woman in his renaissance version anticipating 'Leda and the Swan'. With regard to Moreau, Fletcher notes that 'sacred marriage rather than rape is prominent' in his version: 'Leda achieves apotheosis; creature is mystically united with creator. [. . .] Yeats could hardly have evaded Moreau's images, yet their feeling is quite polar from the violence and sensuality in the sonnet.' Still, the annunciation motif is more clearly obvious in Moreau's version than most others, and Fletcher concludes that Yeats 'rectifies Moreau's passive vision by viewing him through Michaelangelo'.[10]

Such similarities and putative influences need to be extrapolated through close interpretation, unlike what is the case with much ekphrastic verse. For Yeats does not acknowledge his sources. Thus many readers to this day are unaware of the complex act of iconic borrowing – an intermedial form of hypertextuality – performed by the poem. This arguably represents an extreme version of the appropriative force typically evident in ekphrastic poetry, as the poet here does not deign to refer (however briefly) to his sources, but rather claims the image as his own – obliterating any overt trace of its originals. As such Yeats's poem presents a forceful embodiment of the paragonal tendency through which, in the words of W. J. T. Mitchell, 'Each art, each type of sign or medium, lays claim to certain things that it is best equipped to mediate, and each grounds its claims in a certain characterization of its "self", its own proper essence.'[11]

This does not mean that the hypertextual relation is entirely one-sided. Yeats's ekphrastic poetry seeks in some ways to accommodate itself to the essence of the artistic image, adjusting its own form to the nature of its visual subject. As we shall see, making a poem like an image is not without its risks. One could say that this kind of ekphrasis makes for particularly 'aesthetic' poetry, in at least two senses. The first sense is provided by Jacques Ranciére, when he says that aesthetics 'means the rupture of the harmony that enabled correspondence between the texture of the work and its efficacy'.[12] Exactly what form this rupture takes will be explored in the remainder of this reading. The second sense is more historical: the choice of the genre of the sonnet for 'Leda and the Swan' is not accidental, as Yeats inherits from Dante Gabriel Rossetti and the Aesthetic movement of the Victorian age a conception of the brief, concentrated form of the sonnet as a means for constructing a 'moment's monument'. In response to artworks that depict the events of a particular moment, the sonnet represents an especially apt formal choice. The way in which 'Leda and the Swan' almost exclusively focusses upon the brief moment of encounter between divine bird and mortal woman bears evidence of a harnessing of the lyric form to the purpose of framing a passing instant of time. Thus Lessing's influential dichotomy between literature's temporality and the visual art's spatiality is occluded or set aside.[13] Yet the concluding question of the sonnet could be said to simultaneously suggest that there is a crucial, underlying difference: 'Did she put on his knowledge with his power / Before the indifferent beak could let her drop?' (ll. 13–14). As verbal artefacts, works of literature have an immediate and essential discursivity that is not to be found in the artworks from which Yeats's poem is taking its bearings. This can be interpreted as an unfortunate limitation on how far literature can take the kind 'rupture' between work and effect Ranciére ascribes to art in general. Traditionally, however, aesthetically hierarchical accounts of the various arts have as a result tended to grant literature a privileged access to epistemological insight: like other art, literature gives us a modicum of sensuous immediacy – but it also provides us with cognitive gains. In short, and linking up to the concluding question of the poem, Yeats's work may indeed be exactly the kind of follower or inheritor that can put on 'knowledge', while the arts would (according to this view) be more limited to attaining the heights of 'power'.

If we move from the archaeology of the relations between 'Leda and the Swan' and its artistic forebears, to its subsequent interpretative frameworks, the question of knowledge – and the possible absence of knowledge – persists. The history of the poem highlights the difficulty of controlling the epistemological outcome of the image, in the process illustrating a problem that Yeats struggled with for much of his career. When an earlier play of Yeats's, *The Countess Cathleen*, provoked a violent reaction among its Dublin audience in 1892, Yeats himself put this down to a basic problem of framing the meaning of the play's images: 'In using what I considered traditional symbols I forgot that in Ireland they are not symbols but realities' (*CW2* 309). By the time he wrote 'Leda and the Swan', Yeats was more inclined to carefully control the reception of his work, but – as we shall see – that would not fully safeguard him against arbitrariness and open-endedness; there still is a tendency towards 'rupture' between the work and its effect.

Yeats originally wrote the poem in response to a request from his old friend George Russell, who had asked for a contribution to his political journal the *Irish Statesman*. This was, however, not to be, and the first publication of the poem, in *The Dial* in June 1924, was accompanied by a metatextual note, where Yeats explained:

> I wrote Leda and the Swan because the editor of a political review asked me for a poem. I thought, 'After the individualist, demagogic movement, founded by Hobbes and popularized by the Encyclopaedists and the French Revolution, we have a soil so exhausted that it cannot grow that crop again for centuries.' Then I thought, 'Nothing is now possible but some movement from above preceded by some violent annunciation.' My fancy began to play with Leda and the Swan for metaphor, and I began this poem; but as I wrote, bird and lady took such possession of the scene that all politics went out of it, and my friend tells me that his 'conservative readers would misunderstand the poem.' (*VP* 828)

One fascinating consequence of the chequered history of 'Leda and the Swan' is that Yeats would later reinscribe the poem in precisely the political context from which he originally extracted it. He later published it not only in the Irish journal *To-morrow*, but also at strategic and over-determined locations: in the celebrated *The Tower* volume (1928) and in *A Vision* (1925, 1937). It stands at the head of the historical section of *A Vision* – a section titled 'Dove or Swan' – and would there seem to reflect the violent transition from the primary civilization of Christianity to a more anti-democratic, antithetical era, which Yeats saw as imminent in his own time.

Owing to Yeats's inclusion of the poem in *A Vision*, such a historical reading of the poem is legitimate. Perhaps it is not much of a stretch, either – given such a context – to move the political setting of the poem to that of the struggle between Ireland and Britain. Late in his career, Yeats wrote of how his hatred for England 'tortures me with love, my love with hate' (*CW5* 211), and as such the traditional understanding of Leda's seduction as being both forced and acquiescent might seem a not completely unfitting vehicle. On this basis, Declan Kiberd has constructed a reading of the poem as a reflection of colonial power relations.[14] Yet the relative facility with which one fits 'Leda and the Swan' into such historical contexts may ultimately stem more from the poem's own detachment than its inherent engagement with given contexts. In the previously cited note in the *Dial*, Yeats wrote that the poem began as 'metaphor', before 'bird and lady took such possession of the scene'. The vehicle of the metaphor took over, ultimately not only occluding its own tenor–of which it presumably would give us some insight or knowledge–but also detaching itself from that tenor. The whole poem might be termed a mangled metaphor or a truncated trope. If Yeats, then, in Fletcher's account acted with appropriative gusto and took free possession of the art historical images that were at his disposal, one can also say that the process of composition seems to have led to an image that subsequently took possession of Yeats's creative act.

How can one interpret such an event of possession? Two immediate contexts suggest themselves. First, it seems relevant to bring in the movement of Imagism here (see the analysis of *The Resurrection* in Chapter 6). Although Yeats never fitted perfectly in with the dogmas of the movement, 'Leda and the Swan' does suit certain imagist tenets better than much of his verse, particularly with regard to the economical style and lack of interpretation. According to Pound's definition, an '"Image" is that which presents an intellectual and emotional complex in an instant of time. [. . .] It is the presentation of such a "complex" instantaneously which gives that sense of sudden liberation; that sense of freedom from time limits and space limits; that sense of sudden growth, which we experience in the presence of the greatest works of art.'[15] Thus it is possible to see Yeats's poem as showing what for him is an unusually acute degree of modernist autonomy, whereby the literary image becomes a freestanding and self-supporting entity of considerable elliptical intensity.

Another context is even closer at hand, though. If one takes a look at a poem no less celebrated than 'Leda and the Swan', namely 'The Second Coming' (*VP* 401–2; *CW1* 189–90), one finds a description of a process in some ways similar. There, Yeats presents the poet as contemplating a contemporary state of disorder, where 'the centre cannot hold' (l. 3). Meditating upon this state of affairs, the poet is gripped by an epiphanic vision – 'a vast image out of *Spiritus Mundi* / Troubles my sight' (ll. 12–13) – before using this vision to frame a concluding question about the beast slouching 'towards Bethlehem to be born' (l. 22). The reference to *Spiritus Mundi* draws upon Yeats's faith in that there is a collective memory available to all artists, upon which all great art draws. Yeats's description of how the imagery of 'Leda and the Swan' took possession of him seems to suggest a similar surrender to collective insight, notwithstanding the fact that this surrender is not explicitly presented as it is in 'The Second Coming'. Are we in

'Leda and the Swan' presented, not with the violent moment of subjection to the image, but rather just with the image itself? The problem with such an interpretation is that it ingenuously ignores the very overt process of violent forcing that is the content of the poem. This is true also of other formalist readings, such as the imagist one suggested above: the way in which the ending of the poem explicitly raises the possibility and problem of force accompanying insight, necessarily also raises the question how form may or may not be embroiled in content. Unsurprisingly, perhaps, content has been privileged in interpretative framings of this poem – Elizabeth Butler Cullingford's reading of the poem via both 'a positive liberal-historicist hermeneutic and a negative feminist one' being especially notable.[16]

My own sketch of both the iconic prehistory and the interpretative afterlife of 'Leda and the Swan' has approached the text from another angle. The aim here has not been to explain, or present a final genealogy for, Yeats's images. Rather, I have sought to own up to the compelling force of the procession of images, each adjusting the other. It is a profound testimony to the poem's power that it will not allow us to rest in any complacent, formalist seclusion, even as its independence troubles the instruments of more matter-of-fact approaches. Between possession and detachment, 'Leda and the Swan' throws us once more onto the inexorable and winding path of the Chameleon. Yeats may want to have escape from the procession of images he felt himself subjected to as a young man, but the aesthetic nature of the ekphrastic genre rebels against any too simple ordering or dominating of the many images evoked by the poem. This is the case even if 'Leda and the Swan' combined the ekphrastic genre with the conventions of the sonnet – or perhaps this combination in fact heightens the aesthetic 'rupture' postulated by Ranciere. In what follows, an even more complex instance of generic overlapping, in a text that operates that within demanding but more spacious formal parameters, will be inspected. In Chapter 6 the manner in which *The Resurrection* combined several dramatic genres was a theme. But is there no limit to such generic profusion in one single text – no point at which a polygeneric stance can reach a state of exhaustion? And is there something specific to Yeats in such combination of many forms in one poem?

One of Yeats's most familiar ekphrastic poems, 'The Municipal Gallery Re-visited' (*VP* 601–4; *CW1* 326–8), brings these questions to a head. It is a poem of many returns and repetitions, effectively working over both thematic concerns and formal schemes which Yeats had made extensive use of for many years. Familiarity lies at the heart of the poem: thrown into the unknown space of the Municipal Gallery, among alien objects, the speaker's main work in the poem is to render the unfamiliar familiar. The 'images of thirty years' (l. 1) are appropriated by him, as he forces them to yield his own story. This reading will single out some of the more conventional and established frameworks in evidence in 'The Municipal Gallery Re-visited'. In addition to ekphrasis, these include the stanzaic form of *ottava rima*, the thematic convention of the poem of friendship, the genre of elegy, the use of a given and accommodating physical setting, and the genre of history writing. Certainly, the interaction between these frameworks is not simple, particularly since each and every one of them is a fairly complex beast in itself. In his study on the concept of genre, John Frow claims that '*formal and rhetorical structures always convey meaning*'.[17] While this is true, the manners in which they express meaning are diverse, and so – more often than not – are the meanings conveyed.

The same might be said of the basic stanzaic grid within which this poem works. As the name indicates, the *ottava rima* form – an eight-line stanza rhyming abababcc – has Italian origins, but that does not mean that it has a univocal or linear history. For Helen Vendler, '*ottava rima* (throughout Yeats) stands for Renaissance courtly achievement, for culture, for civilization, for "monuments of unageing intellect", for an achieved artifice (either of eternity or of time).'[18] Contrary to a scholar like Cairns Craig – who has documented how Herbert Grierson's scholarly work on Byron influenced Yeats – Vendler dismisses any suggestion that Yeats might be building on the precedent of Byron's ironic deployment of this stanzaic form.[19] In the case of the Municipal gallery poem, the context makes it fitting to see the use of rhyme, in particular, as both playing on a sense of civilized achievement *and* undercutting irony. The confident assertion latent in the final couplet rhyme of 'ends' and 'friends' thus finds its counterpoint in other, imperfect end rhymes in stanzas three and six. The poise and symmetry of the *ottava rima* form in general, is further in contrast to the oddly incomplete, seven-line format of stanza five – seven also being the total number of stanzas in the poem.

Thus classicism is coupled with crookedness in the basic formal schema of the poem. On a more thematic level, the use of the friendship motif is also accompanied by tension. There is tension between the traditional, literary treatment of friendship and the rather tight form for which Yeats has opted here. The eighteenth-century epistle, for instance, is a very loose form, in which the generosity and freedom often associated with modern ideals of friendship are given room to roam. But perhaps Yeats has a more formal kind of friendship in mind in 'The Municipal Gallery Re-visited'? His thoughts on friendship in the poem come after finding images of Lady Gregory, her son (Robert Gregory), Hugh Lane and John Synge among 'the images of thirty years' (l. 1). These were all figures who stood by Yeats's side in the struggles of the Irish Literary Revival in the first decades of the twentieth century, supporting his desire to develop Ireland into a prominent nation in European culture. Most of them were also his associates in the more specific battle to establish a first-class art gallery in the centre of Dublin, building on Hugh Lane's bequest of impressionist art. Yeats presents them with a weighty accolade when he concludes the poem with the celebrated lines: 'Think where man's glory most begins and ends / And say my glory was I had such friends' (ll. 54–5). It is hard, though, to not feel that this statement is something of an exaggeration. Friendship is seldom explicitly addressed in Yeats's poetry – compared to for instance love and hate, it is a very minor theme. The poem as a whole also seems too publicly oriented to convincingly deal with the private relations we today associate with friendship. R. F. Foster has another objection: he claims that 'the ending rings hollow', since Yeats 'was aware that his glory would reside in his books, not in the roll-call of his acquaintance.'[20] Sceptical readings of this kind tend to take for granted, though, that the poem's use of the word 'friendship' is synonymous with our contemporary, everyday meaning. Explicit allusions to Spenser and Shakespeare should suffice, however, to alert the reader that this poem is casting its net relatively deep into the ocean of tradition. More specifically, Yeats's statement on friendship might be taken as an echo of Henry Bolingbroke's claim, in the second act of *Richard II*, that 'I count myself in nothing else so happy / As in a soul rememb'ring my good friends' (II, iii, 46–7).[21] The more classical, civic kind of friendship that was the hallmark of the Early Modern period – as an affinity that could easily include relations of patronage – arguably contradicts the informal and affective relations currently associated with the term.[22]

The third framework I want to address is that of the genre of elegy.[23] 'The Municipal Gallery Re-visited' is both a group elegy for Yeats's deceased friends and an elegy for Yeats himself. Insofar as elegy deals with the dead by way of repeatedly returning to present traces of a past existence, its content touches upon the haunting of ghosts and more gothic territory. A poem such as 'All Soul's Night' uses this similarity as a structuring conceit. Even if an early draft anticipates of Hugh Lane that his 'ghost here will haunt / their empty walls' (*NPMM* 319),[24] the final version of 'The Municipal Gallery Re-visited' renders the ghosts of the past less as supernatural beings – less like the harassing familiars of folklore and gothic fiction – in that their shadowy afterlife is mediated by works of art. The elegiac insistence remains, however; as we are told in stanza four, 'time may bring / Approved patterns of women or of men, / But not that selfsame excellence again' (ll. 30–2).

This poem is not unique in combining these elements, as elegy coexists with both a set of regular and relatively lengthy stanzas and the topic of friendship also in other celebrated poems written by Yeats. In both 'In Memory of Major Robert Gregory' (first published in 1918) and 'All Soul's Night' (1924), for instance, Yeats has created elaborate celebrations of deceased friends in poetic structures not unlike that of 'The Municipal Gallery Re-visited'. Helen Vendler has also linked the second poem of 'The Tower' sequence to these, and one could easily argue that 'Among School Children' takes place in a similar terrain – what with its use of *ottava rima*, emphasis on ageing and his relationship to Maud Gonne, as well the sudden, erotic flashback similar to that found in the second stanza of the Municipal gallery poem. In all of these poems an elegiac or compensatory memory provides the impetus for meditation: loss triggers a wealth of self-discovery and exploration. There are lots of differences at hand, yet nevertheless these poems share the kind of family resemblance that is distinctive of genre. They also provide an interesting glimpse of the creative and developing nature of poetic genre, from within the confines of the *oeuvre* of a single poet. David Duff has pointed out that 'the perception that literary genres are dynamic rather than static entities – that they change or "evolve" across time – is the single most important factor separating modern from earlier genre theory.'[25] From one poem to another in this group, we can see Yeats solidifying and revising a fairly consistent structure that contains both formal and thematic elements.

Vendler remarks upon the inner freedom of the speaker of these poems, identifying in them 'a powerful new genre of Yeatsian lyric' that allows for '"realistic" autobiographical meditation' building on 'sweeping and (putatively) random reminiscence'.[26] It might be added that the speaker's freedom is predicated upon the existence of a fairly flexible setting. In 'The Municipal Gallery Re-visited', we are conscious of the speaker wandering from picture to picture in the tacitly suggested space of the gallery. As Catherine Paul's reading of the poem points out, the museum's space is particularly facilitating in this regard.[27] But also the spaces of the tower in the elegy to Robert Gregory and the private room of 'All Soul's Night' ground their speakers' wandering thoughts in similar fashion. If Yeats summons insubstantial familiars, then the basis of a given and in some ways more solid setting is essential. With respect to how they anchor their wandering musings in a given space, Yeats's poems of friendship remembered build on a familiar template. Romantic texts such as 'Tintern Abbey' and Coleridge's conversation poems, which again were based upon the eighteenth-century loco-descriptive poem, work in a similar way. For Yeats, however, the space that enables the establishment of what a draft calls 'the Ireland – of my mind' (*NPMM* 321) is an embattled and vulnerable site. In stanza five of 'The Municipal Gallery Re-visited', we are told that 'all lacking found' in a particular physical setting (l. 35): loss finds consolation and riches in Lady Gregory's 'household where / Honour had lived so long' (ll. 34–5). Yet whereas Gregory's Big House in Coole Park will soon be demolished, new places facilitating meditation and art are coming into being. Figures mentioned both in draft (such as another co-founder of the Abbey Theatre, Frank Fay) and final versions, indicate that the Abbey Theatre is a tacit alternative at this juncture. But more clearly and explicitly, the Municipal Gallery – 'this hallowed place' to which Yeats invites his audience to come, in the final stanza (l. 51) – is cast as a new Big House of sorts by the poem.[28] Not only is it presented as a monument to the past created by Synge, Gregory and Yeats, it is also portrayed as a receptive space capable of nurturing new acts of creation and national self-definition.

The collective force of just about everything discussed so far in this chapter would seem to suggest that 'The Municipal Gallery Re-visited' is, in important respects, a poem that presents itself as a decidedly *familiar* performance within Yeats's collected works. It utilizes the frameworks of ottava rima, friendship, elegy and space in a way that is recognizably Yeatsian. Sure enough, this sense of overfamiliarity has led to sceptical responses among some critics, who have found this to be an uncharacteristically jaded effort on Yeats's part. Thomas Parkinson, for instance, has censored the poem for 'certif[ying] meanings already habitual' for Yeats.[29] Such a reading grasps only part of the whole story, though, and definitely fails to capture what makes 'The Municipal Gallery Re-visited' a singular performance. For this is a poem that immerses itself in familiarity and the habitual to the point of excess, but in the process establishes itself as a singular performance – and a distinctive exploration of how literature can negotiate with habits and familiarity. The previously mentioned allusions to Shakespeare (in the reference to Hugh Lane as the 'onlie begetter' of the gallery's artworks in line 22, as well as the concluding couplet) and to 'Spenser and the common tongue' (in line 40) highlight the sense of borrowing and belatedness, for instance. And of course the ekphrastic framework of the poem is not new either: Wayne Chapman has argued that the poet in the gallery *topos* builds on seventeenth-century precedent, particularly in the poetry of Edmund Waller.[30]

The poetic response to pictures is however a new addition to the distinctively Yeatsian genre in which this poem participates. One does not find ekphrasis in the elegy to Robert Gregory, the second part of 'The Tower', or any of the other poems that have been mentioned. In Alastair Fowler's taxonomy of forms of generic transformation, this fits in with the category of inclusion. Fowler's main example of this can indeed be considered part of the genealogy of the kind of poem Yeats is working on: namely, Marvell's combination of 'the local descriptive and estate poems with the retirement poem [. . .], to produce a complex form adumbrating the eighteenth-century poem of retirement.'[31] The manner in which Yeats's friendship elegies steadily increase in formal sophistication, combining new forms in an ongoing process of assimilation, suggests that this is one of his most developed responses to what he saw as the hegemony of the novel in dealing with the deeper problems of everyday life on a large scale. His gradually widening conception of what this kind of poem can encompass contradicts Mikhail Bakhtin's influential contrasting of the novel's 'extreme receptivity to other genres', with a view of lyric poetry as exclusionary.[32]

Catherine Paul and Elizabeth Bergmann Loizeaux have recently contributed instructive new readings of how Yeats uses ekphrasis in 'The Municipal Gallery Re-visited', particularly stressing its institutional stakes. Loizeaux is surely correct when she claims that the 'paragonal strain of ekphrasis', as defined by scholars such as W. J. T. Mitchell and James Heffernan, is present throughout the poem.[33] In other words, the literary work is entering into a competition or struggle, of sorts, with the visual arts. Something of this struggle is evident in stanza four, which questions whether painting could render the 'pride' and 'humility' of Lady Gregory (l. 29). Also the summary of Hazel Lavery's pictorial presentation in the words 'As though some ballad singer had sung it all,' in the preceding stanza (l. 24), can be interpreted as tilting the scales towards the art of words. The most striking evidence of the word dominating and appropriating the territory of the image, however, is found behind the scenes – in the compositional history of the poem. A speech given at a banquet of the Irish Academy of Letters, prior to the writing of the poem, summarizes a visit to the gallery as giving him an experience of 'Ireland not as she is displayed in guidebook or history, but, Ireland seen because of the magnificent vitality of her painters, in the glory of her passions.'[34] This obviously is the basis of part of stanza two, but the Ireland of the painters has been replaced by 'an Ireland / The poets have imagined' (ll. 11–12).

Where once there were pictures, now there are words. Like most appropriative gestures, Yeats's version of *ut pictura poesis* functions not only through self-empowerment but also elision. Art suffers a determinate negation as motifs and (in some cases) artists are mentioned, but not the titles of the art works – obscuring, in some cases, exactly which works are being addressed. Thus while we definitely know that Yeats's poem refers to Antonio Mancini's painting *Augusta, Lady Gregory* (1908) and to John Butler Yeats's *John Millington Synge* (1912), other acts of identification are more difficult.[35] Commentators have been especially challenged by the 'Beautiful and gentle' woman mentioned in the second stanza: Hazel Lavery, Lady Beresford and the *fin du siècle* model Ryllis Hacon have all been suggested referents,[36] in what is a quietly burgeoning field of biographical speculation. Many such questions will most likely never be settled, due to the simple fact that Yeats's poem does not give us enough to go on. Perhaps one can even see a sly, winking anticipation of this in the quoting of the 'onlie begetter' dedication to Shakespeare's sonnets in the subsequent stanza (l. 22), since the patron referred to in that dedication has similarly been very hard to identify.[37]

By virtue of being an ekphrastic poem, 'The Municipal Gallery Re-visited' takes its place beside other Yeatsian poems about pictures, including the very different 'Leda and the Swan'. By returning to the issue of Hugh Lane's gallery and pictures, the former also links up thematically with earlier efforts such as 'To a Wealthy Patron' and 'Coole Park, 1929'. At the same time, this poem also represents – as I hope to have shown here – a widening and developing of Yeats's own genre of meditative group elegies set in a quasi-realistic setting. Thus the generic placing of a poem such as this is a complex affair, more suggestive of a complicated network of connections than a row of tightly separated pigeonholes. In light of this, one could say that Yeats's poem on the Municipal Gallery both reveals and conceals its own generic status. By adding ekphrasis to the mix, it masks or makes contentious the very existence of a loosely coherent set of group elegies. At the same time the poem is overloaded with generic ore. The multiplicity of relevant thematic and formal frameworks thrusts the conventional nature of such a text to the fore, emphasizing the work's constructed nature. This is particularly relevant with regard to ekphrasis, since Yeats's discussing of the art works' verisimilitude, force and meaning inevitably reflects back on his own poetic practice. The poem defamiliarizes its own constructed and artificial nature.[38]

Yet even as this happens, Yeats's poem insists upon its own power and extra-aesthetic validity. Unlike what narrowly conceived formalist theories have led us to expect, the way in which 'The Municipal Gallery Re-visited' defamiliarizes its own poetic essence does not lead to an insistence upon artistic autonomy. Instead, it validates the poem's relation to the public sphere – via the institutional framework of the art gallery – and the political constitution of the Irish State (through the themes of the paintings). This is of course evident from the very beginning of the poem, where the speaker utilizes the motifs of the paintings to question the values and narratives of the new nation. In doing so, it links up with yet another genre: namely, history. 'The Municipal Gallery Re-visited' is also a work of history, even if it is one of a peculiarly subjective and partisan kind. Even if the strong Ascendancy colouring of Yeats's version of history may seem not only quaint or self-serving, but also decidedly misguided, today, the poem's engagement on this terrain still is impressive – and it crowns what is an almost virtuoso performance in the intermixing of genres. Unmistakably familiar, yet also oddly unfamiliar, 'The Municipal Gallery Re-visited' shows what happens when generic multiplicity becomes unshackled. As such, its achievement is comparable to, if different from, that of 'Leda and the Swan': the visual richness of the latter makes it, too, difficult to pin down. In these two texts, ekphrasis does not come across as a matter of poetry's appropriation of tangible solidity, or the attainment of a restful simplicity borrowed from art. Rather, these poems show Yeats's lifelong investment in images leading him to construct a challenging form of poetry characterized by dizzying excess.

Shakespeare, Sonnets and Sonnetic Monstrosities

In *Yeats and Violence,* Michael Wood dismisses what he terms the 'imminent return of formalism' as 'one of the great myths of contemporary literary study.'[1] He does not refer to many specific instances of Yeats scholarship, and seems to be mainly alluding to formalist tendencies in other fields of contemporary criticism. Certainly, formalism has hardly been a dominant force in Yeats studies the last few years, being largely overshadowed by biographical approaches, implicitly or explicitly postcolonial readings, and interpretations emphasizing the material production and reception of Yeats's texts.[2] References to formal issues have tended to be cursory, or have amounted to paying lip service to a respected but unfashionable ideal. The recent study *W. B. Yeats in Context* is a characteristic instance of this. In their introduction to the essay collection, the editors David Holdeman and Ben Levitas claim that 'If Yeats is influential, it is an influence borne of technical mastery, and that in turn sits in particular relation to literary traditions. His verse must be contextualized fully within the literary field if we are to consider fully its purchase in the realm of social and cultural thought.'[3] Their essay collection is a fine contribution to Yeats Studies, featuring contributions from many eminent scholars, but this particular dimension of Yeats's writings cannot be said to be particularly well served in its 38 short articles. A stress on context tends to effect a downplaying of specifically textual matters, and – perhaps necessarily given the title and aims of the collection – there are sections on 'Personalities', 'Themes', 'Philosophies', and 'Arts', but none on 'Forms', 'Genres', or anything related.

A concern with thematic or biographical matters need not necessarily exclude an emphasis on, say, the rhythms, rhymes or genres of the poetry, but in practice the critics that place a major stress on the formal properties of Yeats's work are few and far between. Matthew Campbell and Peter McDonald have yet to produce book-length studies of this poet, but their work would arguably fit into this category.[4] Nicholas Grene's book on *Yeats's Poetic Codes* presents many worthwhile observations, but he is anxious that his title should not be misunderstood: 'This is not, in fact, a formalist study in that it has little to say about the genre or stylistic technique of individual poems or indeed of the collections that Yeats took so much care to shape.'[5]

Pure formalism, then, is hard to find in current work on Yeats. There is, however, one commanding work of recent criticism that surely qualifies as formalist: Helen

Vendler's pioneering monograph, *Our Secret Discipline: Yeats and Lyric Form*. One might counter that in addition to being – for the time being, at least – a fairly isolated instance of a particular approach, even her work is relatively far from embracing the kind of formalist autonomy derided by Wood: she is not concerned with form for form's sake. Yet Vendler faces more squarely than most the question of *how* Yeats's texts mean what they do, rather than just dwelling on *what* they mean. In the painstaking thoroughness with which she maps out textual structures, she is in fact an exemplary formalist critic, and very much an inspiration for studies – such as this one – that seek to grasp something of the formal articulation of Yeats's work. Vendler presents her study as 'in every sense a preliminary clearing of the ground of Yeatsian stylistics',[6] and this chapter will attempt to both (a) build on the ground cleared by her, as well as (b) question some of the premises of her foundational work. Vendler's insistence upon the necessary correlation between form and content will be ratified in what follows: form is of importance because it impacts on content, just as content always – in literary texts, at least – responds to formal pressures. This link becomes all the more important, and inescapable, when one deals with matters of genre, since genres not infrequently link particular kinds of content to specific formal features. This chapter will deal with Yeats's sonnets and his poems related to the sonnet, following Vendler's rewarding suggestion that many of Yeats's poems are generically akin to the sonnet, even if they are not identifiably sonnets in a narrow sense. The first part of this chapter will use Vendler's writings on Shakespeare and Yeats to question the Irish poet's relationship to the Shakespearean sonnet. Here the degree to which Vendler takes historical development into account when dealing with literary form will be a key issue, in a way parallel to how Chapters 3 and 4 questioned R. F. Foster's sensitivity to issues of literary form in his historically oriented biography of the poet. The concluding part of this chapter will use Vendler's work on Yeats and the sonnet more affirmatively, as a means to explore a surprisingly consistent thematic pattern.

In 1997 Vendler published *The Art of Shakespeare's Sonnets*, a blow-by-blow reading of all 154 of Shakespeare's sonnets over more than 650 pages. The introduction spells out some of the most important premises for her approach. The most prominent and controversial of these premises is the degree to which she stresses textual autonomy – thus self-consciously distancing herself from the more dominant modes of contemporary criticism. In her own words: 'Contemporary emphasis on the participation of literature in a social matrix balks at acknowledging how lyric, though it may *refer to* the social, remains the genre that directs its *mimesis* toward the performance of the mind in *solitary* speech.'[7] Vendler also remarks that Shakespeareans tend to misread the sonnets for a related reason: they project the play's contextual investments and dramatic qualities onto a kind of writing that is generically heterogeneous to such concerns. When she stresses that 'a poem is not an essay' and its 'paraphrasable propositional content' is not 'merely the jumping-off place for its real work',[8] we recognize the survival of New Critical beliefs. A version of New Criticism might also be assumed to be lurking behind Vendler's stress on poetry as a psychological spectacle: for her the important questions are 'How well does the structure of this poem mimic the structure of thinking?' and 'How well does the linguistic play of the poem embody that structural mimesis?'[9]

With regard to Shakespeare's sonnets, the evident structure of thinking is manifest in the poems' formal architecture. For Vendler, these sonnets exist in basic opposition to the precedent of the earlier Italian, or Petrarchan, sonnet. Whereas the Italian form is dual, through its linking octave and sestet together via a transitional *volta*, the Shakespearean equivalent is more manifold and unpredictable. Take for instance sonnet number 8, 'Music to hear, why hear'st thou music sadly?' Interpreting this poem, Vendler defends the poet's many variations of a conceit whereby the addressee's reluctance to fall in love is compared to the concord and discord of music. She utilizes a diagram in order to make an inventory of 'Shakespeare's strategies for unifying sonnet-parts into a true *concord . . . by unions married*.'[10] Underlying this organized plurality is what she calls an 'aesthetic principle': 'the resolution of many part in one unison', in the vehicle of the musical metaphor, 'is of obvious relevance as an aesthetic principle for the Shakespearean sonnet, which, because of its four discrete parts, runs an inherently greater risk of disunity than does the Italian sonnet.'[11]

For readers familiar with the basic architecture and history of the sonnet, Vendler's distinction between Shakespeare's aesthetic principle and that of the Italian sonnet may come as something of a surprise: conventional wisdom allows for both of these forms to be seen as either divisible by two or four. Traditionally, the English form has been seen as limited by the temptation to use the closing couplet as a vehicle for aphoristic *sententiae*, a kind of closure that invites our conceiving of the whole poem as primarily an argumentative vehicle – something which is at odds with the open-ended structures of meaning cultivated in modern poetry. Vendler, however, insists that because the Shakespearean sonnet, in her view, 'has four parts – three isomorphic ones (the quatrains) and one anomalous one (the couplet), it is far more flexible than the two-part Italian sonnet.'[12] This claim might have been more persuasive were it backed up actual readings of Petrarch or other representative instances of the Italian form.[13] In any case, the fairly exhaustive nature of Vendler's close readings of Shakespeare has the virtue of highlighting the diversity of her chosen texts: the thesis underlying and justifying her study as a whole – namely, that Shakespeare's *Sonnets* 'deserve detailed and particular commentary because they comprise a virtual anthology of lyric possibility' – is convincingly borne out.[14]

The relationship with the Italian precedent is also important for Vendler, due to the way in which it relates to the poet's self-conscious positioning of himself in relation to literary tradition. She sees this positioning as an act of active differentiation, claiming that:

> Because he is especially occupied with literary consolidation (resuming the topics, the images, the consecrated adjectives, and the repertoire of tones of previous sonneteers), one can miss his subversive moves: the 'shocking' elements of the sonnets in both subsequences: the parodies, by indirect quotation, of Petrarchan praise in sonnets 21 and 130 [. . .].[15]

Vendler is keen to stress the excellence of Shakespeare's sonnets, at one point calling him 'a master of aesthetic strategy'.[16] As a result, she tends to reprimand attempts from other critics to identify shortcomings or limitations in the sonnets' discourse or unfolding. For her, these poems are the finished article, and there is no question of mistaking their speaker's frequent bewilderment, hesitation or inconstancy of opinion as indicative of any kind of authorial lapse. In a way that brings to mind the typical retrospective, first person narration of the modern *Bildungsroman*, she insists that

> the author, who is arranging the whole poem, has from the moment of conception a relation of irony to his fictive persona. The persona lives in the 'real time' of the poem, in which he feels, thinks, and changes his mind; the author has planned the whole evolution of the poem before writing the first line, and 'knows' conceptually the gyrations which he plans to represent taking place over time in his fictive speaker.[17]

Given this position, one would expect Vendler to revel in the ironic and developmental possibilities provided by the sonnet sequence as a whole. After all, as John Kerrigan has pointed out, it is the 'subtle modulation of material from poem to poem into the form of the whole which makes reading Shakespeare's Sonnets such a concentrated yet essentially cumulative experience.'[18] As a matter of fact, though, Vendler tends to only register sequential structures in passing: apart from some notable summaries, her main concern is usually the individual poem as an autonomous verbal and psychological structure.

That act of aesthetic delimitation requires some vigilance. Despite having some common points with the interpretative practice of Paul De Man, Vendler is for instance very far removed from his insistence upon pursuing the effects of poetry's connotative connections. In a critique of Hans-Robert Jauss, De Man once noted the potentially vertiginous effects were one to pursue all the dissonant connotations of the name 'Boucher' in Baudelaire's 'Spleen II', insisting that 'it becomes very hard to stop'.[19] For Vendler, it is very important to stop – for a poem needs an external border, if one is to prevent it from spilling over into its surrounding frameworks. Thus she is adamant that Shakespeare's use of seasonal imagery is not to be over-interpreted. Commenting on sonnet number 5 and its claim that 'never-resting time leads summer on / To hideous winter and confounds him there' (lines 5–6), she makes a more general point:

> It cannot be too strongly emphasized that nothing can be said to happen in a poem which is not there suggested. If *summer is confounded in hideous winter*, one is not permitted to add, irrelevantly, 'But can spring be far behind?' If the poet had wanted to provoke such an extrapolation, he would by some means have suggested it.[20]

'[N]othing can be said to happen in a poem which is not there suggested': this ascetic injunction is one of the means by which Vendler defends her own approach to the sonnets against the claims of other alternatives – particularly Joel Fineman's psychoanalytic reading is singled out as deserving a rebuttal.[21] Yet one might doubt whether Vendler always follows this rule herself.

Indeed, if we turn from Vendler's study of Shakespeare to her reading of Yeats, we will soon enough find evidence of a less puritan approach. Much of her book

Our Secret Discipline: Yeats and Lyric Form (2007) was written while she was also at work on the study of Shakespeare. The book on Yeats shares with the earlier study an intense and unmitigated interest in lyric form, but focuses to a large degree on the structures and developments of *genres*, rather than just on specific poems. Its sixth chapter, entitled 'Troubling the Tradition: Yeats at Sonnets', is of particular interest here. Vendler sees Yeats's relation to the sonnet as one of continuous maturation from an early state of uncertain apprenticeship. Written when he was almost 70, 'Meru' is the great culmination of this process. After this bravado performance, Vendler implies that the only possible follow-up was to question or parody the form: with the 1938 poem 'High Talk', she sees Yeats as effectively deconstructing the entire genre. Before that, though, she interprets Yeats's sonnets and sonnet-related poems as a series of negotiations with both the Italian and English forms of the genre. Interestingly, she identifies the sonnet form as being latently present in Yeats's *oeuvre*, even in texts where one would not obviously look for it. Yeats, she claims, was innately attracted to the sonnet, but frequently tended to stray away from the form in the final version of his poems, often using the *douzain* form, consisting of three rhyming quatrains, instead. Thus her chapter on Yeats's sonnets not only looks at obvious candidates such as 'Leda and the Swan', 'Meru', and 'High Talk', but also argues relatively convincingly for the presence of sonnet-like structures in less obvious places, like 'When You are Old' and 'The Sorrows of Love'.

Vendler claims that Yeats associated the sonnet with certain values: it was (a) a distinctively written (rather than oral) form, (b) unabashedly artificial, (c) acutely self-conscious and (d) expressly English. With regard to the Englishness, she claims that precisely 'because of its centrality to English literature, the sonnet compelled from Yeats both his literary allegiance and his nationalist disobedience.'[22] She goes on to state that when 'we wonder why Yeats wrote so few "proper" sonnets, we can find the answer, I think, in his distinctive mixture of that allegiance and that disobedience.'[23] Vendler's interpolation of the words 'I think' here indicates, I think, that she has had to go beyond the textual evidence of the sonnets themselves in order to find her explanation. She is, in other words, trespassing against the injunction she placed against extra-textual evidence in her book on Shakespeare's sonnets.

Where would she find grounds for such conjecture? One way of justifying this reading would be to follow up on Vendler's fascinating hint about the *douzain* form. The latter is, as its name implies, a French genre – utilized by figures such as Ronsard, Hugo and de Vigny, and frequently by Verlaine and other symbolists whom were important for the early Yeats – and is as such rarely found in English poetry. The use of the sonnet's 14-line form can, then, more easily be interpreted as fitting in with English literary tradition than the alternative utilization of the 12-line form imported from France. The manner in which a tetrameter version of the *douzain* was favoured in the early poetry of Yeats's compatriot and close friend A. E. (i.e. George Russell) might be interpreted as a parallel case, which probably also involved an element of emulation and competition.

Still, this far from proves Vendler's thesis. Not only does the Frenchness of the *douzain* not decisively establish the Englishness of Yeats's conception of the sonnet – it does not provide any basis at all for establishing why Yeats might be tempted to avoid artistic links with Shakespeare and Englishness in the first place. One possible source for establishing such an aversion or repulsion would be Yeats's highly ambivalent description of his relationship to England: 'my hatred tortures me with love, my love with hate' (*CW5* 211). He also states: 'I owe my soul to Shakespeare, to Spenser and to Blake, perhaps to William Morris, and to the English language in which I think, speak and write' (*CW5* 211). Strong emotions and ambivalence are certainly on show here. Yet one might notice that Yeats does not express any kind of reservation with regard to the literary tradition embodied by Shakespeare, nor is there any evidence that Yeats saw his work as marked by British imperial views on Ireland. The same goes for the sonnet: Yeats nowhere expressly identifies the genre as an English one. Take for instance a letter to Dorothy Wellesley, dated 8 January 1937, where Yeats makes, in passing, a principled pronouncement about this genre in the context of giving some paternal advice: 'Your son wants a framework of action', he writes, 'much as a man who feels that his poetry is vague & loose will take to writing sonnets' (*CL Intelex* 6771). Notice that while the value of the sonnet might be construed of as being circumscribed here – as a mere means to sharpen poetic craftsmanship, rather than a worthy end in itself – there is no hint of any inherently national orientation. Rather than seeing the sonnet as an instrument of nationalism, Clive Scott has observed that 'national and international traditions [. . .] have increasingly interfered with each other and the structure of the sonnet has acquired a peculiarly "esperanto" flavour.'[24] There is no indication that Yeats – writing at a time when English poets, for instance, frequently favoured the Petrarchan form – is a particular exception to this trend.

In more recent times, another Irish poet, Seamus Heaney, *has* in fact made an associative link between the sonnet and English imperial history, and explained that this link was the cause of his feeling less than at home in the genre – but Heaney is not Yeats.[25] The latter never denunciates Shakespeare for any alleged imperial affiliations. As Rupin W. Desai has shown, there is instead a career-long process of influence and interpretation.[26] Early on in his career, Yeats writes mythological drama in blank verse in a conscious effort to transport his idiom to an Irish context. His early essay on Shakespeare, 'At Stratford on Avon' (1901), is very much a celebration. Written at a period when Yeats, in his own words, spent 'hours reading the plays, and the wise and foolish things men have said of them' (*CW4* 73), this essay not only puts Shakespeare on something of a pedestal, but does the same with his version of England: an England 'made by her adventurers, by her people of wildness and imagination and eccentricity' (*CW4* 78). Further, Yeats contrasts this past era of Merry England with the present's 'imperialistic enthusiasm' embodied in 'the practical ideals of the modern age' (*CW4* 79). In the use of Shakespearean's heroes in some of his later poetry, Yeats frequently finds constructive precedent for his own writing, causing T. McAlindon to claim that Yeats 'managed to achieve a remarkable degree of identification with Shakespeare.'[27] Thus Vendler's simple equation between sonnet form, Shakespeare and the ideology of empire in Yeats's mind seems questionable.

Vendler also tends towards essentializing the historical forms of the sonnet in her reading. The Italian and the English sonnet forms may be useful taxonomic tools, and rough guides to determine some of the more basic workings of the genre, but like all other genres the sonnet is subject to historical variation. By not drawing attention to this, Vendler is in line with an old, classic study like Walter Mönch's *Das Sonnet*, but even he – like Paul Fussell in another classical account – at least admits the added nuance of allowing for three rather than two basic forms.[28] A more historically attuned approach is needed: the sonnet genre is not a mere given and static vehicle, but rather an active framing device that itself is framed by outside contingencies and emphases. Stuart Curran has encapsulated this nicely: 'However extensive the generic line or obvious its pressure', he writes,

> the poetic genres are never mere abstractions: they are always individually recreated in a particularized time and place, and to discuss that recreation attentively requires both immersion in its historical setting and sensitivity to the ways in which great literature spans time.[29]

The ahistorical nature of Vendler's understanding of genre is particularly evident when she writes of the 'true sonnet', which she links to a textual structure that is characterized by a strong sense of antithetical conflict.

A related problem with Vendler's approach lies in how she tends to construct seemingly immediate connections between Shakespeare and Yeats. Here one must surely take into account forms of mediation similar to those we identified, in Chapter 5, as existing between Yeats and classical Greek philosophy: born roughly 300 years after Shakespeare, Yeats could not but approach his writings via the accounts and interpretations given of his work by others. Thus, in another context, Wayne Chapman has claimed that Yeats's 'regard for the Renaissance and its multi-faceted personalities ("Renaissance men")' was 'derived initially and substantially from influential others'– specifically Victorian others –'such as Arnold, Pater, and the elder Yeats'.[30] Though we know Yeats dismissed the scholar Edward Dowden as his own 'legitimate enemy' and as someone who was representative of what he called 'the middle class movement' (to Lady Gregory, 25 April 1901, *CL3* 61), Dowden still influenced Yeats's reading of Shakespeare. Another close friend of Yeats's, Thomas Sturge Moore, published an edition of Shakespeare's sonnets in 1899. In addition, the whole nineteenth-century development of the sonnet is relevant in this context, making it problematical to see Yeats's work as engaged in an exclusive interaction with Shakespearean and Petrarchan essences established long before. For instance, Vendler's interesting claim of there being shortened forms of the sonnet in Yeats's writings – even in cases where the link to the sonnet is not immediately obvious – could be productively linked with the explorations of caudate and curtailed forms of the sonnet in the writings of poets such as Hopkins and Meredith. Beyond that, Yeats was a close reader of a figure such as Dante Gabriel Rossetti and early on the editor of the Victorian anthology *Sonnets of this Century*, William Sharp, was an important ally.

In Vendler's account, Yeats becomes a better sonnet writer the more distant he gets from the Victorians. We are presented with a rigorously linear narrative of maturation, whereby the early Yeats basically does not understand the true nature of the form. Gradually, Yeats will approach the nature of the 'true sonnet', and in 'Meru' we finally find an instantiation of it. After that, only 'High Talk' remains as a late deconstruction of the entire form. While this narrative has much to say for it in terms of transparency and unity, it is less than closely attuned to historical nuance. As such it closely echoes Vendler's book titled *Coming of Age as a Poet*, where the careers of Milton, Keats, T. S. Eliot and Plath are similarly read in terms of straightforwardly teleological narratives.[31] If we inspect Vendler's analysis of Yeats the sonneteer more closely, we find that her basic premise is that in opposition to the 'true sonnet' discovered late in his career, Yeats's early Victorian work built on a conception of the form that was simplistically unified. Thus the 1886 Petrarchan sonnet 'Remembrance' is described as a 'dreamy early sonnet' which has 'almost no thought-content'.[32] For Vendler, such a 'creation of coherent emotional "atmosphere", rising, climaxing, and falling [. . .] continues to be Yeats's aim in the nineties.'[33] She acknowledges that unity was Yeats's aim, but understands this aim to be an aberration, since it does not agree with what she stipulates to be the authentic essence of the sonnet. It is implied that Yeats can only seek the alternative form out of weakness:

> The true inner quarrel of the binary Petrarchan sonnet is too much for him, as are the conflicting perspectives of the four-part Shakespearean sonnet. He therefore continues with the more manageably unifiable pentameter douzain, a form to which he returns (with variable rhyming) all his life, down to the year before his death.[34]

Here Vendler offers us not only an essentialist account of literary history, but also what one might call a monotheistic one. Yeats is not to have any other gods than Shakespeare, and Vendler – it is implied – has seen the single form in which Shakespeare's sonnets have their essence.

If one casts a glance back at the sonnet's nineteenth-century history, some of the problems with this view become evident. Jennifer Ann Wagner's account of the nineteenth-century sonnet starts off with Wordsworth's rediscovery of Milton's political sonnets in 1802. Wagner shows that this discovery entails the emergence of what she calls

> a third possibility for a model of form – the 'unitary' model. [. . .] the Miltonic sonnet, with its tendency toward enjambment and toward overrunning the sonnet's turn, offers the possibility of a unitary model that allows for an opposition or turn but subordinates that opposition to a final assertion of completeness. This assertion overrides any internal divisions not only formally but also – and this is the crucial matter – conceptually.[35]

Joseph Phelan's more recent study of the nineteenth-century sonnet shows how the political and almost phallic emphasis of the Miltonic–Wordsworthian sonnet were displaced by the amatory values espoused by writers like Dante Gabriel Rossetti.[36] What he does not account for, however, is the surprising and significant confluence in structure between Wordsworth's spherically unified ideal and Yeats's, 1890s symbolist efforts. Wagner's account has the advantage of showing that history itself is fluid, multiple and rich – in fact, as such it is much like the Shakespearean sonnet itself.

Vendler's readings of individual poems are almost invariably suggestive and worked out in impressive detail, but problems concerning context – that is, relating to how she frames those readings – recur. While her account of the beginnings of Yeats's sonnetteering invites objections of this kind, her interpretation of its ending is no less problematical. In this latter case, the problem is not the inability to acknowledge the validity of the aesthetic models different from the Shakespearean one, but rather a neglect of the inherent similarities between a sceptical, modern use of the sonnet and what we find happening in the 1609 quarto edition. If one resists reducing Shakespeare's sonnets to a monolithic and given context, and grants that they provide a later poet such as Yeats with a poetic framework of some heterogeneity, then a different reading becomes possible. Take, for instance, Yeats's 'High Talk':

> Processions that lack high stilts have nothing that catches the eye.
> What if my great-granddad had a pair that were twenty foot high,
> And mine were but fifteen foot, no mortal stalks upon higher,
> Some rogue of the world stole them to patch up a fence or a fire.
> Because piebald ponies, led bears, caged lions, make but poor shows,
> Because children demand Daddy-long-legs upon his timber toes,
> Because women in the upper stories demand a face at the pane
> That patching old heels they may shriek, I take to chisel and plane.
> Malachi Stilt-Jack am I, whatever I learned has run wild,
> From collar to collar, from stilt to stilt, from father to child.
> All metaphor, Malachi, stilts and all. A barnacle-goose
> Far up in the stretches of the night; night splits and the dawn breaks loose;
> I, through the terrible novelty of light, stalk on, stalk on;
> Those great sea-horses bare their teeth and laugh at the dawn.
>
> (*VP* 622–3; *CW1* 351)

Vendler points out that this poem 'belongs thematically to the conventional sonnet-tradition because its topic is its own aesthetic', and claims that Yeats developed this self-conscious stance 'with the example of Sidney and Shakespeare' before him.[37] She nevertheless quickly brands 'High Talk' an anomaly: its 'rough hexameters' and wildness of tone effectively place Yeats beyond the pale of sonnet tradition. This is, in her view, the result of a willed transgression that makes a very specific statement within literary history:

> 'High Talk', by means of its forms 'run wild', voices Yeats's view that the 'high' rhetoric of the sonnet tradition had collapsed with the rest of European culture in the interwar period. We understand Yeats's cultural commentary here only if we see Malachi's apocalyptical images, his primitive couplets, his aberrant prosody, and his exultant despair as the formal ruination of the courtly European sonnet by a new primitivism.[38]

Here, again, Vendler seems to be going beyond the remit allowed by her New Critical precepts. The contextual evidence necessary to convert this poem into an apocalyptical parody of contemporary history is not readily available, unless one, say, stipulates that Yeats's draft version of 'The Second Coming', written many years earlier, is also effectively a draft version of 'High Talk'.[39] Further, one might question why Vendler is less prone to see an ironic relationship to the poet's persona in such a poem, than what is the case when she interprets Shakespeare's sonnets.

Setting aside the cultural content of Vendler's reading, the generic dimension of her interpretation also seems vulnerable. For does this poem really spell the 'formal ruination' of the sonnet tradition? Romantic forerunners such as Keats and Shelley provide a significant precedent for the manner in which this poem reassembles the constituent elements of the sonnet. Perhaps, though, the earlier, august example of Shakespeare might be also justly seen as belonging to a tradition that is not essentially alien to Yeats's *modus operandi* in 'High Talk'? For even if Vendler tends to operate with a monolithic understanding of what a Shakespearean sonnet is, the 1609 quarto edition includes several poems that markedly depart from the standard template. Sonnet number 145, for instance, is written in tetrameters rather than pentameters. Number 99 errs in being expansive rather than elliptical: it consists of 15 lines. A more important forerunner for 'High Talk' is Shakespeare's one-hundred-and-twenty-sixth sonnet, which similarly consists solely of rhyming couplets – though there are six rather than seven of them. In addition, number 126 – 'O thou my lovely boy, who in thy power' – also deviates rhythmically: as Vendler points out, 'the poem falls into a trochaic and amphibracic rather than an iambic pattern.'[40]

Given his documented familiarity with the sonnets,[41] we can presume that Yeats knew of all these deviations from Shakespeare's norm. Further, we also know that one of Shakespeare's more unusual sonnets held a special importance for him. Writing to Dorothy Wellesley on 21 January 1937, during what was a difficult time for Yeats, he stressed how important a particular sonnet of Shakespeare's was for him: 'Everything seems exaggerated [sic] – I had not a symptom of illness yet I had to take to my bed. I kept repeating that Sonnet of Shakespeare's about "Captive good" – I felt I was in an utter solitude' (*CL Intelex* 6785). The sonnet in question is number 66, 'Tired with all these, for restful death I cry', a poem which Yeats had quoted in its entirety in his 'At Stratford-on-Avon' essay 36 years earlier. Interestingly, Yeats's seeking comfort at this juncture was at least partially caused by the controversy around Roger Casement's diaries, a source of considerable acrimony in Anglo-Irish relations at the time.[42] While he was driven to one of his most outspokenly anti-imperial utterances in 'The Ghost of Roger Casement' by this contentious issue, this letter of Yeats's shows that he also sought – and found – solace in a particular Shakespearean sonnet. If he ever wished to avoid all connections with Shakespeare due to some perceived, inextricable link with British imperialism, then this surely would be the time for it.

Shakespeare's sonnet number 66 contains a paratactic catalogue of wrongs that have driven the speaker to the brink. Vendler describes the poem as 'wearily reiterative and syntactically poverty-stricken [. . .]. It is so tired, and so tongue-tied, that it sounds repetitive and anticlimactic.'[43] She acknowledges, though, that the poem cannot be interpreted as a failure: its faults are intended, supplied to emphasize its underlying message. The same is of course the case with regard to Yeats's poem. If 'High Talk' is more histrionic than sonnet 66, both are poems of dejection and disgust. In another context Yeats claimed that, for him, the 'strength and weight of Shakespeare' came from his 'preoccupation with evil' (*CW5* 42), and certainly these poems show the two writers in question sharing a sense of defiant opposition in the face of almost crippling adversity. Whereas Yeats's Malachi chooses theatrical exaggeration as a defence, Shakespeare's speaker can only keep going due to his love for his interlocutor: 'Tired with all these, from these would I be gone, / Save that to die, I leave my love alone.' Despite such a difference, it seems evident that Yeats is not all that far from the Elizabethan forerunner here, after all. Combining the shared, hyperbolic dejection of number 66 with the unconventional couplet form of sonnet 126, the Irishman has certainly made a unique poem all of his own – but not, for all that, one that is a fundamental negation of the Shakespearean precedent. As mentioned earlier, Vendler insists upon Shakespeare's 'subversive moves' with regard to the sonnet tradition: insofar as Yeats makes subversive moves of his own, he is actually reinforcing the validity of that precedent, rather than simply attempting to tear it down.

It is easier to agree with Vendler when she claims that the final lines of 'Meru' – 'That day brings round the night, that before dawn / His glory and monuments are gone' (*VP* 563, ll. 13–14; *CW1* 295) – are very much in line with the author of the 1609 *Sonnets*. Here we have a 'Shakespearean couplet', and here too, the 'dynastic word "monuments" [. . .] is conspicuously Shakespearean.' One might add that the contrast between form and content in 'Meru' is also conspicuously Shakespearean, at least if we permit ourselves to see Shakespeare as Yeats saw him. For in *A Vision*, Yeats writes: 'Shakespeare showed through a style, full of joy, a melancholy vision sought from afar' (*CW13* 81).[44] Yeats's hermits have also found their tragic irony, their 'melancholy vision', at a solitary place – far from home – and their vision, too, is compensatingly embodied in a style that is 'full of joy'. So, yes, the monument is indeed Shakespearean. One might also add, with such a powerful Victorian poem such as 'A Sonnet is a moment's monument' in mind, that it is also in part, for instance, Rossettian.[45] Yeats neither negates Shakespeare, nor ignores the weight of the sonnet tradition between him and his most elevated forerunner. A true master's monument does not just exist in solitude, doing one thing and the same, but rather it is able to play in 10,000 places.

If we now move away from the question of Yeats's relationship to Shakespeare – as well as issues concerning the historical development of the sonnet – and home more squarely in on close textual details concerning Yeats's dealings with the sonnet form, then a more positive use of Vendler's work becomes possible. By arguing that a number of Yeats's poems – not all 14 lines in length, and many obeying rhyme schemes not in tune with sonnet tradition – should be read in terms of how they address the genre of the sonnet, Vendler has effectively constituted a new group of texts. The following argument will build on, and dwell on, the group she discovers. Two preparatory remarks need to be made, however. First of all, I wish to note that this expanded group seems to relate to the sonnet proper as mode relates to genre or kind. As Fowler points out, 'modal terms never imply a complete external form. Modes have always an incomplete repertoire, a selection only of the corresponding kind's features, and one from which overall external structure is absent.'[46] The development of modal forms – a process he calls modulation – is, according to Fowler, one of the most important ways in which genres develop. As was mentioned in Chapter 7, the establishment of the 'tragic' on the basis of the dramatic genre of tragedy is typical of this process, in which a more general (and less formally defined) adjectival term evolves out of a genre described with a substantive term. On this basis, I propose that the adjective 'sonnetic' can be used to encapsulate the more broad sense of sonnet-like features established by Vendler. The second point I want to make here relates to how such adjectival terms typically modify a new substantive, which indicates a subgenre. In what follows, a thematic pattern consistently linked with the same sonnetic template will be established. As this thematic pattern involves consistent use of animal imagery, frequently with apocalyptical or bestial overtones, the subgenre in question might be given the appellation 'sonnetic monstrosity'.

This subgenre is particularly linked to the ending of sonnets and sonnetic poems. Take 'The Fascination of What's Difficult' (*VP* 260; *CW1* 92), a sonnet-related poem according to Vendler, even if it is one line short (in consisting of 13 rather than the sonnet's standard 14 lines). In this poem a hallowed, traditional symbol for the poetical vocation – the mythical horse Pegasus – is deployed. In a short, lyrical effusion on how Yeats's poetical gift has had to be manhandled in order to contribute to the establishment of an Irish theatre, the animal and the human are treated in a similar fashion. After three-and-a-half lines about the speaker's personal struggle, the poem segues into a metaphorical description of the travails of the mythical creature. The seamlessness of this transition is sanctioned by the force of tradition: Yeats can take for granted that his readers are not put out by the identification of the poet with the horse. The link enables an extended conceit, as well as a subtle shift at the end of the poem, where the speaker's alienation from his own gift is figured as the relationship between rider (or owner) and horse. The final two lines envisage a dramatic turnaround for both of them: 'I swear before the dawn comes round again / I'll find the stable and pull out the bolt' (ll. 12–13). This ending provides a sudden change in tempo, as all of the preceding sentences of the poem are substantially longer. The altered speed signifies dispatch: the speaker is foreseeing a moment of decisiveness, whereby the horse's travails are set aside for a new freedom. The final two lines' enjambed sentence, devoid of any grammatical pause, mimes this liberation as it contrasts not only with how the preceding three lines are end-stopped, but also with the extreme stress signified both thematically and formally in 'Shiver under the lash, strain, sweat and jolt / As though it dragged road-metal' (ll. 7–8). In a September 1909 note that provides the first, prose draft of the content of the poem, Yeats refers to the uninhibited horse as 'the wild-winged and unbroken colt' (*Mem* 229).

Earlier in 'The Fascination of What's Difficult', Pegasus is described as leaping 'from cloud to cloud' (l. 6) on Olympus. Although this being is a remnant of classical mythology, Yeats is concerned with removing from it any association with the merely staid and harmonious. As such, there is a subterranean link with the seemingly very different creature that appears in the celebrated vision that concludes 'The Second Coming', another poem linked by critics such as Vendler and Seamus Deane with the sonnet form: 'what rough beast, its hour come round at last, / Slouches towards Bethlehem to be born?' (*VP* 401–2, ll. 21–2; *CW1* 189–90). This is of course a far less benevolent being than Pegasus: Nicholas Grene has eloquently described it as 'a rough beast that monstrously mimics the roughest of human characteristics'.[47] An inaugurator of a new age, the rough beast is an Egyptian sphinx 'with lion body and the head of a man, / A gaze blank and pitiless as the sun' (ll. 14–15). Despite being associated with the implacability of the sun, though, this is a figure of obscurity: only the poet's visionary genius can tap into the collective mind and gain access to this 'vast image' (l. 12). As such, the rough beast is akin to Pegasus, since also the true nature of the Olympic horse is out of reach under some circumstances. During 'the day's war with every knave and dolt' (l. 10), only the constricted colt is apparent in 'The Fascination of What's Difficult'. In an early draft, Yeats toyed with the idea of having the poet still struggling during the night: he would only release Pegasus, 'if but there is no moon tonight' (*Mem* 243). This scenario is still tacitly present in the published ending of the poem, where the poet must act while daylight is still at an arm's length: he has to act 'before the dawn comes round again' (l. 12).

The verbal echo in this last line is perhaps the closest link between the endings of these two poems. If another poet had written 'The Fascination of What's Difficult', it would be natural to say that 'The Second Coming' constituted a conscious allusion to the earlier poem. For 'comes round at last' is a very close cousin, or even sibling, of 'comes round again'. Both poems celebrate long-awaited returns, unleashing primal energies. The speakers' positions are manifestly different: where the poet in 'Fascination' obviously relishes freeing the pent-up force of inspiration, in 'The Second Coming' he seems to be intrigued but also – as is made clear by the opening eight lines – repelled by the spectacle presented by his vision. The obvious fascination felt by the speaker of 'The Second Coming' has nevertheless led some critics to read the poem against the grain, as an endorsement of the cold, new antithetical age that is being ushered in. Yvor Winters was one of the first proponents of such a view: he claimed that 'we may find the beast terrifying, but Yeats finds him satisfying – he is Yeats's judgment upon all that we regard as civilized. Yeats approves of this kind of brutality.'[48] Reading the poem as a kind of palimpsest upon a pattern already established by 'The Fascination of What's Difficult' can only strengthen the basis for this view. It is as if Yeats is hinting that the rough beast 'slouching towards Bethlehem to be born' is, in fact, an image of the rebirth of his own imagination – an imagination with inherently demonic and apocalyptical potential. Alternatively, one could interpret this echo as something less significant: as a more elaborate version of a verbal tic. The limitedness of Yeats's vocabulary is occasionally noted by critics; perhaps this echo can be explained as more of a poetic habit, say, than a consciously chosen instance of technique?

Whether this repetition is conscious or not, it is in fact part of a more encompassing pattern. In a preface written later in his career, to the play *The Resurrection*, Yeats wrote of the long-term presence of a seemingly related beast: 'Had I begun *On Baile's Strand* or not when I began to imagine, as always at my left side just out of the range of the sight, a brazen winged beast that I associated with laughing, ecstatic destruction?' In a note to this passage, Yeats stated that the beast in question was 'Afterwards described in my poem "The Second Coming"' (*CW2* 723). We have encountered this passage before, in the discussion of *The Resurrection* in Chapter 6, and there as here the articulation of a heterogeneous space was involved. This idea of a beast just out of sight – just around the corner of the available visual field – gains added relevance if one links it with the structural architectonics of the poems that have been discussed in this chapter. Here the critical framing of both 'The Fascination of What's Difficult' and 'The Second Coming' as being sonnetic – through seeing the former as a shortened sonnet and the latter as an extended one – becomes relevant. Both of the endings we have looked at function, according to this perspective, like the concluding couplet of a sonnet. Although this genre typically has an argumentative twist after the opening octave, it not infrequently has a similar volte-face in its concluding couplet in its Shakespearean version.

At one stage Vendler refers to such an effect as providing the 'bite' of the concluding couplet,[49] and the metaphor is all the more apt if one looks at some of the other poems that belong to the same generic terrain: for if there is a gnashing of teeth at the end of Yeats's sonnets and sonnetic poems, it is frequently brought to pass by the sudden appearance of an animal. The concluding couplet is where Yeats's sonnets turn the corner, bringing into full or partial vision the wild animals that are only dimly sensed or hinted at in the preceding lines. Take the concluding poem of *Responsibilities,* 'While I, from that reed-throated whisperer' (*VP* 320–1; *CW1* 127). There the vaguely bird-like opening description of poetic inspiration finds its contrast in the blunt, final intrusion of far more everyday, lowly animals: 'till all my priceless things / Are but a post the passing dogs defile' (ll. 13–14). These canine creatures – reputedly inspired by George Moore's satirical put-downs of Yeats[50] – do not gnash their teeth. But there are fangs on display also in 'High Talk', discussed earlier in this chapter, which concludes a wild detour into natural terrain in its final two lines: 'I, through the terrible novelty of light, stalk on, stalk on, / Those great sea-horses bare their teeth and laugh at the dawn' (*VP* 623; *CW1* 352). Here again the sudden intrusion of animalistic energy is linked with morning, albeit in a more melodramatically sinister guise than in the other instances discussed so far.

These are all self-conscious poems, more or less openly raising fundamental questions about the nature of poetry. As such they manifest one of the traits Vendler considers characteristic of Yeats's dealings with sonnets. The complete list of traits is as follows:

> What the sonnet meant to Yeats, historically speaking, was verse consciously aware of itself as written, not oral; verse from a European court tradition; verse knowing itself to be artifice, and often speaking about its own art; verse (although of Italian origin) associated with the essential English lyric tradition, from Wyatt and Surrey through Shakespeare, Milton, Wordsworth, and Keats.[51]

Earlier in this chapter, I questioned the nation-based premises of Vendler's reading of this group of poems. In this particular context, the question of 'artifice' is thrust to the fore. In their self-conscious dealings with the art of poetry (and imagination), the group of texts we are addressing seem to be not only about artifice – but also about the bestial underpinnings of, or provocations bringing about, artifice. The very line between artifice and its opposite has become blurred. At a structural level, this is particularly clear in how an entirely conventional feature – the tendency to end the sonnet with a gnomic summary or surprising turn of reasoning – is both repeated and made the systematic instrument of an irruption of animal energies.

This is most forcefully brought to the surface in 'Leda and the Swan' (*VP* 441; *CW1* 218), which has no final couplet presenting a sudden appearance of an animal, but rather a sustained meditation over that very same phenomenon. The opening words – 'A sudden blow' – highlight the fact that this poem functions like a slow-motion exploration of the dramatic encounter with animality; a sonnet *volta* writ large. As yet another meditation on epochal change, 'Leda and the Swan' can be – and has been – interpreted in a number of ways. At one level the poem's ending spells out the challenge of form. If Zeus disguised as a swan embodies the uncontrollable force of form, the poem would seem to insist that that force need not be accompanied by insight: 'Did she put on his knowledge with his power / Before the indifferent beak could let her drop?' (ll. 13–14) The coupling of form and content is itself a monstrosity, a hybrid: for despite the mutual influence the two have on one another, they do not fuse into an organic unity bringing together power and knowledge. Yeats presented another version of this claim when he, towards the very end of his life, came up with the adage that 'Man can embody truth but he cannot know it' (letter to Elizabeth Pelham, 4 January 1939, *CL Intelex* 7362).

Approached from this perspective, poetic composition is more like a monstrous conception forced upon the poet by divinity, than a narcissistic reproductive process where thematic content appropriates to itself an apposite form. Genre is more a matter of impenetrable, habit-like structures, than a deliberate exercise in finding a rational embodiment for an established position. The formal features of language and genre are not so much fitting and convenient vehicles for an already established content as the ministries of an ineluctable obsession. It is, however, possible to go further, challenging Vendler's use of the sonnet as a kind of teleological goal for Yeats's use of douzains, 13-line poems and other texts of a roughly similar format. Perhaps it is not so much a matter of Yeats expanding the sonnet's reach – or of escaping or unintentionally seeking what Vendler on occasion calls 'the true sonnet' – as immersing the sonnet in a larger, more disparate and hard-to-map network of forms and possibilities? In other words, what if the poems scrutinized in this chapter do not constitute more or less successful approximations of one single norm – that norm being identified with what Vendler calls the 'true sonnet' – rather than a disparate exploration of various formal techniques and kinds of poems? Such is the logical consequence if one follows the lead of Alastair Fowler, one of several critics who have claimed that genres should not be identified in terms of definitions based on necessary characteristics, but rather on the basis of Wittgensteinian family likenesses (whereby no single trait need be shared by all members of a genre).[52] Thus sonnets may be of 14 lines, including an octave, a sestet and a *volta*, as well as being written in iambic pentameter, and be about love (as in Petrarch and Shakespeare) or politics (as in Milton and Wordsworth). Many poems, however, which we think of sonnets do not fit this pattern perfectly; they share some of these features with poems that adhere more narrowly to the mould, and are nevertheless admitted into the genre due to their 'brotherhood' or 'sisterhood' with the latter.

With Yeats and the sonnet, something more radical seems to be taking place, as the central group adhering to the alleged norm is outnumbered by its sonnetic brothers, sisters and cousins. Rather than operating with one central entity and a few peripheral ones, there is a structure more akin to an archipelago of related but non-identical forms. This should have consequences for how one erects, or resists the erection of, normative ideals. Thus one can say that the early symbolist Yeats wrote intensely unified poems, without any clear argumentative turn, as faithful embodiments of a particular kind of aesthetic ideal. Later poems would have other aims. While a critic may well enjoy 'Meru' more than Yeats's or Wordsworth's instantiations of the former ideal, literary history is not so straightforward or linear as to simply confirm that the latter ideal is superior. If any poem questions simple historical schemas, and the western privileging of will and rationality, then surely it is 'Meru': the poem shows how mankind's 'Ravening, raging, and uprooting' leads to the 'desolation of reality', rather than the production of any lasting monuments of civilization (*VP* 563, ll. 6–7; *CW1* 295). Does this message mean that 'Meru' is, in fact, nostalgic for a less willed, and indeed more intensely unified, state of being? The passivity of the hermits 'Caverned in night under the drifted snow' (l. 10) at the end of the poem, may signify as much. If so, then the message of the poem – broadly in line with the posthumanist gist of much recent poetry and criticism – would indeed be pointing us back, nostalgically, to the more immersive and less analytical ideal of Yeats's earlier douzains.

Could it be that the 'true' form of the Yeatsian sonnets is the douzain, rather than the other way around? Perhaps the reason why he stuck by the douzain so consistently is that it entailed an ideal – an international ideal, embraced by Irish, English and French writers – which he would not relinquish? Attractive as it may be, I do not want to embrace such a possibility unreservedly here. Rather, a more inclusive approach – where douzains, sonnets, curtailed sonnets and other short lyric forms overlap and intermix – seems more cognizant of the complex generic maneuverings of Yeats's poetry. This is perhaps one of the extremes at which Yeats can be meaningfully linked with the modern desire to transcend genre altogether[53]: for if no genre is pure, and every poem tentatively placed within a genre is related to poems in other genres, then the idea of definite classes has yielded to a more dizzying notion of an all-inclusive (but not totalizable) network. At that point one has perhaps entered into the impure regions of generic monstrosity.

11

Coda: Yeats and the Transcendence of Genre

Genre does not have the best of reputations. For some the term conjures up the prescriptive strictures of neoclassicism,[1] while others happily dismiss all generic issues as dry-as-dust distractions from the real and vital business of literature. Like the notion of the everyday, genre tends to be saddled with pejorative associations of being merely automatic and habitual. Although French structuralism has come up with invaluable contributions to the modern understanding of literary genres, its tendency to indulge in taxonomic nit-picking has perhaps strengthened such prejudice. As an outstanding representative of this movement, the work of Gérard Genette has been used in this study as an aid to terminological clarity. Although not all these concepts roll equally smoothly off the tongue, Genette's terms intertextuality, paratextuality, metatextuality, architextuality and (less frequently) hypertextuality have been deployed in order to bring some clarity and sense of overview to the ways in which Yeats's texts relate to external or internal frameworks. All of these concepts belong under the more general category of transtextuality. In a fictional interview with himself that concludes *The Architext: An Introduction*, Genette defines his interest in the latter as deriving from an interest in '*textual transcendence* – namely, everything that brings [the text] into relation (manifest or hidden) with other texts.'[2] Later, in *Palimpsests*, he defines transtextuality as 'the textual transcendence of the text'.[3] Here one can observe both a structuralist insistence upon purely textual relationships and – in another gesture not untypical of structuralism – a kind of ironical deflating of the metaphysical heft of the term 'transcendence'. With regard to both these tendencies, we are a far cry from much of what we associate with William Butler Yeats's writings. If Genette is helpful for studies (such as this one) that concern themselves with literary genre, and much less relevant for metaphysical speculation about extratextual forms of transcendence, Yeats would seem to inhabit a rather different literary universe.

It has been an underlying premise of this book, though, that genre and other forms of transtextuality coexist with, and indeed relate to, extra-literary forms of transcendence in Yeats's writings. Providing a historically oriented reading of genre and allusion in Yeats's poetry, prose and drama, I have not stopped with taxonomies or internal textual relations, but have also explored questions concerning, for instance, personal, political, linguistic and metaphysical transcendence. Bakhtin's expanded sense of genre has been utilized to show how the literary text relates to the conventions of everyday speech and opinion (particularly in Chapter 8). Other key, recurring concerns have been knowledge, transformation and unity. Through his interaction with genres and other authors, Yeats does not just play a literary game, as it were, but also seeks to appropriate (or outbid) the knowledge of the traditions with which he engages. The acquisition of knowledge is, at least in part, linked to an aspiration for a higher form of identity. In the use of genre, Yeats thus submits himself to a transformative process that aims for a purification of the self – and also of the Irish nation. At the same time, however, transcendence also means leaving the narrow, everyday confines of the self and nation behind. Where both the empirical self and contemporary opinion in Ireland appear to be fluctuating and limited, Yeats seeks to reach a higher plane by immersing himself in the forms of literature. This higher self frequently involves a philosophical transcendence, which this study has been linked not only to the Great Memory or Neo-Platonic philosophy (as in Chapter 5), but also to classical aesthetics. At this level, where a 'distance' must be 'firmly held against a pushing world' (*CW4* 165), Yeats's texts would ideally transcend not only the self (and narrow national interests) but also the specifics of literary genres – as has been shown in the discussion of Yeats's modulations of tragedy (in Chapter 7) and the sonnet (in Chapter 10). Although Yeats's accomplishments are astounding, it must however be pointed out that the texts do not necessarily fulfil his ambitions. In line with this, I have questioned how far an ideal literary self can actually be said to leave the messy details and distractions of the everyday behind (in Chapter 2), and whether or not the errant behaviour of images and the autonomy of aesthetics might not rebel against Yeats's ambitions in his ekphrastic poetry (in Chapter 9). The readings of *The Resurrection*, *The Player Queen* and 'Easter, 1916' have also revealed that political dissension – frequently presented as an unruly mixture of warring and culturally heterogeneous factions – is present in the framing of the Yeatsian text or space.

In a recent defence of Modernism, Gabriel Josipovici has identified the transcendence of genre – or what he calls a 'denial of genre' – as one of the essential features of this movement.[4] This agrees nicely with the popularly held conception of Modernism as an avant-garde phenomenon that leaves behind the hackneyed traditions of the past. A whole movement of art, according to this view, was primarily about innovation and radical newness. Genres imply those very conventions of the past that the modernists had to renounce, and it is no accident that key theoretical critiques of genre – belonging to figures such as Benedetto Croce and Maurice Blanchot – take place in roughly the same historical period. Fredric Jameson has indeed linked this theoretical critique with what he calls 'the ideology of modernism'.[5] By identifying such denunciation as an ideology, however, Jameson suggests that it entails an obfuscation of the truth. One might also question whether it is an ideology that is exclusively distinctive of Modernism. Josipovici, for instance, is aware of the fact that the denunciation of genre is not specific to Modernism: he traces the roots of this transcendence in Romanticism, using Wordsworth and the German painter Caspar David Friedrich as privileged examples.[6] Not only these artists, but also romantic theorists aspired to a transcendence of literary genre: particularly Friedrich Schlegel and the Jena romantics explored the exhaustion of the neo-classical regime of genres, and suggested that the highest forms of art might not only mix but also ultimately go beyond genre.[7]

In this sense, Yeats's dealings with genre come across as distinctively romantic: for he seeks both to combine and transcend genres, often in a complex engagement with philosophical positions (associated with both withdrawal and comprehension) that is also typical of central romantic texts. Recent ground-breaking work on British romanticism and genre by scholars such as Stuart Curran and David Duff helps fill out this picture,[8] demonstrating that mixture and transcendence are also accompanied by ceaseless transformation of inherited genres. Curran and Duff have shown that Romantic literature is thoroughly informed by genre, and that the development of genre is intrinsic to Romanticism. Duff has dismissed what he calls 'the anti-generic hypothesis' concerning that time period: that is, 'the belief that Romanticism was fundamentally hostile to genre, or interested in genres only for the purposes of dissolving or transcending them.'[9] The absence of a similarly sustained meditation on the role of genre in modernist literature may provide part of the reason why a similar thesis is tacitly held also for Modernism. Recent scholarship has revealed that the genre-mixing of Romanticism continues into the Victorian era,[10] and surely future work will demonstrate that many of the same issues and forms extend into Modernism, too. In *The Fantastic*, in 1970, Genette's fellow structuralist Tzvetan Todorov opined that 'it is doubtful that contemporary literature is entirely exempt from generic distinctions; it is only that these distinctions no longer correspond to the notions bequeathed by the literary theories of the past.'[11] Surely the same is true of the literature of the opening decades of the twentieth century. Already some of the key monuments of Modernism are indissolubly linked to literary genre. To cite some of the most obvious examples: what would *The Waste Land* be without romance – or *Ulysses* without epic? And how would 'In a Station at the Metro' have come about without the precedent of haiku? Recent work on the modernist epic poem indicates that scholarship is starting to tap into the potential riches of this field,[12] yet much work surely remains before the study of Modernism reaches anything approaching the level of generic sophistication already attained by romantic scholars.

In the continued absence of any kind of overview of Modernism's relationship to genre, ideology and prejudice are not easily dismissed. Thus it is not simple to straightforwardly determine whether Yeats's generic practices qualify or disqualify him for inclusion in literary Modernism. The same goes for his allusions. Does the unearthing of obscure allusions to Oliver Wendell Holmes (in Chapter 2) and W. S. Gilbert (in Chapter 8) strengthen Yeats's modernist case? Particularly thanks to *The Waste Land* and *Ulysses*, it has long been thought that the obscure, almost private, nature of modernist allusion provides a distinctive formal feature of the movement. Referring to the allusive practices of T. S. Eliot, Pound and Joyce, John Hollander has countered that although 'the tendency of modernism was almost to claim this ironic mode of allusion as purely its own', the fact remains that 'the various engines of allusion have always been central to the poetic record and the poetic procedure.'[13] This study has not sought to dismiss the obvious fact of Yeats's indebtedness to, and respect for, literary tradition. Chapter 10, for instance, revealed that even while Yeats was moving the sonnet into territory hitherto uncharted by literary criticism, he was nonetheless in close communication with the precedents of both Shakespeare and Victorian poetry. Indeed, I have repeatedly returned to Yeats's inheritance from the 1890s – for instance relating to *Salomé* or the douzain form – in order to contextualize his texts' transtextual positionings.

I have also made use of Wayne Chapman's notion of 'adaptive complexes' to plot some of the detail of Yeats's transtextual relationships. Close readings of key works and concepts have been selectively pursued, rather than the kind of overview promised by structuralist poetics. Not only has little attention been given to Yeats's work prior to about 1910, but – more crucially perhaps – several of Yeats's genres have either been broached in passing or not at all. This includes, for instance, not only many of the lyric genres explored by Helen Vendler in *Our Secret Discipline* or more singular extra-literary genres such as the radio broadcast and senate speech, but also the whole field of narrative fiction (comprising texts such as *John Sherman, Stories of Red Hanrahan*, 'The Adoration of the Magi', the unfinished novel *The Speckled Bird* and so on). Modern genre theory insists upon the fact that genres are strongly influenced by their siblings, and particularly so when their brothers or sisters occupy a dominant position. In accordance with this, I have stressed that some of Yeats's choices must be seen as either negating the ground of the novel (see Chapter 2), or indeed competing with the novel's generic inclusiveness (as in the reading of 'The Municipal Gallery Re-visited' in Chapter 9). Yet a more thorough reckoning of the novel's importance for Yeats would surely also include a detailed inspection of his own forays into narrative prose – as well as an account of his attempts at narrative verse.[14]

Certainly much remains to be done in the exploration of genre's role in post-romantic literature. Given the wealth of available material, it might seem hard to know where to start. According to Alastair Fowler, what we 'have to do, in approaching recent literature, is to explore new groupings. But these will have taken their departure from earlier groupings. We are far less likely to find or understand them if we abandon the study of genres.'[15] It is in this light Yeats might prove to be, if not quite *sui generis,* then at least an exemplary figure. As the preceding chapters have shown, Yeats develops new and arresting generic constructions on the basis of given forms such as autobiography, scholarly literature, tragedy, mystery plays, Japanese Noh, elegy, the ekphrastic poem and the sonnet. The results are often quite complex, and he seldom settles down into one mould for long. Such, however, are the vicissitudes of literary genres: always in flux, they nevertheless constitute a bridge between past and future. As a traditionalist who was always keen to try out new forms, Yeats is a distinctive figure – a key bridging author between traditional genres and authors and the literatures of the twentieth and twenty-first centuries. Like the golden bird of 'Sailing to Byzantium', he sings of 'what is past, or passing, or to come' (*VP* 408; *CW1* 198) – and the way in which that song accompanies, and inflects, the modern development of genres is one of its many significant achievements.

Notes

Chapter 1

1 Patrick J. Keane, *Yeats's Interactions with Tradition.* Columbia: University of Minnesota Press, 1987, xv.
2 Travel is of course also a privileged trope on several accounts. Metaphor itself is a form of transport, as witnessed by etymology: the Greek *metapherein* meant to transfer. Travel is given a privileged place in the cognitive account of metaphor provided by George Lakoff and Mark Johnson in *Metaphors We Live By* (Chicago: University of Chicago Press, 2003).
3 Gérard Genette, *The Architext: An Introduction,* translated by Jane E. Lewin. Berkeley and Los Angeles: University of California Press, 1992, 81.
4 The five forms of transtextuality are presented in Gérard Genette, *Palimpsests: Literature in the Second Degree,* translated by Channa Newman and Claude Doubinsky. Lincoln and London: University of Nebraska Press, 1997, 1–7. A handy overview is also provided in Richard Macksey, 'Foreword', in Gérard Genette, *Paratexts: Thresholds of Interpretation,* translated by Jane E. Lewin. Cambridge: Cambridge University Press, 1997, xviii–xix.
5 On 'pre-texts', see Gérard Genette, *Paratexts: Thresholds of Interpretation,* translated by Jane E. Lewin. Cambridge: Cambridge University Press, 1997, 395–403.
6 Ibid., 8.
7 Jonathan Culler, *Framing the Sign: Criticism and its Institutions.* Oxford: Blackwell, 1988, ix.
8 Jacques Derrida, *The Truth in Painting,* translated by Geoff Bennington and Ian McLeod. Chicago and London: The University of Chicago Press, 1987, 63. For a reading of Yeats that is in part informed by Derrida's theories, see Edward Larrissy, *Yeats the Poet: The Measures of Difference.* Hemel Hempstead: Harvester Wheatsheaf, 1994.
9 Marjorie Levinson, 'What is New Formalism?' *PMLA,* 122(2), (2007), 559.
10 Helen Vendler, *Our Secret Discipline: Yeats on Lyric Form.* Oxford: Oxford University Press, 2007. Another difference from Vendler's work lies in the fact that I will address not only Yeats's poetry, but also his prose and drama.
11 Amy J. Devitt, *Writing Genres.* Carbondale: Southern Illinois University Press, 2004, 9–10.
12 Alastair Fowler, *Kinds of Literature: An Introduction to the Theory of Genres and Modes.* Oxford: Clarendon, 1982, 56.
13 Ibid., 23.
14 Ibid., 107.
15 Richard Ellmann, *Eminent Domain: Yeats among Wilde, Joyce, Pound, Eliot and Auden.* New York: Oxford University Press, 1967, 8.
16 Ibid., 3. It is hard not to hear an echo of T. S. Eliot here: 'Immature poets imitate; mature poets steal' (*The Sacred Wood: Essays on Poetry and Criticism.* London: Faber

and Faber, 1997, 105). Bloom's most well-known account of literary influence is to be
found in *The Anxiety of Influence* (New York: Oxford University Press, 1997).

17 Ellmann, *Eminent Domain*, 8.

18 Harold Bloom, *Yeats*. New York: Oxford University Press, 1970, 24.

19 For an opposing view of literary influence, see for instance Christopher Ricks,
    Allusion to the Poets. Oxford: Oxford University Press, 2002. George Watson shows
    how Victorianism 'shaped Yeats's sensibility in profound ways' in 'Yeats, Victorianism,
    and the 1890s', 36, in Marjorie Howes and John Kelly (eds), *The Cambridge
    Companion to W. B. Yeats*. Cambridge: Cambridge University Press, 2006.

20 See Michael McAteer's *Yeats and European Drama* (Cambridge: Cambridge
    University Press, 2010) and chapter two in Irene Ruppo Malone's *Ibsen and the Irish
    Revival* (Basingstoke: Palgrave Macmillan, 2010).

21 To be fair to Genette, he states clearly in a section of *Palimpsests* entitled 'A few
    precautions' that 'one must not view the five types of transtextuality as separate and
    absolute categories without any reciprocal contact or overlapping. On the contrary,
    their relationships to one another are numerous and often crucial. For example,
    generic architextuality is, historically, almost always constituted by way of imitation
    (Virgil imitates Homer, Mateo Aleman's *Guzman* imitates the anonymous *Lazarillo*),
    hence by way of hypertextuality' (Genette, *Palimpsests*, 7).

22 John Frow, *Genre*. London and New York: Routledge, 2006, 49.

23 Kristeva introduced the concept of '*inter-textuality*' to denote the 'transposition of
    one (or several) sign system(s) into another'. She immediately added a caveat: 'since
    this term has often been understood in the banal sense of "study of sources", we prefer
    the term *transposition* because it specifies that the passage from one signifying system
    to another demands a new articulation of the thetic – of enunciative and denotative
    positionality' (Julia Kristeva, *Revolution in Poetic Language*, translated by Margaret
    Waller. New York: Columbia University Press, 1984, 59–60). In the essay 'Word,
    Dialogue and Novel', Kristeva acknowledged a debt to Mikhail Bakhtin on this issue:
    'what appears as a lack of rigour is in fact an insight first introduced into literary
    theory by Bakhtin: any text is constructed as a mosaic of quotations; any text is the
    absorption and transformation of another. The notion of *intertextuality* replaces that
    of intersubjectivity' (*The Kristeva Reader*, edited by Toril Moi. Oxford: Blackwell,
    1986, 37). For a perceptive comparative reading of the relationship between Kristeva
    and Bakhtin, see David Duff, 'Intertextuality versus Genre Theory: Bakhtin, Kristeva
    and the Question of Genre', *Paragraph*, 25(1), (2002), 54–73.

24 Wayne K. Chapman, *Yeats and English Renaissance Literature*. Basingstoke:
    Macmillan, 1991, 10.

25 Ibid., xii.

26 Ibid., 69.

27 Hans-Georg Gadamer, *Truth and Method*, 2nd edn, translated by Joel Weinsheimer
    and Donald G. Marshall. London: Sheed & Ward, 1989, 306.

28 Edmund Wilson, *Axel's Castle: A Study in the Imaginative Literature of 1870 to 1930*.
    New York: Charles Scribner's Sons, 1931, 24.

29 Daniel Albright, 'Yeats and Modernism', 75, in Marjorie Howes and John Kelly
    (eds), *The Cambridge Companion to W. B. Yeats*. Cambridge: Cambridge University
    Press, 2006. My account of the relationship between Yeats and Modernism in this
    introduction is brief and selective. For a presentation that quotes and summarizes
    some key statements on this question – from figures such as Pound, Edmund Wilson,
    Frank Kermode, Harold Bloom, F. R. Leavis, C. K. Stead, Richard Ellmann, Thomas

Parkinson and James Longenbach – see chapter three in Michael Flaherty (ed.), *The Poetry of W. B. Yeats: A Reader's Guide to Essential Criticism*. Basingstoke: Palgrave Macmillan, 2005.

30 Michael Levenson, 'Introduction', 2–3, in Michael Levenson (ed.), *The Cambridge Companion to Modernism*. Cambridge: Cambridge University Press, 1999.

31 James Longenbach, 'Modern Poetry', 110, in Michael Levenson (ed.), *The Cambridge Companion to Modernism*. Cambridge: Cambridge University Press, 1999.

32 James Longenbach, *Stone Cottage: Pound, Yeats and Modernism*. New York and Oxford: Oxford University Press, 1988, 254.

33 James Longenbach, 'Modern Poetry', 327, in David Holdeman and Ben Levitas (eds), *W. B. Yeats in Context*. Cambridge: Cambridge University Press, 2010.

34 Steven Matthews, *Yeats as Precursor: Readings in Irish, British and American Poetry*. Basingstoke: Macmillan, 2000, 21. In a related vein, David Young refers to how 'Yeats's varied cultural allegiances [. . .] brought differing aesthetic commitments into direct conflict' (*Troubled Mirror: A Study of Yeats's 'The Tower'*. Iowa City: University of Iowa Press, 1987, 3).

35 Douglas Archibald, 'John Butler Yeats', in David Holdeman and Ben Levitas (eds), *W. B. Yeats in Context*. Cambridge: Cambridge University Press, 2010, 111.

36 David Holdeman goes as far as to claim that, due to the pre-textual material available today, 'anyone who writes about Yeats's poems or plays without considering their histories of composition has no excuse but sheer laziness' (Holdeman, 'Manuscripts and Revisions', 365, in David Holdeman and Ben Levitas (eds), *W. B. Yeats in Context*. Cambridge: Cambridge University Press, 2010).

Chapter 2

1 Derrida, *The Truth in Painting*, 61.

2 Charles Taylor, *Sources of the Self: The Making of the Modern Identity*. Cambridge: Cambridge University, 1989, 14.

3 Yuriko Saito, *Everyday Aesthetics*. Oxford: Oxford University Press, 2007, 28.

4 Liesl Olson's study on *Modernism and the Ordinary* (Oxford: Oxford University Press, 2009) devotes its first chapter to Joyce and its second chapter to Woolf.

5 Virginia Woolf, *A Moment's Liberty: The Shorter Diary*, abridged and edited by Anne Olivier Bell. London: Pimlico, 1997, 289.

6 Genette, *Paratexts*, 173.

7 Jacques Rancière, *The Future of the Image*, translated by Gregory Elliott. London and New York: Verso, 2007, 120.

8 Jacques Rancière, *The Emancipated Spectator*, translated by Gregory Elliott. London and New York: Verso, 2011, 69.

9 Quoted in Michael Sheringham, *Everyday Life: Theories and Practices from Surrealism to the Present*. Oxford: Oxford University Press, 2006, 148.

10 Oscar Wilde, *The Works*. London: Collins, 1931, 181.

11 George Moore, *Hail and Farewell: Ave, Salve, Vale,* edited by Richard Cave. Toronto: Macmillan of Canada, 1976, 244.

12 Andrea Broomfield, *Food and Cooking in Victorian England: A History*. Santa Barbara: Praeger, 2007, 26.

13 David R. Clark (ed.), '"The Poet and the Actress": An Unpublished Dialogue by W. B. Yeats', *YA8* (1991), 133.

14   Compare this comment: 'Mr. Shane Leslie thinks that Swift's relation to Vanessa was
      not platonic, and that whenever his letters speak of a cup of coffee they mean the
      sexual act; whether the letters seem to bear him out I do not know, for those letters
      bore me' (*VPl* 966–7; *CW2* 717).
15   Honoré de Balzac, 'The Pleasures and Pains of Coffee', translated by Robert Onopa.
      Accessed on 22 November 2012 at: www.blissbat.net/balzac.html.
16   Digestion per se is a distraction. In a letter to John Quinn on 23 July 1918, Yeats
      justified his use of the conventions of Japanese Noh theatre as a means to arrive at
      a form whereby he would be able 'to escape the press, and people digesting their
      dinners, and to write for my friends' (*CL Intelex* 3468). Yeats's adaptation of Noh
      conventions will be discussed in Chapter 6.
17   Sheringham, *Everyday Life*, 180.
18   Yeats's distaste for ephemeral news is not all that atypical. Jahan Ramazani observes
      that if 'we take our cues from [William Carlos] Williams, [W. H.] Auden, and
      [Walter] Benjamin, one approach to the impossibly general question, "what is
      poetry?", is the almost equally general answer: under modernity, poetry is what it is
      by virtue of not being the news' ('"To Get the News from Poems": Poetry as Genre', 6,
      in Erik Martiny (ed.), *A Companion to Poetic Genre*. Oxford: Wiley-Blackwell, 2012).
19   Arthur Henry Hallam, 'On Some Characteristics of Modern Poetry', in *The Writings
      of Arthur Hallam*, edited by T. H. Vail Motter. New York: MLA, 1943, 190.
20   In a programme note dated 21 November 1907, Yeats uses the same concept of the
      'heterogeneous' to justify the rewriting of the play *Where There is Nothing* into *The
      Unicorn from the Stars*. The original version of the play, he wrote, 'had too much of
      heterogeneous life for artistic unity' (cited in Liam Miller, *The Noble Art of
      W. B. Yeats*. Dublin: The Dolmen Press, 1977, 136).
21   On the link between *The King's Threshold* and political fasting in Ireland, see for
      instance McAteer, *Yeats and European Drama*, 47.
22   Saito, *Everyday Aesthetics*, 50.
23   Sheringham, *Everyday Life*, 136.
24   Richard Kirkland, *Literature and Culture in Northern Ireland since 1965: Moments of
      Danger*. London and New York: Longman, 1996, 21.
25   See R. F. Foster, *W. B. Yeats, A Life, I: The Apprentice Mage*. Oxford: Oxford University
      Press, 1997, 305, 447.
26   The reference is to the poem 'The Deacon's Masterpiece: Or, the Wonderful
      "One-Hoss Shay"' (see Oliver Wendell Holmes, *The Poetical Works*, volume II. Boston
      and New York: Houghton Mifflin and Company, 1895, 131–5).
27   Oliver Wendell Holmes, *The Poet at the Breakfast-Table*. Boston: James R. Osgood
      and Company, 1872, 9–10.
28   Ibid., 227.
29   Ibid., 37.
30   Ibid., 289.
31   Ibid., 32.
32   Ibid., 11.
33   Ibid., 128.
34   Patrick J. Keane, *Emerson, Romanticism, and Intuitive Reason: The Transatlantic 'Light
      of All our Day'*. University of Missouri Press, 2005, 325–6.
35   Helen Vendler, 'A. Norman Jeffares, *W. B. Yeats: A New Biography*', *YA9*, 1992, 328.

Chapter 3

1   R. F. Foster, *W. B. Yeats: A Life, II: The Arch-Poet*. Oxford: Oxford University Press, 2003, xix–xx, 516.
2   Ibid., xx.
3   Yeats cited in Richard Ellmann, *Yeats: The Man and the Masks*. New York and London: Norton, 1999 (1948), 5.
4   See, for instance, Peter Levi, *Tennyson*. London: Macmillan, 1991, 284.
5   Boris Tomashevskij, 'Literature and Biography', in Ladislav Matejka and Krystyna Pomorska (eds), *Readings in Russian Poetics: Formalist and Structuralist Views*. Cambridge, MA: The MIT Press, 1971.
6   See Foster, *W. B. Yeats: A Life*, II, xix. Terence Brown, *The Life of W. B. Yeats: A Critical Biography*. Oxford: Blackwell, 2001.
7   O'Donoghue claims that the title of the second volume 'places a more determined emphasis on the poetry [than in the first volume].' He goes on to say that 'Foster is an admirable reader of the poems, and his *Life* – especially the second volume – will now be one of the authoritative contexts for interpretation as well as for source study' ('Hearing the Right Voices', in *The Guardian*, 27 September 2003, 9).
8   Foster, *W. B. Yeats: A Life*, I, xxx.
9   Foster, *W. B. Yeats: A Life*, II, 348.
10 Ibid., 349.
11 On this topic, see Charles I. Armstrong, *Figures of Memory: Poetry, Space, and the Past*. Basingstoke: Palgrave Macmillan, 2009, 85–97.
12 John Banville, 'The Rescue of W. B. Yeats', in *The New York Review*, 26 February 2004, 14.
13 See Gadamer, *Truth and Method*, 277–307.
14 Richard Holmes, *Footsteps: Adventures of a Romantic Biographer*. London: Flamingo, 1995, 67, 264.
15 René Wellek and Austin Warren, *Theory of Literature*. New York: Penguin Books, 1983 (1949), 75.
16 Foster, *W. B. Yeats: A Life*, II, xxi.
17 Hackett quoted in ibid., xix.
18 Ellmann, *The Man and the Mask*, 169.
19 Ibid., 165.
20 Richard Ellmann, *The Identity of Yeats*. London: Faber and Faber, 1964 (1954), xxv.
21 Ibid., 5. David Holdeman makes use of a similar tripartite arrangement in his introductory volume to Yeats's career as a writer, separating that career into phases that last (1) from the 1880s to 1899, (2) from 1900 to 1915 and (3) from 1916 to the end of Yeats's life (*The Cambridge Introduction to W. B. Yeats*. Cambridge: Cambridge University Press, 2006, ix).
22 Brenda Maddox, *George's Ghosts: A New Life of W. B. Yeats*. London: Picador, 1999. For an insightful treatment of Yeats's relationship to his mother, see Deirdre Toomey, 'Away', *YA10* 3–32.
23 Brenda Maddox, *Nora: Biography of Nora Joyce*. London: Hamish Hamilton, 1988; Ann Thwaite, *Emily Tennyson: The Poet's Wife*. London: Faber and Faber, 1996; Claire Tomalin, *The Invisible Woman: The Story of Nelly Ternan and Charles Dickens*. London: Penguin, 1991.

24   For a different reading of the poem's publication history, see Wayne K. Chapman,
     Yeats's Poetry in the Making: Sing Whatever is Well Made. Basingstoke: Palgrave
     Macmillan, 2010, 79–87.

25   R. F. Foster, *The Irish Story: Telling Tales and Making it up in Ireland.* London:
     Penguin, 2001, xiii.

26   Foster, *W. B. Yeats: A Life,* I, xxix.

27   Foster, *W. B. Yeats: A Life,* II, 411.

28   For a more recent treatment of this topic, see R. F. Foster, 'Fascism', in David
     Holdeman and Ben Levitas (eds), *W. B. Yeats in Context.* Cambridge: Cambridge
     University Press, 2010, 213–23.

29   Foster, *W. B. Yeats: A Life,* I, xxxi.

30   Ellmann, *The Man and the Masks,* 73.

31   Foster, *W. B. Yeats: A Life,* I, xxvii.

32   'The form of biography, then, is countenancing experiments comparable to those of
     the novel and poem. It cannot be so mobile as those forms because it is associated
     with history, and must retain a chronological pattern, though not necessarily a simple
     one' (Richard Ellmann, *Golden Codgers: Biographical Speculations.* London: Oxford
     University Press, 1973, 15).

33   Foster, *W. B. Yeats: A Life,* II, xxiii.

34   Ibid., 353.

35   Andrew Brown, 'Interpreter of Myths', in *The Guardian,* 13 September 2003, 22.

36   Michel de Certeau, *The Writing of History,* translated by Tom Conley. New York:
     Columbia University Press, 1988, 119.

37   Some of Foster's comments on modern literary theory do, however, make it clear that
     his is a rather traditional historicism in this respect. He has recently welcomed what
     he calls a 'movement within English studies away from literary theory and towards
     literary history', and also claimed that 'the contributions of a highly politicized
     literary criticism may obscure more than they clarify' (Foster, *Words Alone: Yeats and
     His Inheritances.* Oxford: Oxford University Press, 2011, 9, 42).

38   Foster, *W. B. Yeats: A Life,* II, 659.

39   Foster, *Words Alone,* xiii, 140.

40   Foster, *W. B. Yeats: A Life,* I, xxix.

41   R. F. Foster, *Lord Randolph Churchill: A Political Life.* Oxford: Clarendon Press, 1981, 4.

42   De Certeau, *The Writing of History,* 11.

43   On the organicism of Gadamer's thought, see chapter eight in Charles I. Armstrong,
     Romantic Organicism: From Idealist Origins to Ambivalent Afterlife. London:
     Macmillan, 2003.

44   Foster, *W. B. Yeats: A Life,* II, xxii.

45   Ibid., 436.

46   Foster, *The Irish Story,* 121.

47   Ibid.

48   Ibid.

49   Foster, *W. B. Yeats: A Life,* I, xxvii–xxviii.

50   R. F. Foster, *Paddy and Mr Punch: Connections in Irish and English History.* London:
     Penguin, 1995, 61.

51   Paula R. Backscheider, *Reflections on Biography.* Oxford: Oxford University Press,
     2001, 150, 202.

52   Foster, *W. B. Yeats: A Life,* II, 615.

53   Ibid., 66.

54 Ibid., 67.
55 Friedrich Nietzsche, *Untimely Meditations*, edited by Daniel Breazeale, translated by R. J. Hollingdale. Cambridge: Cambridge University Press, 1997, 94.
56 Foster, *W. B. Yeats: A Life*, II, 67.
57 Pierre Nora, 'General Introduction: Between Memory and History', 3, in Nora (ed.), *Realms of Memory: Rethinking the French Past*, volume I, edited by Lawrence D. Kritzman, translated by Arthur Goldhammer. New York: Columbia University Press, 1996.
58 Ibid.
59 On some of the individual traits associated with the Celtic Tiger, see Carmen Kuhling and Kieran Keohane, *Cosmopolitan Ireland: Globalisation and Quality of Life*. London and Ann Arbor: Pluto Press, 2007, 5.
60 George Russell, quoted in Foster, *W. B. Yeats: A Life*, II, 339.
61 Foster, *W. B. Yeats: A Life*, II, 217.
62 Foster quoted in Andrew Brown, 'Interpreter of Myths', 21. At the end of the introduction to his biography of Churchill, Foster claims that his subject 'did his best to behave like a character in a classical English political novel, and his career involves all the trappings of romance, opportunism and triviality characteristic of the genre. But it is no less part of English political history for that' (Foster, *Lord Randoph Churchill*, 7).
63 Hayden White, *Metahistory: The Historical Imagination in Nineteenth-Century Europe*. Baltimore and London: The Johns Hopkins University Press, 1973, 8n. 6.

Chapter 4

1 Hayden White, *Metahistory*, 31.
2 Yeats's scruples concerning the depiction of the living also surfaces in the preface to *The Trembling of the Veil*, which is dated May 1922: 'Except in one or two trivial details, where I have the warrant of old friendship, I have not, without permission, quoted conversation or described occurrence from the private life of named or recognizable living persons' (*CW3* 111).
3 'Je est un autre' was pronounced by Rimbaud in letters to Georges Izambard (on 13 May 1871) and Paul Demeny (two days later). See Arthur Rimbaud, *Complete Works*, translated by Paul Schmidt. Reading: Picador, 1975, 100, 102.
4 *The Prelude* (1805), book II, lines 31–3, in William Wordsworth, *The Prelude: 1799, 1805, 1850*, edited by Jonathan Wordsworth, M. H. Abrams, and Stephen Gill. New York and London: Norton, 1979, 66.
5 Pater's story is alluded to in Yeats's account (see *Mem* 96).
6 Brown claims, for instance, that Pater's study of the Renaissance was 'a series of impressionistic meditations in art history and literary criticism [that] were an elaborately disguised paean to an equivocal aestheticized eroticism, at its most narcotic in his prose poem on the famously enigmatic smile of the *Mona Lisa*' (*The Life of W. B. Yeats*, 41). Brown insists – conveniently enough for readers of Yeats – that the aesthetic movement was a mere transitional phase, preparing the ground for later developments, and insists that Yeats 'catches the quintessence of the Decadence' in one single autobiographical anecdote (ibid., 59). For a more generous and nuanced account, focusing on Symons and Yeats, see Ellmann's 'Discovering Symbolism' in *Golden Codgers*, 101–12. Daniel T. O'Hara's reading stresses that all of

Yeats's friends and associates are 'completed images of his own latent and potentially disastrous tendencies' in the autobiographical writings (*Tragic Knowledge: Yeats's 'Autobiography' and Hermeneutics*. New York: Columbia University Press, 1981, 85).

7   Coleridge's criticism of mechanical unities is explicitly cited, and used to criticize the Irish Agrarian movement, in Yeats's *Autobiographies* (see *CW3* 270).

8   On the topic of organicism in German Idealism and British Romanticism, see parts I and II of Armstrong, *Romantic Organicism*.

9   See Paul Ricoeur, *Time and Narrative*, volume I, translated by Kathleen McLaughlin and David Pellauer. Chicago and London: The University of Chicago Press, 1984.

10 Yeats quoted in Foster, *W. B. Yeats: A Life*, II, 22.

11 Moore, *Hail and Farewell*, 547.

12 Ibid., 460.

13 Genette, *Palimpsests*, 1.

14 Claire Lynch's approach is akin to the one pursued here, in that she counters Foster's 'historical' focus on Yeats's autobiographical writings with one 'more focused on literary technique' (*Irish Autobiography: Stories of Self in the Narrative of a Nation*. Bern: Peter Lang, 2009). Her specific interest in a national tradition, though, leads her to place the autobiographical writings of Yeats and other members of the Irish Revival in the context of (mainly later) works by Irish-language writers (see ibid., chapters 2 and 3).

15 Harold Nicolson cited in David Novarr, *The Lines of Life: Theories of Biography, 1880–1970*. West Lafayette: Purdue University Press, 1986, 49.

16 Virginia Woolf, *The Crowded Dance of Modern Life*. London: Penguin, 1993, 145.

17 Linda H. Peterson, *Victorian Autobiography: The Tradition of Self-Interpretation*. New Haven and London: Yale University Press, 1986, 189.

18 Ibid., 182.

19 Ibid., 159.

20 Ian Fletcher, 'Rhythm and Pattern in *Autobiographies*', 80, in Harold Bloom (ed.), *William Butler Yeats: Modern Critical Views*. New York and Philadelphia: Chelsea House, 1986.

21 'The Child in the House', 1, in Walter Pater, *Selected Writings*, edited by Harold Bloom. New York: Columbia University Press, 1974.

22 Foster is of course far from alone in this respect. Ben Pimlott has claimed that 'there is a strong argument for saying that, despite Lytton Strachey and a century of supposed biographical iconoclasm, the Victorian tome still reigns' ('Picture this . . .', in *The Guardian Review*, 28 August 2004, 22).

23 Fletcher, 'Rhythm and Pattern in *Autobiographies*', 73.

24 Lynch, *Irish Autobiography*, 82.

25 Edward S. Casey, *Remembering: A Phenomenological Study*. Bloomington and Indianapolis: Indiana University Press, 2000, 44.

26 Roland Barthes, *Roland Barthes*, translated by Richard Howard. Berkeley and Los Angeles: University of California Press, 1977, 151.

27 Yeats, quoted in Foster, *W. B. Yeats: A Life*, II, 400.

28 Foster, *W. B. Yeats: A Life*, II, 440.

29 The link between Yeats's own relationship to memory and his theories concerning the dead is addressed in the second chapter of Peter McDonald's *Serious Poetry: Form and Authority from Yeats to Hill* (Oxford: Oxford University Press, 2002). See also Charles I. Armstrong, 'Ghost Memories: Yeats on Individual and Collective Pasts', in *Nordic Irish Studies*, 11(1), (2012), 175–84.

30 Ian Fletcher comments on this passage: 'A middle-aged bore, bowed down with the weight of "a precious, an incommunicable past", he may stop buttonholing strangers. But the deeper meaning suggests the cathartic; final responsibility to the past involves not rejection but transcendence: liberation from guilt, self-pity, historical necessity, the inescapable folly of art, multiplicity and indirection, that "wilderness of mirrors", whether of Wilde's competing gifts or Magian temptations' (Fletcher, 'Rhythm and Pattern in *Autobiographies*', 81).

31 Foster, *W. B. Yeats: A Life*, II, 180.

32 Jacques Derrida, *Archive Fever: A Freudian Impression*, translated by Eric Prenowitz. Chicago and London: The University of Chicago Press, 1996, 91.

33 Foster, *Paddy and Mr Punch*, 229.

34 Ibid., 94.

35 Compare this with the Paterian 'privileged moment' in *Per Amica Silentia Lunae*: 'It seems as if the vehicle had suddenly grown pure and far extended and so luminous that the images from *Anima Mundi*, embodied there and drunk with that sweetness, would, like a country drunkard who has thrown a wisp into his own thatch, burn up time' (*Myth* 365).

Chapter 5

1 Culler, *Framing the Sign*, ix.

2 As early as 17 October 1918, the instructors were advising Yeats to spend 'half an hour a day reading philosophic literature' (*YVP2* 82).

3 For a discussion of this episode, see George Mills Harper, *The Making of Yeats's 'A Vision': A Study of the Automatic Script*, Volume 1. London: Macmillan, 1987, 9–12, as well as his *W. B. Yeats and W. T. Horton: The Record of an Occult Friendship*. London and Basingstoke: Macmillan, 1980, 59–63.

4 Phaedrus, 246a, in Plato, *Euthyphro, Apology, Crito, Phaedo, Phaedrus*, translated by Harold North Fowler, Loeb Classical Library. Cambridge, MA: Harvard University Press, 1914, 471.

5 Hazard Adams, *The Book of Yeats's Vision: Romantic Modernism and Antithetical Tradition*. Ann Arbor: University of Michigan Press, 1995, 70.

6 Blake played an important role in the first version of *A Vision*, and George Mills Harper's commentaries on the automatic script point out several important parallels from the very beginning; see Harper, *The Making of Yeats's 'A Vision'* and *YVP1*.

7 Matthew DeForrest, 'Philosophical Differences and Yeats's Corroborative System in *A Vision*', in *The South Carolina Review*, Vol. 32, no. 1, Fall 1999, 224.

8 James Olney, *The Rhizome and the Flower: The Perennial Philosophy – Yeats and Jung*. Berkeley: University of California Press, 1980, 150.

9 Rosemary Puglia Ritvo, 'A Vision B: The Plotinian Metaphysical Basis', *Review of English Studies*, New Series, 26(101), (1975), 34–46.

10 Ibid., 35n. Although Ritvo does not contextualize her reading, it is most likely Yeats's receptivity to romantic tenets that makes possible an agreement with what Pierre Hadot has called 'Plotinus' central intuition: the human self is *not* irrevocably separated from its eternal model, as the latter exists within divine Thought' (*Plotinus, or The Simplicity of Vision*, translated by Michael Chase. Chicago: University of Chicago Press, 1993, 27).

11   Brian Arkins, *Builders of My Soul: Greek and Roman Themes in Yeats*. Gerrards Cross:
      Colin Smythe, 1990, 35.
12   Matthew Gibson, 'Classical Philosophy', in David Holdeman and Ben Levitas (eds),
      W. B. Yeats in Context. Cambridge: Cambridge University Press, 2010, 276–87. In
      personal correspondence with the author, Gibson has also pointed out how Yeats's
      use of his sources regarding the concept of the Eternal Return changes. While it is
      presented as a mainly Nietzschean idea in the first edition (*CW13* 142), Yeats takes
      the concept back to ancient Greek thought in the second.
13   Genette defines metatextuality, one of his five types of transtextuality, as 'the
      relationship most often labelled "commentary". It unites a given text to another,
      of which it speaks without necessarily citing it (without summoning it), in fact
      sometimes even without naming it. Thus does Hegel, in *The Phenomenology of Mind*,
      allusively and almost silently evoke Denis Diderot's *Neveu de Rameau*. This is the
      critical relationship par excellence' (Genette, *Palimpsests*, 4).
14   Walter Pater, *Plato and Platonism: A Series of Lectures*. Amsterdam: Fredonia Books,
      2002, 2.
15   See, for instance, Catherine H. Zuckert, *Postmodern Platos: Nietzsche, Heidegger,
      Gadamer, Strauss, Derrida*. Chicago and London: University of Chicago Press, 1996.
16   Olney, *The Rhizome and the Flower*, 226.
17   Thomas Parkinson, 'This Extraordinary Book' (*YA1* [1982] 195).
18   Genette, *Paratexts*, 410.
19   Plato's *Phaedrus* as quoted in 'Introduction and headnotes to *Fairy and Folk Tales
      of the Irish Peasantry*, edited by W. B. Yeats (1888)', (*CW6* 9). The same passage is
      referred to again in 'Enchanted Woods' in *The Celtic Twilight* (see *Myth* 63).
20   Margaret Mills Harper, *Wisdom of Two: The Spiritual and Literary Collaboration of
      George and W. B. Yeats*. Oxford: Oxford University Press, 2006, 135.
21   Derrida, *The Truth in Painting*, 73.
22   Pater, *Plato and Platonism*, 64. Yeats presents Platonic anamnesis as 'a relation to the
      timeless' in John Aherne's letter (*AVB* 54).
23   H. P. Blavatsky, *The Secret Doctrine: The Synthesis of Science, Religion, and Philosophy*,
      2 vols. London: Theosophical Publishing Company, 1888, 1:77.
24   See S. L. MacGregor Mathers, *The Kabbalah Unveiled*. Henley: Routledge & Kegan
      Paul, 1981, 21, 214n.
25   Graham Hough, *The Mystery Religion of W. B. Yeats*. Brighton: Harvester Press, 1984.
26   Interestingly, two of Yeats's most important scholarly sources – A. E. Taylor and John
      Burnet – pointed in opposite directions. According to Frank M. Turner, in Taylor's
      work 'both Socrates and Plato emerged as proto-Christians who had been primarily
      concerned with the tendance of the soul, which Taylor equated with the modern
      concept of "the development of 'moral personality'"' (Turner, *The Greek Heritage
      in Victorian Britain*. New Haven and London: Yale University Press, 1981, 382).
      On the other hand, John Burnet's work on Plato and Socrates – concurrent, in this
      respect, with his later work on early Greek philosophy – was 'part and parcel of the
      more general late-Victorian and Edwardian effort to examine sympathetically those
      features of Greek religion, philosophy and society that earlier rationalist authors had
      largely discounted in order to discover an ancient positivistic age' (ibid., 317). Richard
      Jenkyns has, however, contradicted the tendency to simplify the Victorian stance
      here: 'it was also characteristic of the age, or of its more enquiring members, to feel
      that between faith in Christianity and the love of Greece there must be a tension' (*The
      Victorians and Ancient Greece*. Oxford: Basil Blackwell, 1980, 70).

27 Yeats's passing, disparaging comparison of Platonic thought to death and Christian asceticism in 'Dove or Swan' (see *CW13* 153; *AVB* 271) is also decidedly Nietzschean in tone; see Otto Bohlmann, *Yeats and Nietzsche: An Exploration of Major Nietzschean Echoes in the Writings of William Butler Yeats*. Totowa: Barnes & Noble Books, 1982, 88–9.

28 See chapter 1 of Sarah Cole, *Modernism, Male Friendship, and the First World War*. Cambridge: Cambridge University Press, 2003.

29 See Claire Nally, *Envisioning Ireland: Occult Nationalism in the Work of W. B. Yeats*. Oxford: Peter Lang, 2009.

30 On the late Yeats as a philosopher-poet, see Matthew Gibson, *Yeats, Coleridge and the Romantic Sage*. Basingstoke: Macmillan, 2000.

31 Walter Pater, *Marius the Epicurean*, edited by Michael Levey. London: Penguin, 1985, 147.

Chapter 6

1 Katharine Worth, *The Irish Drama of Europe from Yeats to Beckett*. London: The Athlone Press, 1978; McAteer, *Yeats and European Drama*.

2 Alan Richardson, *A Mental Theatre: Poetic Drama and Consciousness in the Romantic Age*. University Park and London: The Pennsylvania State University Press, 1988.

3 For recent summaries of Yeats's poetic relation to the romantics, see Matthew Campbell's 'The English Romantic Symbolists' (in David Holdeman and Ben Levitas (eds), *W. B. Yeats in Context*. Cambridge: Cambridge University Press, 2010) and George Bornstein's 'Yeats and Romanticism' (in Marjorie Howes and John Kelly (eds), *The Cambridge Companion to W. B. Yeats*. Cambridge: Cambridge University Press, 2006).

4 See, for instance, chapter 8 of James Longenbach, *Stone Cottage*.

5 Yury Tynjanov, 'The Literary Fact', in David Duff (ed.), *Modern Genre Theory*. Harlow: Pearson Education, 2000, 39.

6 Here the formalists' insistence upon unified traditions might seem to be too narrow, however. Looking outside Western traditions, Yeats and Pound – and other modernists such as Picasso – engaged in a cross-cultural dialogue more amenable to the theories of Mikhail Bakhtin. Bakhtin's account of linguistic genres will be utilized in Chapter 8.

7 Augustine Martin, 'Yeats's Noh: The Dancer and the Dance', xiv, in Masaru Sekine and Christopher Murray, *Yeats and the Noh: A Comparative Study*, with contributions by Augustine Martin, Peter Davidson, Colleen Hanrahan and Katharine Worth. Savage, Maryland: Barnes & Nobel Books, 1990. David R. Clark has pointed out that Yeats also was selective in his approach to the subgenres of Noh: 'Of the five sorts of Noh plays, Yeats and Pound were especially interested in only one – the Noh of spirits' (David R. Clark, with Rosalind Clark, *W. B. Yeats and the Theatre of Desolate Reality*, revised edition. Washington, DC: The Catholic University of America Press, 1993, 192).

8 Andrew Parkin, 'Introduction', xxix, in W. B. Yeats, *At the Hawk's Well* and *The Cat and the Moon: Manuscript Materials*, edited by Andrew Parkin. Ithaca and London: Cornell University Press, 2010. Hiro Ishabishi takes a more sceptical stance, claiming that the Yeats's adaptation may have resulted in 'high art' but was 'born of a misunderstanding' of the Japanese form ('Yeats and the Noh: Types of Japanese Beauty and their Reflection in Yeats's Plays', in *The Dolmen Press Yeats Centenary*

Papers, MCMLXV, 1966, 151). Harold Bloom has of course later claimed that all
'strong' poets appropriate their role models for themselves, through a process of
misinterpretation: see *The Anxiety of Influence.*

9 See the comparative readings included in Masaru Sekine and Christopher Murray's
Yeats and the Noh: A Comparative Study (with contributions by Augustine Martin,
Peter Davidson, Colleen Hanrahan and Katharine Worth. Savage, Maryland: Barnes &
Nobel Books, 1990), as well as chapter 4 of Richard Taylor, *The Drama of W. B. Yeats:
Irish Myth and the Japanese Nō.* New Haven and London: Yale University Press,
1976.

10 Parkin, 'Introduction', xxvii.

11 Ernest Fenollosa and Ezra Pound, *'Noh' or Accomplishment: A Study of the Classical
Stage of Japan.* Gretna: Pelican Publishing Company, 1999, 101.

12 Sekine and Murray, *Yeats and the Noh,* 55.

13 For the formal continuity between *On Baile's Strand* and Yeats's dance plays, see Sylvia
C. Ellis, *The Plays of W. B. Yeats: Yeats and the Dancer.* Basingstoke: Macmillan, 1999,
277–80.

14 See McAteer, *Yeats and European Drama.*

15 David Duff, *Romanticism and the Uses of Genre.* Oxford: Oxford University Press,
1999, 178.

16 Miller, *The Noble Drama of W. B. Yeats,* 261–2.

17 Bloom, *Yeats,* 337.

18 Ibid., 318.

19 On Yeats's part in the centenary commemoration of the 1798 rising, see for instance
Brown, *The Life of W. B. Yeats,* 101–2.

20 Gail Marshall, 'Introduction', in Marshall (ed.), *The Cambridge Companion to the Fin
de Siècle.* Cambridge: Cambridge University Press, 2007, 4.

21 Noreen Doody, 'An Echo of Some One Else's Music: The Influence of Oscar Wilde
on W. B. Yeats', in Uwe Böker, Richard Corballis and Julie A. Hibbard (eds), *The
Importance of Reinventing Oscar: Versions of Wilde during the Last 100 Years.*
Amsterdam: Rodopi, 2002, 175–82. While I believe that *Salomé* is the most salient
modern forerunner for the way in which Yeats adopts Biblical material in *The
Resurrection,* this is not to say that there are not many other significant influences.
In *Biblical Drama in England: From the Middle Ages to the Present Day* (London:
Faber and Faber, 1968), Murray Roston anticipates part of the argument of this
chapter in arguing that *The Resurrection* 'betrays in Yeats a certain hankering after
the old dispensation, the glory and might which must pass at the advent of the new
era' (273). Roston also demonstrates that Biblical drama was very much in the air
at the time, and that significant plays of this kind were written by associates and
acquaintances of Yeats, such as John Masefield, Thomas Sturge Moore and George
Bernard Shaw.

22 See Foster, *W. B. Yeats: A Life,* II, 372–7.

23 Richard Ellmann, *Oscar Wilde.* London: Penguin, 1987, 338.

24 See Jarlath Killeen, *The Faiths of Oscar Wilde: Catholicism, Folklore and Ireland.*
Basingstoke: Palgrave Macmillan, 2005, 62.

25 W. B. Yeats, *The Resurrection: Manuscript Materials,* edited by Jared Curtis and Selina
Guinness. Ithaca and London: Cornell University Press, 2011, 501.

26 Early on in Wilde's play, a soldier mocks how the Jews always 'are disputing about
their religion' (Oscar Wilde, *Salomé.* Boston: Branden Publishing Company, 1996, 1).
Peter Ure describes *The Resurrection* as 'a play of ideas' where '[s]ome of the ideas

are directly expressed in the debates between the characters' (*Yeats the Playwright: A Commentary on Character and Design in the Major Plays.* London: Routledge & Kegan Paul, 1963, 120).

27   Wilde, *Salomé,* 23.
28   McAteer, *Yeats and European Drama,* 52.
29   See E. R. Dodds, *The Greeks and the Irrational.* Berkeley: University of California Press, 1951.
30   Letter to George Yeats, 19 May 1925. *CL Intelex* 4732 gives this as 'asiatic gong & rattle', while the wording cited above is to be found in W. B. Yeats and George Yeats, *The Letters,* edited by Ann Saddlemyer. Oxford: Oxford University Press, 2011, 161.
31   Brown, *The Life of W. B. Yeats,* 348. For Frazer on the link between Christian resurrection and paganism, see chapter 37 of *The Golden Bough: A Study of Magic and Religion.* London: Papermac, 1987.
32   Ellmann, *The Identity of Yeats,* 261. Ellmann's reading of the 'Two Songs from a Play' also establishes their link with Frazer's *Golden Bough.*
33   Jared Curtis and Selina Guinness, 'Introduction', xix, in W. B. Yeats, *The Resurrection: Manuscript Materials.* Ithaca and London: Cornell University Press, 2011.
34   Letter from Georgie Yeats to W. B. Yeats, 13 June 1937, in W. B. Yeats and George Yeats, *The Letters,* 473.
35   Helen Vendler, *Yeats's Vision and the Later Plays.* Cambridge, MA: Harvard University Press, 1963, 184–5.
36   Ibid., 179.
37   Sylvia C. Ellis has stressed this connection, describing *The Resurrection* as 'a dance play without a dance' (*The Plays of W. B. Yeats,* 300).
38   These terms are taken from Rick Altman's discussion of mixed genres in cinema, Rick Altman, *Film/Genre.* London: Palgrave Macmillan, 2012 (1999), 136.
39   Martin, 'Introduction', xiv.
40   Parkin, 'Introduction', xxxi.
41   Miller, *The Noble Drama of W. B. Yeats,* 216.
42   Ibid., 223.
43   As Steven Putzel has shown, not only the actual folding and unfolding of the cloth, but also the accompanying words 'help define the role that spectators will play' in *Four Plays for Dancers* ('Poetic Ritual and Audience Response: Yeats and the Nō', 120, in Leonard Orr (ed.), *Yeats and Postmodernism.* Syracuse: Syracuse University Press, 1991). Richard Taylor suggests that such measures were not enough: 'However well-suited to his subject matter and theatrical aims, the non-realistic and expressive staging of the dance dramas was not yet acceptable to the theatre-going public and proved to be still another stumbling block to the reception of his work' (*The Drama of W. B. Yeats,* 119–20).
44   See chapter 4 of Altman, *Film/Genre.*
45   Peter Ure may have been hinting at this ancestral link, when he entitled his study of these two texts 'Yeats's Christian Mystery Plays'. See Peter Ure, 'Yeats's Christian Mystery Plays', *The Review of English Studies,* New Series, 11(42), (May 1960), 171–82. The hint of a connection disappeared three years later when the same reading was presented as the sixth chapter, now entitled 'For Reason, Miracle' in *Yeats the Playwright.*
46   The performance is mentioned in Yeats's letter to Lady Gregory, 10 November 1911 (*CL Intelex* 1767). See also the references in John S. Kelly, *A W. B. Yeats Chronology.* Basingstoke: Palgrave Macmillan, 2003, 152, 203.

47 Peter Happé, 'Introduction', in Happé (ed.), *English Mystery Plays: A Selection*. London: Penguin, 1988 (1975), 32.

48 Richard Beadle and Pamela M. King (eds), *York Mystery Plays: A Selection in Modern Spelling*. Oxford: Oxford University Press, 2009 (1984), 264. The wording in the Resurrection pageant of the Towneley cycle is very much the same: see Peter Happé (ed.), *English Mystery Plays: A Selection*. London: Penguin, 1988 (1975), 587.

49 Vendler, *Yeats's Vision and the Later Plays*, 181–2.

50 Richard Beadle and Pamela M. King, 'General Introduction', in Beadle and King (eds), *York Mystery Plays: A Selection in Modern Spelling*. Oxford: Oxford University Press, 2009 (1984), xi.

Chapter 7

1 See, for instance, pages 771–3 of Daniel Albright's notes, in W. B. Yeats, *The Poems*, edited and introduced by Daniel Albright. London: Everyman, 1990. For the influence of classical Greece on Yeats, see Arkins, *Builders of My Soul*.

2 See, for instance, Fowler, *Kinds of Literature*, 106–7.

3 Nicholas Grene, 'J. M. Synge', in David Holdeman and Ben Levitas (eds), *W. B. Yeats in Context*. Cambridge: Cambridge University Press, 2010, 143.

4 John Millington Synge, *Plays, Poems and Prose*, edited by Micheál Mac Liammóir. London: Dent, 1968, 215.

5 See Aristotle, *Poetics*, translated and with a commentary by George Whalley. Montreal: McGill-Queen's University Press, 1997, 87–91.

6 Lee Oser distinguishes Yeats's conception of tragedy from that of Aristotle on the basis of the former's strong emphasis on passion: see *The Ethics of Modernism: Moral Ideas in Yeats, Eliot, Joyce, Woolf, and Beckett*. Cambridge: Cambridge University Press, 2007, 33–4.

7 Scott Brewster, *Lyric*. London and New York: Routledge, 2009, 1. Brewster opposes this understanding of the lyric, advocating that the genre ultimately transcends the subject. In this respect, he is in line with Yeats's tendency to stress the impersonal nature of his poetry.

8 Yeats had already written of 'tragic joy' a few years prior to the essay on 'The Tragic Theatre': see the 1904 *Samhain* (*CW8* 72).

9 See Bohlmann, *Yeats and Nietzsche*, 42, 46.

10 See Jeffrey Perl, *The Tradition of Return: The Implicit History of Modern Literature*. Princeton: Princeton University Press, 1984.

11 Michael McAteer writes with great acumen about the importance of farce in later Yeats: see, for instance, pages 170–4 of *Yeats and European Drama*.

12 Foster, *W. B. Yeats: A Life*, II, 25.

13 See Bradford's comments in *WTPQ* 254, where it is suggested that 'Yeats seems to be starting more hares than he can pursue.'

14 Raymond Williams, *Modern Tragedy*, edited by Pamela McCallum. Peterborough, Ontario: Broadview, 2006, 88.

15 In draft 16, for instance, we are 'in the country of Surrico, which is unknown to history though known to legend'. The rebels are dressed in clothes that 'vaguely suggest the middle of the 15th century' (*MTPQ* 191).

16 See for instance Aristotle, *The Poetics*, 93–5.

17   See Edna Longley, 'Helicon and ni Houlihan: *Michael Robartes and the Dancer*', 212, in Jonathan Allison (ed.), *Yeats's Political Identities: Selected Essays*. Ann Arbor: The University of Michigan Press, 1996.

18   Daniel T. O'Hara, *Tragic Knowledge*, 47.

19   George Steiner, *The Death of Tragedy*, quoted in John Drakakis and Naomi Conn Liebler (eds), *Tragedy*. London and New York: Longman, 1998, 146.

20   Ibid.

21   Terry Eagleton, *Sweet Violence: The Idea of the Tragic*. Oxford: Blackwell, 2003, 124.

22   See Michael Wood, *Yeats and Violence: The Clarendon Lectures in English 2008*. Oxford: Oxford University Press, 2010.

23   Michael Valdez Moses, 'Nietzsche', in David Holdeman and Ben Levitas (eds), *W. B. Yeats in Context*. Cambridge: Cambridge University Press, 2010, 274.

24   Edward Engelberg, *The Vast Design: Patters in W. B. Yeats's Aesthetic*, second edition, expanded. Washington, DC: The Catholic University of America Press, 1988, 174.

25   Jon Stallworthy, *Vision and Revision in Yeats's 'Last Poems'*. Oxford: Clarendon Press, 1969, 43.

Chapter 8

1   On knowledge in the early Yeats, see Allen R. Grossman, *Poetic Knowledge in the Early Yeats: A Study of 'The Wind among the Reeds'*. Charlottesville: University Press of Virginia, 1969.

2   M. M. Bakhtin, *Speech Genres and Other Late Essays*, edited by Caryl Emerson and Michael Holquist, translated by Vern W. McGee. Austin: University of Texas Press, 1986, 66.

3   Ibid., 65.

4   See, for instance, Wolfgang Iser, *The Act of Reading: A Theory of Aesthetic Response*. Baltimore and London: Johns Hopkins University Press, 1978, 210.

5   For a cognitive account of auditory memory, see, for instance, S. E. Gathercole, 'The Nature and Uses of Working Memory', in Peter Morris and Michael Gruneberg (eds), *Theoretical Aspects of Memory*, 2nd edn. London and New York: Routledge, 1994, 50–78.

6   While pointing to the similarities between Yeats and Mallarmé, George Moore insisted that the Irishman's affinity for folk literature separated the two: see Moore, *Hail and Farewell*, 545.

7   See, for instance, Colin Meir, *The Ballads and Songs of W. B. Yeats: The Anglo-Irish Heritage in Subject and Style*. London: Macmillan, 1974.

8   'Digging' in Seamus Heaney, *Death of a Naturalist*. London: Faber and Faber, 1991 (1966), 1–2.

9   In a Bakhtinian reading of orality in Yeats's writings, R. B. Kershner makes a point of John Butler Yeats's importance for his son. See R. B. Kershner, 'Yeats/Bakhtin/Orality/Dyslexia', 176, in Leonard Orr (ed.), *Yeats and Postmodernism*. New York: Syracuse University Press, 1991.

10   Elizabeth Butler Cullingford, *Gender and History in Yeats's Love Poetry*. New York: Syracuse University Poetry, 1996, 17.

11   See Jean-Jacques Rousseau and Johann Gottfried Herder, *On the Origin of Language*, translated by John H. Moran and Alexander Gode. Chicago and London: The University of Chicago Press, 1966.

12 Foster, *W. B. Yeats: A Life*, II, 61.
13 Longley, 'Helicon and ni Houlihan: *Michael Robartes and the Dancer*', 214.
14 Bakhtin, *Speech Genres and Other Late Essays*, 62.
15 Jahan Ramazani, *Yeats and the Poetry of Death: Elegy, Self-Elegy, and the Sublime*. New Haven and London: Yale University Press, 1990, 64.
16 De Certeau, *The Writing of History*, 5–6.
17 Charles Townshend, *Easter 1916: The Irish Rebellion*. London: Penguin, 2005, 202.
18 Williams, *Modern Tragedy*, 89.
19 Ibid.
20 For an account of how Yeats sought to both transcend and immerse himself in history, see Thomas R. Whitaker, *Swan and Shadow: Yeats's Dialogue with History*, revised edition. Washington, DC: Catholic University of America Press, 1989.
21 Paul de Man, *The Rhetoric of Romanticism*. New York: Columbia University Press, 1984, 151. See also Hazard Adams, 'Constituting Yeats's Poems as a Book', in David Pierce (ed.), *W. B. Yeats; Critical Assessments, Volume IV. Assessments: 1980–2000*. Mountfield: Helm Information, 2000.
22 McDiarmid's emphasis, however, differs from mine when she writes: 'In lyric poems written after 1914, however, writing – particularly the physical activity of writing – begins to appear as a primary source of value. Particularly in the poems that describe and defend his metier, Yeats emerges as a cosmopolitan, lettered poet writing in a classical, European tradition, not a poet of the people' (Lucy McDiarmid, 'Yeats and the Lettered Page', in W. B. Yeats, *Yeats's Poetry, Drama, and Prose*, edited by James Pethica. New York: Norton, 2000, 371).
23 Edna Longley, 'Helicon and ni Houlihan: *Michael Robartes and the Dancer*', 212.
24 Eliot, *The Sacred Wood*, 43.
25 R. F. Foster, *W. B. Yeats: A Life. II*, 217.
26 Declan Kiberd, *Ulysses and Us: The Art of Everyday Living*. London: Faber and Faber, 2009, 54.
27 James Joyce, *Ulysses*, London and New York: Everyman, 1997, 41.
28 For a classic account of the relationship between Yeats and Joyce, see chapter 3 of Richard Ellmann, *Eminent Domain*.
29 Joyce, *Ulysses*, 43.
30 Ibid., 52.
31 Frank Kermode, *Romantic Image*. London and New York: Routledge, 2002 (1957), 100.
32 Donald T. Torchiana, '"Among School Children" and the Education of the Irish Spirit', 141, in A. Norman Jeffares and K. G. W. Cross (eds), *In Excited Reverie: A Centenary Tribute to William Butler Yeats, 1865–1939*. New York: St. Martin's Press, 1965. In addition to the Montessori link, Torchiana also draws on Yeats's interest in the educational philosophy of Giovanni Gentile.
33 Bakhtin, *Speech Genres and Other Late Essays*, 93.
34 *The Complete Annotated Gilbert and Sullivan*, introduced and edited by Ian Bradley. Oxford: Oxford University Press, 1996, 513–15.
35 Genette, *Palimpsests*, 212.
36 Ibid., 367. Strictly speaking, the relationship between 'Among School Children' and *Princess Ida* is one of intertextuality rather than hypertextuality (according to Genette's terminology), since the former is not strongly dependent upon the existence of the latter. Nonetheless, the specific hypertextual phenomenon of transvaluation is relevant to this case.

37 Geraldine Higgins, 'Popular Culture', 406, in David Holdeman and Ben Levitas (eds), *W. B. Yeats in Context*. Cambridge: Cambridge University Press, 2010.

38 On January 2, 1889, he and his brother Jack attended *The Yeomen of the Guard*, and we also know that Yeats saw a performance of Gilbert's early play *The Palace of Truth* in May 1905. See Kelly, *A W. B. Yeats Chronology*, 15, 100.

39 Joseph Darracott, *The World of Charles Ricketts*. New York and Toronto: Methuen, 1980, 187–91.

40 *The Complete Annotated Gilbert and Sullivan*, 463. The phrase 'In my mind's eye' derives from *Hamlet*, act I, scene ii, line 184 (William Shakespeare, *Hamlet*, edited by Bernard Lott. Harlow: Longman, 1968, 21). Compare the opening lines of *At the Hawk's Well*: 'I call to the eye of the mind / A well long choked up and dry' (*VPl* 399; *CW2* 297).

41 *The Complete Annotated Gilbert and Sullivan*, 479.

42 Ibid.

43 There is also indirect criticism of the use of classical exemplars in education, via the use of Greek and Roman casts in art, in 'The Child and the State', Yeats's speech made to the Irish Literary Society in November 1925. See *SS* 171. On the classics' role in Yeats's own education, see Arkins, *Builders of My Soul*, 1–5.

44 Sean Farren, *The Politics of Irish Education, 1920–65*. Belfast: The Institute of Irish Studies, 1995, 113.

45 Cullingford, *Gender and History in Yeats's Love Poetry*, 201.

46 Such a symbolist context provides the grounding of Frank Kermode's reading of the poem in *Romantic Image*, 99–103.

47 Alfred, Lord Tennyson, *A Selected Edition*, edited by Christopher Ricks. Harlow: Longman, 1989 (1969), 328.

48 Carolyn Williams, *Gilbert and Sullivan: Gender, Genre, Parody*. New York: Columbia University Press, 2011, 243.

Chapter 9

1 On Yeats's family and the arts, see Hilary Pyle, *Yeats: Portrait of an Artistic Family*. London: National Gallery of Ireland in association with Merrell Holberton, 1997, *passim*.

2 Jacques Rancière, *The Politics of Aesthetics*, translated by Gabriel Rockhill. London: Continuum, 2004, 26.

3 Jacques Rancière, *The Future of the Image*, translated by Gregory Elliott. London: Verso, 2007, 43.

4 James A. W. Heffernan, *Museum of Words: The Poetics of Ekphrasis from Homer to Ashbery*. Chicago and London: The University of Chicago Press, 1993, 3.

5 In addition to Heffernan's *Museum of Words*, see for instance Barbara K. Fischer, *Museum Mediations: Reframing Ekphrasis in Contemporary American Poetry* (New York: Routledge, 2006) and Catherine Paul, *Poetry in the Museums of Modernism: Yeats, Pound, Moore, Stein*. Ann Arbor: The University of Michigan Press, 2002.

6 Elizabeth Bergmann Loizeaux, *Yeats and the Visual Arts*. New York: Syracuse University Press, 2003.

7 Ibid., 171.

8   'Michael Robartes and the Dancer' is one of several ekphrastic poems discussed in
    Elizabeth Bergmann Loizeaux, 'Yeats's Poems on Pictures', *The Yeats Journal of Korea*,
    38, (summer 2012), 11–31.

9   See Giorgio Melchiori, *The Whole Mystery of Art*. London: Routledge and Kegan
    Paul, 1959, 159.

10 Ian Fletcher, ' "Leda and the Swan" as Iconic Poem', *YA1* (1982) 96–7.

11 W. J. T. Mitchell, *Iconology: Image, Text, Ideology*. Chicago: The University of Chicago
    Press, 1986, 47.

12 Rancière, *The Emancipated Spectator*, 62.

13 G. E. Lessing, *Laocoon: An Essay on the Limits of Painting and Poetry*, translated by
    Edward Allen McCormick. Baltimore: Johns Hopkins University Press, 1984.

14 Declan Kiberd, *Inventing Ireland: The Literature of a Modern Nation*. London:
    Vintage, 1996, 315.

15 Ezra Pound, 'A Few Don'ts by an Imagiste', in Peter Jones (ed.), *Imagist Poetry*.
    London: Penguin, 1972, 130.

16 Cullingford, *Gender and History in Yeats's Love Poetry*, 164.

17 Frow, *Genre*, 76.

18 Vendler, *Our Secret Discipline*, 66.

19 Ibid., 262. On the influence of Grierson's Byron on Yeats, see Cairns Craig, 'The Last
    Romantics: How the scholarship of Herbert Grierson influenced Modernist poetry',
    in *Times Literary Supplement*, 15 January 2010, 14–15. The stanzaic form of 'The
    Municipal Gallery Re-visited' is said be 'derived from Byron' in Chapman, *Yeats's
    Poetry in the Making*, 207.

20 Foster, *W. B. Yeats: A Life*, II, 598.

21 Yeats's rhyme indicates that the fourth epistle of Pope's *An Essay of Man* may also
    have been an influence. The speaker of Pope's poem says the following of fame: 'All
    that we feel of it begins and ends / In the small circle of our friends' (lines 241–2 of
    Epistle IV in Alexander Pope, *'The Rape of the Lock' and Other Major Writings*, edited
    by Leo Damrosch. London: Penguin, 2011, 130).

22 On Early Modern friendship, see Tom MacFaul, *Male Friendship in Shakespeare and
    his Contemporaries*. Cambridge: Cambridge University Press, 2007.

23 There is a lot of outstanding scholarship on Yeats and elegy. The following two studies
    are notable for placing Yeats's elegiac work in the context of the genre's history: Peter
    M. Sacks, *The English Elegy: Studies in the Genre from Spenser to Yeats*. Baltimore
    and London: The Johns Hopkins University Press, 1985; Jahan Ramazani, *Poetry of
    Mourning: The Modern Elegy from Hardy to Heaney*. Chicago: University of Chicago
    Press, 1994.

24 In his text for the catalogue *Yeats at the Municipal Gallery*, Arland Ussher commented
    that 'Few ghostly gatherings have had such a host to make the introductions' (Ussher
    quoted in Paul, *Poetry in the Museums of Modernism*, 56).

25 David Duff (ed.), *Modern Genre Theory*. Harlow: Pearson, 2000, 232.

26 Vendler, *Our Secret Discipline*, 295.

27 Paul, *Poetry in the Museums of Modernism*, 42.

28 Elizabeth Bergmann Loizeaux also makes this connection: 'Behind the idea of the
    Municipal Gallery as a physical place lies the example of Lady Gregory's house at
    Coole Park, which she had opened up and given over to Yeats, Synge and other
    writers and artists of the Irish Renaissance' (*Twentieth-Century Poetry and the Visual
    Arts*. Cambridge: Cambridge University Press, 2008, 43).

29 Thomas Parkinson, *W. B. Yeats, Self-Critic: A Study of His Early Verse, and the Later Poetry*. Berkeley: University of California Press, 1971, 170–1.

30 Chapman, *Yeats's Poetry in the Making*, 207.

31 Fowler, *Kinds of Literature*, 171.

32 Duff, 'Intertextuality versus Genre Theory', 66.

33 Loizeaux, *Twentieth-Century Poetry and the Visual Arts*, 38.

34 Yeats quoted in Chapman, *Yeats's Poetry in the Making*, 187.

35 For photographic reproductions of Lane's collection, as well as instructive essays on him and the Municipal Gallery, see Barbara Dawson (ed.), *Hugh Lane: Founder of a Gallery of Modern Art for Ireland*. London: Scala, 2008.

36 See, for instance, Deirdre Toomey, '"Amaryllis in the Shade": The Municipal Gallery Revisited', in Warwick Gould (ed.), *Poems and Contexts* (*YA16* [2005]) 131–59.

37 Here another genre relevant to 'The Municipal Gallery Re-visited' might be mentioned. Yeats's poem is unlike most acts of art criticism in that leaves out such information, yet it is still like art criticism in the way it mentions works of art, assessing their significance and value in the process. Such an overlap between literature and its aesthetic cousin is a common feature of most ekphrastic poetry, but perhaps particularly relevant in Yeats's case: he included, for instance, a versified rendition of Walter Pater's interpretation of the Mona Lisa (from *The Renaissance*) as the opening poem to his 1936 edition of *The Oxford Book of Modern Verse*, thus decisively blurring the generic boundary between poetry and art criticism.

38 I am alluding to the concept of defamiliarization or making strange (*ostranenie*) developed by Russian Formalism.

Chapter 10

1 Wood, *Yeats and Violence*, 87.

2 In addition to studies cited earlier in this book, the following undoubtedly deserve to be mentioned: George Bornstein, *Material Modernism: The Politics of the Page*. Cambridge: Cambridge University Press, 2001; Yug Mohit Chaudhry, *Yeats: The Irish Literary Revival and the Politics of Print*. Cork: Cork University Press, 2001; David Holdeman, *Much Labouring: The Texts and Authors of Yeats's First Modernist Books*. Ann Arbor: The University of Michigan Press, 1997; Marjorie Howes, *Yeats's Nations: Gender, Class, and Irishness*. Cambridge: Cambridge University Press, 1996; W. J. McCormack, *Blood Kindred: W. B. Yeats. The Life, the Death, the Politics*. London: Pimlico, 2005; 'W. B. Yeats: A Postcolonial Poet?' in Jahan Ramazani, *The Hybrid Muse: Postcolonial Poetry in English*. Chicago and London: The University of Chicago Press, 2001.

3 David Holdeman and Ben Levitas (eds), *W. B. Yeats in Context*. Cambridge: Cambridge University Press, 2010, 9–10.

4 For examples of their criticism on Yeats, see chapter six in Peter McDonald, *Serious Poetry* and Matthew Campbell, 'Yeats in the Coming Times', *Essays in Criticism*, 53(1), (January 2003), 10–32.

5 Nicholas Grene, *Yeats's Poetic Codes*. Oxford: Oxford University Press, 2008, 3. See also Vereen M. Bell's *Yeats and the Logic of Formalism* (Columbia and London: University of Missouri Press, 2006) which distinguishes its own 'existential' focus on formal issues from more traditional ones (7).

6   Vendler, *Our Secret Discipline*, xiv.
7   Helen Vendler, *The Art of Shakespeare's Sonnets*. Cambridge, MA: Belknap Press, 1997, 1–2. Compare this to Scott Brewster's claim that 'lyric, far from presenting the unmediated thoughts and feelings of an isolated individual, centres on the relationship between the self and others, the self and history, and the self and language' (*Lyric*, 14).
8   Vendler, *The Art of Shakespeare's Sonnets*, xiii.
9   Ibid., 3.
10 Ibid., 81.
11 Ibid., 80.
12 Ibid., 22.
13 For a structural reading of Shakespeare's sonnets that pays detailed attention to Italian precedent, see Roy T. Eriksen, 'Shaping the Sonnet Italian Style: Petrarch, Tasso, Daniel and Shakespeare', in Sonja Fielitz (ed.), *Shakespeare's Sonnets: Loves, Layers, Languages*. Heidelberg: Universitätsverlag Winter, 2010, 55–73.
14 Vendler, *The Art of Shakespeare's Sonnets*, 12.
15 Ibid., 28.
16 Ibid., xiv.
17 Ibid., 26.
18 John Kerrigan, 'Introduction', in William Shakespeare, *'The Sonnets' and 'A Lover's Complaint'*, edited by John Kerrigan. London: Penguin, 2009 (1995), xii.
19 Paul de Man, 'Lyrical Voice in Contemporary Theory: Riffaterre and Jauss', in Chaviva Hosek and Patricia Parker (eds), *Lyric Poetry: Beyond New Criticism*. Ithaca and London: Cornell University Press, 1985, 66.
20 Vendler, *The Art of Shakespeare's Sonnets*, 69.
21 See Joel Fineman, *Shakespeare's Perjured Eye*. Berkeley: University of California Press, 1986.
22 Vendler, *Our Secret Discipline*,147.
23 Ibid.
24 Clive Scott, *French Verse-Art: A Study*. Cambridge: Cambridge University Press, 1980, 172.
25 For a critical view on Heaney's stance, see Jason David Hall, 'Form and Process: Seamus Heaney's "A New Life" into "Act of Union"', in Frank Beardow and Alison O'Malley-Younger (eds), *Representing Ireland: Past, Present and Future*. Sunderland: University of Sunderland Press, 2005, 153–64.
26 Rupin W. Desai, *Yeats's Shakespeare*. Evanston: Northwestern University Press, 1971. For a more recent reading of Yeats's relationship to Shakespeare, see chapters 1 and 2 in Neil Corcoran, *Shakespeare and the Modern Poet*. Cambridge: Cambridge University Press, 2010.
27 T. McAlindon, 'Yeats and the English Renaissance', *PMLA*, 82(2) (May 1967), 164.
28 See Walter Mönch, *Das Sonett: Gestalt und Geschichte* (Kerle: Heidelberg, 1955) and Paul Fussell, *Poetic Metre and Poetic Form* (London: McGraw-Hill, 1979).
29 Stuart Curran, *Poetic Form and British Romanticism*. Oxford: Oxford University Press, 1990, 8. Alastair Fowler makes a similar point: 'There is a good deal to say about Attic tragedy, Elizabethan tragedy, perhaps even modern tragedy, but not much that makes sense about all tragedy. Without some historical localization, discussion of genre tends towards the vacuous' (*Kinds of Literature*, 47).
30 Chapman, *Yeats and English Renaissance Literature*, 32.

31 Helen Vendler, *Coming of Age as a Poet: Milton, Keats, Eliot, Plath*. Cambridge, MA: Harvard University Press, 2003.

32 Vendler, *Our Secret Discipline*, 148, 149.

33 Ibid., 154.

34 Ibid.

35 Jennifer Ann Wagner, *A Moment's Monument: Revisionary Poetics and the Nineteenth-Century Sonnet*. London: Associated University Presses, 1996, 14.

36 Joseph Phelan, *The Nineteenth-Century Sonnet*. Basingstoke: Palgrave Macmillan, 2005.

37 Vendler, *The Art of Shakespeare's Sonnets*, 150, 152.

38 Ibid., 152.

39 The drafts of 'The Second Coming' are more politically explicit than its final version. See, for instance, Jon Stallworthy's discussion of these drafts in the first chapter of *Between the Lines: Yeats's Poetry in the Making*. Oxford: Clarendon Press, 1963.

40 Vendler, *The Art of Shakespeare's Sonnets*, 535.

41 Desai's *Yeats's Shakespeare* includes an appendix that lists in detail all of Yeats's references to Shakespeare's works. For the various editions that were in Yeats's possession, see Edward O'Shea, *A Descriptive Catalog of W. B. Yeats's Library*. New York and London: Garland, 1985.

42 For an account of how the controversy affected Yeats, see R. F. Foster, *W. B. Yeats: A Life*, II, 568–75.

43 Vendler, *The Art of Shakespeare's Sonnets*, 310.

44 Although Yeats found much to disagree with in Edward Dowden's view on Shakespeare, on this particular point he seems to concur with parts of the interpretation presented by the friend of his father. Dowden reads Shakespeare's sonnets as developing an artistic credo of distance through suffering. In his introduction to the sonnets, Dowden writes of 'a time in his life when the springs of faith and hope had almost cease to flow; and he recovered these not by flying from reality and life, but by driving his shafts deeper towards the centre of things' (*The Sonnets of William Shakspere*, edited by Edward Dowden. London: Kegan Paul, Trench & Co., 1883, xxv). He also presents a similar view in a monograph on Shakespeare; in the sonnets, he claims, 'we may perhaps discover the sorrow which first roused his heart and imagination to their long inquisition of evil and grief, and which, sinking down into his great soul, and remaining there until all bitterness had passed away, bore fruit in the most mature of Shakespeare's writings' (*Shakspere: A Critical Study of His Mind and Art*. London: Kegan Paul, Trench & Co., 1889, 394).

45 Compare Dante Gabriel Rossetti's 'A Sonnet is a Moment's Monument', which is given a useful analysis in chapter five of Wagner, *A Moment's Monument*.

46 Fowler, *Kinds of Literature*, 107.

47 Grene, *Yeats's Poetic Codes*, 106.

48 Yvor Winters, 'The Poetry of W. B. Yeats', *Twentieth Century Literature*, 6(1), (April 1960), 10.

49 Vendler, *Our Secret Discipline*, 155.

50 Foster, *W. B. Yeats: A Life*, I, 509.

51 Vendler, *Our Secret Discipline*, 147.

52 See chapter three of Fowler, *Kinds of Literature*. Hans Robert Jauss states that 'literary genres are to be understood not as *genera* (classes) in the logical senses, but rather as *groups* or *historical families*' (*Toward an Aesthetic of Reception*, translated by Timothy Bahti. Minneapolis: University of Minnesota Press, 1982, 79–80).

53 'All that matters is the book, such as it is, far away from genres, outside the
     categories – prose, poetry, novel, chronicle – with which it refuses to align itself, and
     whose power to impose its place and determine its form it denies. A book no longer
     belongs to a genre, every book pertains to literature alone' (Maurice Blanchot, *The
     Blanchot Reader*, edited by Michael Holland. Oxford: Blackwell, 1995, 141). David
     Duff writes perceptively of the challenged mounted by Blanchot and other twentieth
     century theorists to the notion of literary genre in his introduction to Duff (ed.),
     Modern Genre Theory.

Chapter 11

1   See, for instance, 'The Law of Genre', in Jacques Derrida, *Acts of Literature*, edited by
     Derek Attridge. New York and London: Routledge, 1992.
2   Genette, *The Architext: An Introduction*, 81.
3   Genette, *Palimpsests*, 1.
4   Gabriel Josipovici, *What Ever Happened to Modernism?* New Haven and London: Yale
     University Press, 2010, 65.
5   Fredric Jameson, 'Magical Narratives: Romance as Genre', *New Literary History*, 7(1),
     (Autumn 1975), 135.
6   See Josipovici, *What Ever Happened to Modernism?*, 48–50.
7   For an excellent discussion of genre in German Romanticism, see chapter 3 of
     Philippe Lacoue-Labarthe and Jean-Luc Nancy, *The Literary Absolute: The Theory of
     Literature in German Romanticism*, translated by Philip Barnard and Cheryl Lester.
     Albany: State University of New York Press, 1988.
8   See Curran, *Poetic Form and British Romanticism* and Duff, *Romanticism and the Uses
     of Genre*.
9   Duff, *Romanticism and the Uses of Genre*, 1.
10 See U. C. Knoepflmacher and Logan D. Browning (eds), *Victorian Hybridities:
     Cultural Anxiety and Formal Innovation*. Baltimore: The Johns Hopkins University
     Press, 2010.
11 Tzvetan Todorov, *The Fantastic: A Structural Approach to a Literary Genre*, translated
     by Richard Howard. Ithaca: Cornell University Press, 1975, 8.
12 See Daniel Gabriel, *Hart Crane and the Modernist Epic: Canon and Genre Formation
     in Crane, Pound, Eliot, and Williams*. Basingstoke: Palgrave Macmillan, 2007.
13 John Hollander, *The Figure of Echo: A Mode of Allusion in Milton and After*. Berkeley
     and Los Angeles: University of California Press, 1981, 72–3.
14 The question whether or not Yeats's narrative poems should be provided a separate
     space, subsequent to his lyrics, has been the perhaps most controversial issue
     regarding the editing of Yeats's collected poems. On this, see for instance chapter 7
     of Richard J. Finneran, *Editing Yeats's Poems: A Reconsideration*. Basingstoke:
     Macmillan, 1990.
15 Fowler, *Kinds of Literature*, 33.

Bibliography

W. B. Yeats – publications

Yeats, William B., *Autobiographies*, edited by William H. O'Donnell, Douglas N. Archibald, J. Fraser Cocks III and Gretchen L. Schwenker. New York: Scribner, 1999.

— *The Collected Letters, Volume I, 1865–1895*, edited by John Kelly and Eric Domville. Oxford: Clarendon Press, 1986.

— *The Collected Letters, Volume III, 1901–1904*, edited by John Kelly and Ronald Schuchard. Oxford: Clarendon Press, 1994.

— *The Collected Letters of W. B. Yeats*, general editor John Kelly. Oxford University Press (Intelex Electronic Edition) 2002.

— *Early Articles and Reviews*, edited by John P. Frayne and Madeleine Marchaterre. New York: Scribner, 2004.

— *Early Essays*, edited by Richard J. Finneran and George Bornstein. New York: Scribner, 2007.

— *Explorations*, selected by Mrs. W. B. Yeats. London: Macmillan, 1962.

— *The Irish Dramatic Movement*, edited by Mary FitzGerald and Richard J. Finneran. New York: Scribner, 2003.

— *John Sherman and Dhoya*, edited by Richard J. Finneran. New York: Macmillan, 1991.

— *Later Articles and Reviews: Uncollected Articles, Reviews, and Radio Broadcasts Written After 1900*, edited by Colton Johnson. New York: Scribner, 2000.

— *Later Essays*, edited by William H. O'Donnell with Elizabeth Bergmann Loizeaux. New York: Scribner, 1994.

— *The Making of 'The Player Queen'*, edited by Curtis Bradford. DeKalb: Northern Illinois University Press, 1977.

— *Memoirs: Autobiography – First Draft: Journal*, transcribed and edited by Denis Donoghue. London: Macmillan, 1972.

— *Mythologies*. London: Macmillan, 1959.

— *New Poems: Manuscript Materials*, edited by J. C. C. Mays and Stephen Parrish. Ithaca and London: Cornell University Press, 2000.

— *The Plays*, edited by David R. Clark and Rosalind E. Clark. New York: Scribner, 2001.

— *The Poems*, 2nd edn, edited by Richard J. Finneran. New York: Scribner, 1997.

— *Prefaces and Introductions*, edited by William H. O'Donnell. New York: Macmillan, 1989.

— *The Resurrection: Manuscript Materials*, edited by Jared Curtis and Selina Guinness. Ithaca and London: Cornell University Press, 2011.

— *The Senate Speeches of W. B. Yeats*, edited by Donald R. Pearce. Bloomington: Indiana University Press, 1960.

— *The Tower (1928): Manuscript Materials*, edited by Richard J. Finneran with Jared Curtis and Ann Saddlemyer. Ithaca and London: Cornell University Press, 2007.

— *The Variorum Edition of the Plays of W. B. Yeats*, edited by Russell K. Alspach assisted by Catherine C. Alspach. London: Macmillan, 1979 (1966).

— *The Variorum Edition of the Poems of W. B. Yeats,* edited by Peter Allt and Russell K. Alspach. New York: Macmillan, 1966 (1957).
— *A Vision.* London: Macmillan, 1962 (1937).
— *'Vision' Papers, Volume 1: The Automatic Script: 5 November 1917–18 June 1918,* edited by Steve L. Adams, Barbara J. Frieling and Sandra L. Sprayberry. London: Macmillan, 1992.
— *'Vision' Papers, Volume 2: The Automatic Script: 25 June 1918–29 March 1920,* edited by Steve L. Adams, Barbara J. Frieling and Sandra L. Sprayberry. London: Macmillan, 1992.
— *'Vision' Papers, Volume 3: Sleep and Dream Notebooks, Vision Notebooks 1 and 2, Card File,* edited by Robert Anthony Martinich and Margaret Mills Harper. London: Macmillan, 1992.
— *A Vision (1925),* edited by Catherine E. Paul and Margaret Mills Harper. New York: Scribner, 2008.
Yeats, William B. and Yeats, George, *The Letters,* edited by Ann Saddlemyer. Oxford: Oxford University Press, 2011.

Other works

Adams, Hazard, *The Book of Yeats's Vision: Romantic Modernism and Antithetical Tradition.* Ann Arbor: University of Michigan Press, 1995.
— 'Constituting Yeats's Poems as a Book', in David Pierce (ed.), *W. B. Yeats: Critical Assessments, Volume IV. Assessments: 1980–2000.* Mountfield: Helm Information, 2000, 230–45.
Albright, Daniel, 'Notes', in W. B. Yeats, *The Poems,* edited and introduced by Daniel Albright. London: Everyman, 1990, 397–845.
— 'Yeats and Modernism', in Marjorie Howes and John Kelly (eds), *The Cambridge Companion to W. B. Yeats.* Cambridge: Cambridge University Press, 2006, 59–76.
Altman, Rick, *Film/Genre.* Basingstoke: Palgrave Macmillan, 2012 (1999).
Archibald, Douglas, 'John Butler Yeats', in David Holdeman and Ben Levitas (eds), *W. B. Yeats in Context.* Cambridge: Cambridge University Press, 2010, 109–18.
Aristotle, *Poetics,* translated and with a commentary by George Whalley. Montreal: McGill-Queen's University Press, 1997.
Arkins, Brian, *Builders of My Soul: Greek and Roman Themes in Yeats.* Gerrards Cross: Colin Smythe, 1990.
Armstrong, Charles I., *Romantic Organicism: From Idealist Origins to Ambivalent Afterlife.* Basingstoke: Macmillan, 2003.
— *Figures of Memory: Poetry, Space, and the Past.* Basingstoke: Palgrave Macmillan, 2009.
— 'Ghost Memories: Yeats on Individual and Collective Pasts', *Nordic Irish Studies,* 11(1), (2012), 175–84.
Backscheider, Paula R., *Reflections on Biography.* Oxford: Oxford University Press, 2001.
Bakhtin, Mikhail M., *Speech Genres and Other Late Essays,* edited by Caryl Emerson and Michael Holquist, translated by Vern W. McGee. Austin: University of Texas Press, 1986.
Balzac, Honore de, 'The Pleasures and Pains of Coffee', translated by Robert Onopa. Accessed on 22 November 2012 at: www.blissbat.net/balzac.html.
Banville, John, 'The Rescue of W. B. Yeats', *The New York Review,* 26 February 2004.

Barthes, Roland, *Roland Barthes*, translated by Richard Howard. Berkeley and Los Angeles: University of California Press, 1977.

Beadle, Richard and King, Pamela M., 'General Introduction', in Richard Beadle and Pamela M. King (eds), *York Mystery Plays: A Selection in Modern Spelling*. Oxford: Oxford University Press, 2009 (1984), ix–xxx.

Beadle, Richard and King, Pamela M. (eds), *York Mystery Plays: A Selection in Modern Spelling*. Oxford: Oxford University Press, 2009 (1984).

Bell, Vereen M., *Yeats and the Logic of Formalism*. Columbia and London: University of Missouri Press, 2006.

Blanchot, Maurice, *The Blanchot Reader*, edited by Michael Holland. Oxford: Blackwell, 1995.

Blavatsky, Helena Petrovna, *The Secret Doctrine: The Synthesis of Science, Religion, and Philosophy*, 2 vols. London: Theosophical Publishing Company, 1888.

Bloom, Harold, *The Anxiety of Influence*, 2nd edn. New York: Oxford University Press, 1997.

— *Yeats*. New York: Oxford University Press, 1970.

Bohlmann, Otto, *Yeats and Nietzsche: An Exploration of Major Nietzschean Echoes in the Writings of William Butler Yeats*. Totowa: Barnes & Noble Books, 1982.

Bornstein, George, *Material Modernism: The Politics of the Page*. Cambridge: Cambridge University Press, 2001.

— 'Yeats and Romanticism', in Marjorie Howes and John Kelly (eds), *The Cambridge Companion to W. B. Yeats*. Cambridge: Cambridge University Press, 2006, 19–35.

Brewster, Scott, *Lyric*. London and New York: Routledge, 2009.

Broomfield, Andrea, *Food and Cooking in Victorian England: A History*. Santa Barbara: Praeger, 2007.

Brown, Andrew, 'Interpreter of Myths',*The Guardian*, 13 September 2003.

Brown, Terence, *The Life of W. B. Yeats: A Critical Biography*. Oxford: Blackwell, 2001.

Campbell, Matthew, 'Yeats in the Coming Times', *Essays in Criticism*, 53(1), (January 2003), 10–32.

— 'The English Romantic Symbolists', in David Holdeman and Ben Levitas (eds), *W. B. Yeats in Context*. Cambridge: Cambridge University Press, 2010, 310–19.

Casey, Edward S., *Remembering: A Phenomenological Study*. Bloomington and Indianapolis: Indiana University Press, 2000.

Chapman, Wayne K., *Yeats and English Renaissance Literature*. Basingstoke: Macmillan, 1991.

— *Yeats's Poetry in the Making: Sing Whatever is Well Made*. Basingstoke: Palgrave Macmillan, 2010.

Chaudhry, Yug Mohit, *Yeats: The Irish Literary Revival and the Politics of Print*. Cork: Cork University Press, 2001.

Clark, David R. (ed.), '"The Poet and the Actress": An Unpublished Dialogue by W. B. Yeats', *Yeats Annual*, edited by Warwick Gould, 8, 1991, 123–43.

Clark, David R. with Clark, Rosalind, *W. B. Yeats and the Theatre of Desolate Reality*, revised edition. Washington, D C: The Catholic University of America Press, 1993.

Cole, Sarah, *Modernism, Male Friendship, and the First World War*. Cambridge: Cambridge University Press, 2003.

Corcoran, Neil, *Shakespeare and the Modern Poet*. Cambridge: Cambridge University Press, 2010.

Craig, Cairns, 'The Last Romantics: How the Scholarship of Herbert Grierson Influenced Modernist Poetry', *Times Literary Supplement*, 15 January 2010.

Culler, Jonathan, *Framing the Sign: Criticism and Its Institutions*. Oxford: Blackwell, 1988.

Cullingford, Elizabeth Butler, *Gender and History in Yeats's Love Poetry*. New York: Syracuse University Poetry, 1996.

Curran, Stuart, *Poetic Form and British Romanticism*. Oxford: Oxford University Press, 1990.

Curtis, Jared and Guinness, Selina, 'Introduction', in W. B. Yeats, *The Resurrection: Manuscript Materials*. Ithaca and London: Cornell University Press, 2011, xix–xliv.

Darracott, Joseph, *The World of Charles Ricketts*. New York and Toronto: Methuen, 1980.

Dawson, Barbara,(ed.), *Hugh Lane: Founder of a Gallery of Modern Art for Ireland*. London: Scala, 2008.

De Certeau, Michel, *The Writing of History*, translated by Tom Conley. New York: Columbia University Press, 1988.

DeForrest, Matthew, 'Philosophical Differences and Yeats's Corroborative System in *A Vision*', *The South Carolina Review*, 32(1), (Fall 1999), 213–32.

De Man, Paul, *The Rhetoric of Romanticism*. New York: Columbia University Press, 1984.

— 'Lyrical Voice in Contemporary Theory: Riffaterre and Jauss', in Chaviva Hosek and Patricia Parker (eds), *Lyric Poetry: Beyond New Criticism*. Ithaca and London: Cornell University Press, 1985, 55–72.

Derrida, Jacques, *The Truth in Painting*, translated by Geoff Bennington and Ian McLeod. Chicago and London: The University of Chicago Press, 1987.

— *Acts of Literature*, edited by Derek Attridge. New York and London: Routledge, 1992.

— *Archive Fever: A Freudian Impression*, translated by Eric Prenowitz. Chicago and London: The University of Chicago Press, 1996.

Desai, Rupin W., *Yeats's Shakespeare*. Evanston: Northwestern University Press, 1971.

Devitt, Amy J., *Writing Genres*. Carbondale: Southern Illinois University Press, 2004.

Dodds, Eric Robertson, *The Greeks and the Irrational*. Berkeley: University of California Press, 1951.

Doody, Noreen, 'An Echo of Some One Else's Music: The Influence of Oscar Wilde on W. B. Yeats', in Uwe Böker, Richard Corballis and Julie A. Hibbard (eds), *The Importance of Reinventing Oscar: Versions of Wilde During the Last 100 Years*. Amsterdam: Rodopi, 2002, 175–82.

Dowden, Edward, *Shakspere: A Critical Study of His Mind and Art*. London: Kegan Paul, Trench & Co., 1889.

Drakakis, John and Liebler, Naomi Conn (eds), *Tragedy*. London and New York: Longman, 1998.

Duff, David, 'Intertextuality versus Genre Theory: Bakhtin, Kristeva and the Question of Genre', *Paragraph*, 25(1), (2002), 54–73.

— *Romanticism and the Uses of Genre*. Oxford: Oxford University Press, 1999.

Duff, David, (ed.), *Modern Genre Theory*. Harlow: Pearson, 2000.

Eagleton, Terry, *Sweet Violence: The Idea of the Tragic*. Oxford: Blackwell, 2003.

Eliot, Thomas Stearns, *The Sacred Wood: Essays on Poetry and Criticism*. London: Faber and Faber, 1997.

Ellis, Sylvia C., *The Plays of W. B. Yeats: Yeats and the Dancer*. Basingstoke: Macmillan, 1999.

Ellmann, Richard, *The Identity of Yeats*. London: Faber and Faber, 1964 (1954).

— *Eminent Domain: Yeats among Wilde, Joyce, Pound, Eliot and Auden*. New York: Oxford University Press, 1967.

— *Golden Codgers: Biographical Speculations*. London: Oxford University Press, 1973.

— *Oscar Wilde*. London: Penguin, 1987.

— *Yeats: The Man and the Masks*. New York and London: Norton, 1999 (1948).

Engelberg, Edward, *The Vast Design: Patters in W. B. Yeats's Aesthetic*, 2nd edn, expanded. Washington, DC: The Catholic University of America Press, 1988.

Eriksen, Roy T., 'Shaping the Sonnet Italian Style: Petrarch, Tasso, Daniel and Shakespeare', in Sonja Fielitz (ed.), *Shakespeare's Sonnets: Loves, Layers, Languages*. Heidelberg: Universitätsverlag Winter, 2010, 55–73.

Farren, Sean, *The Politics of Irish Education, 1920–65*. Belfast: The Institute of Irish Studies, 1995.

Fenollosa, Ernest and Pound, Ezra, *'Noh' or Accomplishment: A Study of the Classical Stage of Japan*. Gretna: Pelican Publishing Company, 1999.

Fineman, Joel, *Shakespeare's Perjured Eye*. Berkeley: University of California Press, 1986.

Finneran, Richard J., *Editing Yeats's Poems: A Reconsideration*. Basingstoke: Macmillan, 1990.

Fischer, Barbara K., *Museum Mediations: Reframing Ekphrasis in Contemporary American Poetry*. New York: Routledge, 2006.

Flaherty, Michael (ed.), *The Poetry of W. B. Yeats: A Reader's Guide to Essential Criticism*. Basingstoke: Palgrave Macmillan, 2005.

Fletcher, Ian, ' "Leda and the Swan" as Iconic Poem', *Yeats Annual*, 1, 1982, 82–113.

— 'Rhythm and Pattern in *Autobiographies*', in Harold Bloom (ed.), *William Butler Yeats: Modern Critical Views*. New York and Philadelphia: Chelsea House, 1986, 73–94.

Foster, Robert Fitzroy, *Lord Randolph Churchill: A Political Life*. Oxford: Clarendon Press, 1981.

— *Paddy and Mr Punch: Connections in Irish and English History*. London: Penguin, 1995.

— *W. B. Yeats, A Life. I: The Apprentice Mage*. Oxford: Oxford University Press, 1997.

— *The Irish Story: Telling Tales and Making It up in Ireland*. London: Penguin, 2001.

— *W. B. Yeats: A Life, II: The Arch-Poet*. Oxford: Oxford University Press, 2003.

— 'Fascism', in David Holdeman and Ben Levitas (eds), *W. B. Yeats in Context*. Cambridge: Cambridge University Press, 2010, 213–23.

— *Words Alone: Yeats and His Inheritances*. Oxford: Oxford University Press, 2011.

Fowler, Alastair, *Kinds of Literature: An Introduction to the Theory of Genres and Modes*. Oxford: Clarendon, 1982.

Frazer, James George, *The Golden Bough: A Study of Magic and Religion*. London: Papermac, 1987.

Frow, John, *Genre*. London and New York: Routledge, 2006.

Fussell, Paul, *Poetic Metre and Poetic Form*. London: McGraw-Hill, 1979.

Gabriel, Dante, *Hart Crane and the Modernist Epic: Canon and Genre Formation in Crane, Pound, Eliot, and Williams*. Basingstoke: Palgrave Macmillan, 2007.

Gadamer, Hans-Georg, *Truth and Method*, 2nd edn, translated by Joel Weinsheimer and Donald G. Marshall. London: Sheed & Ward, 1989.

Gathercole, Susan E., 'The Nature and Uses of Working Memory', in Peter Morris and Michael Gruneberg (eds), *Theoretical Aspects of Memory*, 2nd edn. London and New York: Routledge, 1994, 50–78.

Genette, Gérard, *The Architext: An Introduction*, translated by Jane E. Lewin. Berkeley and Los Angeles: University of California Press, 1992.

— *Palimpsests: Literature in the Second Degree*, translated by Channa Newman and Claude Doubinsky. Lincoln and London: University of Nebraska Press, 1997.

— *Paratexts: Thresholds of Interpretation*, translated by Jane E. Lewin. Cambridge: Cambridge University Press, 1997.

Gibson, Matthew, *Yeats, Coleridge and the Romantic Sage*. Basingstoke: Macmillan, 2000.

— 'Classical Philosophy', in David Holdeman and Ben Levitas (eds), *W. B. Yeats in Context.* Cambridge: Cambridge University Press, 2010, 276–87.

Gilbert, William Schwenk and Sullivan, Arthur, *The Complete Annotated Gilbert and Sullivan,* introduced and edited by Ian Bradley. Oxford: Oxford University Press, 1996.

Grene, Nicholas, *Yeats's Poetic Codes.* Oxford: Oxford University Press, 2008.

— 'J. M. Synge', in David Holdeman and Ben Levitas (eds), *W. B. Yeats in Context.* Cambridge: Cambridge University Press, 2010, 139–47.

Grossman, Allen R., *Poetic Knowledge in the Early Yeats: A Study of 'The Wind among the Reeds'.* Charlottesville: University Press of Virginia, 1969.

Hadot, Pierre, *Plotinus, or the Simplicity of Vision,* translated by Michael Chase. Chicago: University of Chicago Press, 1993.

Hall, Jason David, 'Form and Process: Seamus Heaney's "A New Life" into "Act of Union"', in Frank Beardow and Alison O'Malley-Younger (eds), *Representing Ireland: Past, Present and Future.* Sunderland: University of Sunderland Press, 2005, 153–63.

Hallam, Arthur Henry, 'On Some Characteristics of Modern Poetry', *The Writings of Arthur Hallam,* edited by T. H. Vail Motter. New York: MLA, 1943.

Happé, Peter, 'Introduction', in Peter Happé (ed.), *English Mystery Plays: A Selection.* London: Penguin, 1988 (1975), 9–35.

— (ed.), *English Mystery Plays: A Selection.* London: Penguin, 1988 (1975).

Harper, George Mills, *W. B. Yeats and W. T. Horton: The Record of an Occult Friendship.* London and Basingstoke: Macmillan, 1980, 59–63.

— *The Making of Yeats's 'A Vision': A Study of the Automatic Script,* Volume 1. London: Macmillan, 1987.

Harper, Margaret Mills, *Wisdom of Two: The Spiritual and Literary Collaboration of George and W. B. Yeats.* Oxford: Oxford University Press, 2006.

Heaney, Seamus, *Death of a Naturalist.* London: Faber and Faber, 1991 (1966).

Heffernan, James A. W., *Museum of Words: The Poetics of Ekphrasis from Homer to Ashbery.* Chicago and London: The University of Chicago Press, 1993.

Higgins, Geraldine, 'Popular Culture', in David Holdeman and Ben Levitas (eds), *W. B. Yeats in Context.* Cambridge: Cambridge University Press, 2010, 406–15.

Holdeman, David, *Much Labouring: The Texts and Authors of Yeats's First Modernist Books.* Ann Arbor: The University of Michigan Press, 1997.

— *The Cambridge Introduction to W. B. Yeats.* Cambridge: Cambridge University Press, 2006.

— 'Manuscripts and Revisions', in David Holdeman and Ben Levitas (eds), *W. B. Yeats in Context.* Cambridge: Cambridge University Press, 2010, 365–75.

Holdeman, David and Levitas, Ben (eds), *W. B. Yeats in Context.* Cambridge: Cambridge University Press, 2010.

Hollander, John, *The Figure of Echo: A Mode of Allusion in Milton and after.* Berkeley and Los Angeles: University of California Press, 1981.

Holmes, Oliver Wendell, *The Poet at the Breakfast-Table.* Boston: James R. Osgood and Company, 1872.

— *The Poetical Works,* Volume II. Boston and New York: Houghton Mifflin and Company, 1895.

Holmes, Richard, *Footsteps: Adventures of a Romantic Biographer.* London: Flamingo, 1995.

Hough, Graham, *The Mystery Religion of W. B. Yeats.* Brighton: Harvester Press, 1984.

Howes, Marjorie, *Yeats's Nations: Gender, Class, and Irishness.* Cambridge: Cambridge University Press, 1996.

Iser, Wolfgang, *The Act of Reading: A Theory of Aesthetic Response*. Baltimore and London: Johns Hopkins University Press, 1978.

Ishabishi, Hiro, *Yeats and the Noh: Types of Japanese Beauty and Their Reflection in Yeats's Plays, The Dolmen Press Yeats Centenary Papers*, MCMLXV, 1966.

Jameson, Fredric, 'Magical Narratives: Romance as Genre', *New Literary History*, 7(1), (Autumn 1975), 135–63.

Jauss, Hans Robert, *Toward an Aesthetic of Reception*, translated by Timothy Bahti. Minneapolis: University of Minnesota Press, 1982.

Jenkyns, Richard, *The Victorians and Ancient Greece*. Oxford: Basil Blackwell, 1980.

Josipovici, Gabriel, *What Ever Happened to Modernism?* New Haven and London: Yale University Press, 2010.

Joyce, James, *Ulysses*, London and New York: Everyman, 1997.

Keane, Patrick J., *Yeats's Interactions with Tradition*. Columbia: University of Minnesota Press, 1987.

— *Emerson, Romanticism, and Intuitive Reason: The Transatlantic 'Light of All our Day'*. University of Missouri Press, 2005.

Kelly, John S., *A W. B. Yeats Chronology*. Basingstoke: Palgrave Macmillan, 2003.

Kermode, Frank, *Romantic Image*. London and New York: Routledge, 2002 (1957).

Kerrigan, John, 'Introduction', in William Shakespeare, *'The Sonnets' and 'A Lover's Complaint'*, edited by John Kerrigan. London: Penguin, 2009 (1995).

Kershner, R. Brandon, 'Yeats/Bakhtin/Orality/Dyslexia', in Leonard Orr (ed.), *Yeats and Postmodernism*. New York: Syracuse University Press, 1991, 167–88.

Kiberd, Declan, *Inventing Ireland: The Literature of a Modern Nation*. London: Vintage, 1996.

— *Ulysses and Us: The Art of Everyday Living*. London: Faber and Faber, 2009.

Killeen, Jarlath, *The Faiths of Oscar Wilde: Catholicism, Folklore and Ireland*. Basingstoke: Palgrave Macmillan, 2005.

Kirkland, Richard, *Literature and Culture in Northern Ireland since 1965: Moments of Danger*. London and New York: Longman, 1996.

Knoepflmacher, Ulrich C. and Browning, Logan D. (eds), *Victorian Hybridities: Cultural Anxiety and Formal Innovation*. Baltimore: The Johns Hopkins University Press, 2010.

Kristeva, Julia, *Revolution in Poetic Language*, translated by Margaret Waller. New York: Columbia University Press, 1984.

— *The Kristeva Reader*, edited by Toril Moi. Oxford: Blackwell, 1986.

Kuhling, Carmen and Keohane, Kieran, *Cosmopolitan Ireland: Globalisation and Quality of Life*. London and Ann Arbor: Pluto Press, 2007.

Lacoue-Labarthe, Philippe and Nancy, Jean-Luc, *The Literary Absolute: The Theory of Literature in German Romanticism*, translated by Philip Barnard and Cheryl Lester. Albany: State University of New York Press, 1988.

Lakoff, George and Johnson, Mark, *Metaphors We Live By*. Chicago: University of Chicago Press, 2003.

Larrissy, Edward, *Yeats the Poet: The Measures of Difference*. Hemel Hempstead: Harvester Wheatsheaf, 1994.

Lessing, Gotthold Ephraim, *Laocoon: An Essay on the Limits of Painting and Poetry*, translated by Edward Allen McCormick. Baltimore: Johns Hopkins University Press, 1984.

Levenson, Michael, 'Introduction', in Michael Levenson (ed.), *The Cambridge Companion to Modernism*. Cambridge: Cambridge University Press, 1999, 1–8.

Levi, Peter, *Tennyson*. London: Macmillan, 1991.

Levinson, Marjorie, 'What is New Formalism?' *PMLA*, 122(2), (2007), 558–69.

Loizeaux, Elizabeth Bergmann, *Yeats and the Visual Arts*. New York: Syracuse University Press, 2003.

— *Twentieth-Century Poetry and the Visual Arts*. Cambridge: Cambridge University Press, 2008.

— 'Yeats's Poems on Pictures', *The Yeats Journal of Korea*, 38, (summer 2012), 11–31.

Longenbach, James, *Stone Cottage: Pound, Yeats and Modernism*. New York and Oxford: Oxford University Press, 1988.

— 'Modern Poetry', in Michael Levenson (ed.), *The Cambridge Companion to Modernism*. Cambridge: Cambridge University Press, 1999, 100–29.

— 'Modern Poetry', in David Holdeman and Ben Levitas (eds), *W. B. Yeats in Context*. Cambridge: Cambridge University Press, 2010, 320–9.

Longley, Edna, 'Helicon and ni Houlihan: *Michael Robartes and the Dancer*', in Jonathan Allison (ed.), *Yeats's Political Identities: Selected Essays*. Ann Arbor: The University of Michigan Press, 1996, 203–20.

Lynch, Claire, *Irish Autobiography: Stories of Self in the Narrative of a Nation*. Bern: Peter Lang, 2009.

MacFaul, Tom, *Male Friendship in Shakespeare and His Contemporaries*. Cambridge: Cambridge University Press, 2007.

Macksey, Richard, 'Foreword', in Gérard Genette, *Paratexts: Thresholds of Interpretation*, translated by Jane E. Lewin. Cambridge: Cambridge University Press, 1997.

Maddox, Brenda, *Nora: Biography of Nora Joyce*. London: Hamish Hamilton, 1988.

— *George's Ghosts: A New Life of W. B. Yeats*. London: Picador, 1999.

Malone, Irene Ruppo, *Ibsen and the Irish Revival*. Basingstoke: Palgrave Macmillan, 2010.

Marshall, Gail, 'Introduction', in Gail Marshall (ed.), *The Cambridge Companion to the Fin de Siècle*. Cambridge: Cambridge University Press, 2007, 1–12.

Martin, Augustine, 'Yeats's Noh: The Dancer and the Dance', in Masaru Sekine and Christopher Murray (eds), *Yeats and the Noh: A Comparative Study*, with contributions by Augustine Martin, Peter Davidson, Colleen Hanrahan and Katharine Worth. Savage, Maryland: Barnes & Nobel Books, 1990, xiii–xviii.

Mathers, S. L. MacGregor, *The Kabbalah Unveiled*. Henley: Routledge & Kegan Paul, 1981.

Matthews, Steven, *Yeats as Precursor: Readings in Irish, British and American Poetry*. Basingstoke: Macmillan, 2000.

McAlindon, Thomas, 'Yeats and the English Renaissance', *PMLA*, 82(2), (May 1967), 157–69.

McAteer, Michael, *Yeats and European Drama*. Cambridge: Cambridge University Press, 2010.

McCormack, William John, *Blood Kindred: W. B. Yeats. The Life, the Death, the Politics*. London: Pimlico, 2005.

McDiarmid, Lucy, 'Yeats and the Lettered Page', in W. B. Yeats, *Yeats's Poetry, Drama, and Prose*, edited by James Pethica. New York: Norton, 2000.

McDonald, Peter, *Serious Poetry: Form and Authority from Yeats to Hill*. Oxford: Oxford University Press, 2002.

Meir, Colin, *The Ballads and Songs of W. B. Yeats: The Anglo-Irish Heritage in Subject and Style*. London: Macmillan, 1974.

Melchiori, Giorgio, *The Whole Mystery of Art*. London: Routledge and Kegan Paul, 1959.

Miller, Liam, *The Noble Art of W. B. Yeats*. Dublin: The Dolmen Press, 1977.

Mitchell, William J. Thomas, *Iconology: Image, Text, Ideology*. Chicago: The University of Chicago Press, 1986.

Mönch, Walter, *Das Sonett: Gestalt und Geschichte*. Kerle: Heidelberg, 1955.

Moore, George, *Hail and Farewell: Ave, Salve, Vale*, edited by Richard Cave. Toronto: Macmillan of Canada, 1976.

Moses, Michael Valdez, 'Nietzsche', in David Holdeman and Ben Levitas (eds), *W. B. Yeats in Context*. Cambridge: Cambridge University Press, 2010, 266–75.

Nally, Claire, *Envisioning Ireland: Occult Nationalism in the Work of W. B. Yeats*. Oxford: Peter Lang, 2009.

Nietzsche, Friedrich, *Untimely Meditations*, edited by Daniel Breazeale, translated by R. J. Hollingdale. Cambridge: Cambridge University Press, 1997.

Nora, Pierre, 'General Introduction: Between Memory and History', in Pierre Nora (ed.), *Realms of Memory: Rethinking the French Past*, Volume I, edited by Lawrence D. Kritzman, translated by Arthur Goldhammer. New York: Columbia University Press, 1996, 1–20.

Novarr, David, *The Lines of Life: Theories of Biography, 1880–1970*. West Lafayette: Purdue University Press, 1986.

O'Donoghue, Bernard, 'Hearing the Right Voices', *The Guardian*, 27 September, 2003.

O'Hara, Daniel T., *Tragic Knowledge: Yeats's 'Autobiography' and Hermeneutics*. New York: Columbia University Press, 1981.

Olney, James, *The Rhizome and the Flower: The Perennial Philosophy – Yeats and Jung*. Berkeley: University of California Press, 1980.

Olson, Liesl, *Modernism and the Ordinary*. Oxford: Oxford University Press, 2009.

Oser, Lee, *The Ethics of Modernism: Moral Ideas in Yeats, Eliot, Joyce, Woolf, and Beckett*. Cambridge: Cambridge University Press, 2007.

O'Shea, Edward, *A Descriptive Catalog of W. B. Yeats's Library*. New York and London: Garland, 1985.

Parkin, Andrew, 'Introduction', in W. B. Yeats, *At the Hawk's Well* and *The Cat and the Moon: Manuscript Materials*, edited by Andrew Parkin. Ithaca and London: Cornell University Press, 2010, xxiii–lv.

Parkinson, Thomas, *W. B. Yeats, Self-Critic: A Study of His Early Verse, and the Later Poetry*. Berkeley: University of California Press, 1971.

— 'This Extraordinary Book', *Yeats Annual*, 1, 1982, 195–206.

Pater, Walter, *Selected Writings*, edited by Harold Bloom. New York: Columbia University Press, 1974.

— *Marius the Epicurean*, edited by Michael Levey. London: Penguin, 1985.

— *Plato and Platonism: A Series of Lectures*. Amsterdam: Fredonia Books, 2002.

Paul, Catherine, *Poetry in the Museums of Modernism: Yeats, Pound, Moore, Stein*. Ann Arbor: The University of Michigan Press, 2002.

Perl, Jeffrey, *The Tradition of Return: The Implicit History of Modern Literature*. Princeton: Princeton University Press, 1984.

Peterson, Linda H., *Victorian Autobiography: The Tradition of Self-Interpretation*. New Haven and London: Yale University Press, 1986.

Phelan, Joseph, *The Nineteenth-Century Sonnet*. Basingstoke: Palgrave Macmillan, 2005.

Pimlott, Ben, 'Picture this . . .', *The Guardian Review*, 28 August 2004.

Plato, *Euthyphro, Apology, Crito, Phaedo, Phaedrus*, translated by Harold North Fowler, Loeb Classical Library. Cambridge, MA: Harvard University Press, 1914.

Pope, Alexander, *'The Rape of the Lock' and Other Major Writings*, edited by Leo Damrosch. London: Penguin, 2011.

Pound, Ezra, 'A Few Don'ts by an Imagiste', in Peter Jones (ed.), *Imagist Poetry*. London: Penguin, 1972, 130–4.

Putzel, Steven, 'Poetic Ritual and Audience Response: Yeats and the Nō', in Leonard Orr (ed.), *Yeats and Postmodernism*. Syracuse: Syracuse University Press, 1991, 105–25.

Pyle, Hilary, *Yeats: Portrait of an Artistic Family*. London: National Gallery of Ireland in association with Merrell Holberton, 1997.

Ramazani, Jahan, *Yeats and the Poetry of Death: Elegy, Self-Elegy, and the Sublime*. New Haven and London: Yale University Press, 1990.

— *Poetry of Mourning: The Modern Elegy from Hardy to Heaney*. Chicago: The University of Chicago Press, 1994.

— *The Hybrid Muse: Postcolonial Poetry in English*. Chicago and London: The University of Chicago Press, 2001.

— '"To Get the News from Poems": Poetry as Genre', in Erik Martiny (ed.), *A Companion to Poetic Genre*. Oxford: Wiley-Blackwell, 2012, 3–16.

Rancière, Jacques, *The Politics of Aesthetics*, translated by Gabriel Rockhill. London: Continuum, 2004.

— *The Future of the Image*, translated by Gregory Elliott. London: Verso, 2007.

— *The Emancipated Spectator*, translated by Gregory Elliott. London and New York: Verso, 2011.

Richardson, Alan, *A Mental Theatre: Poetic Drama and Consciousness in the Romantic Age*. University Park and London: The Pennsylvania State University Press, 1988.

Ricks, Christopher, *Allusion to the Poets*. Oxford: Oxford University Press, 2002.

Ricoeur, Paul, *Time and Narrative*, Volume I, translated by Kathleen McLaughlin and David Pellauer. Chicago and London: The University of Chicago Press, 1984.

Rimbaud, Arthur, *Complete Works*, translated by Paul Schmidt. Reading: Picador, 1975.

Ritvo, Rosemary Puglia, '*A Vision* B: The Plotinian Metaphysical Basis', *Review of English Studies*, New Series, 26(101), (1975), 34–46.

Roston, Murray, *Biblical Drama in England: From the Middle Ages to the Present Day*. London: Faber and Faber, 1968.

Rousseau, Jean-Jacques and Herder, Johann Gottfried, *On the Origin of Language*, translated by John H. Moran and Alexander Gode. Chicago and London: The University of Chicago Press, 1966.

Sacks, Peter M., *The English Elegy: Studies in the Genre from Spenser to Yeats*. Baltimore and London: The Johns Hopkins University Press, 1985.

Saito, Yuriko, *Everyday Aesthetics*. Oxford: Oxford University Press, 2007.

Scott, Clive, *French Verse-Art: A Study*. Cambridge: Cambridge University Press, 1980.

Sekine, Masaru and Murray, Christopher, *Yeats and the Noh: A Comparative Study*, with contributions by Augustine Martin, Peter Davidson, Colleen Hanrahan and Katharine Worth. Savage, Maryland: Barnes & Nobel Books, 1990.

Shakespeare, William, *The Sonnets of William Shakspere*, edited by Edward Dowden. London: Kegan Paul, Trench & Co., 1883.

— *Hamlet*, edited by Bernard Lott. Harlow: Longman, 1968.

Sheringham, Michael, *Everyday Life: Theories and Practices from Surrealism to the Present*. Oxford: Oxford University Press, 2006.

Stallworthy, Jon, *Between the Lines: Yeats's Poetry in the Making*. Oxford: Clarendon Press, 1963.

— *Vision and Revision in Yeats's 'Last Poems'*. Oxford: Clarendon Press, 1969.

Synge, John Millington, *Plays, Poems and Prose*, edited by Micheál Mac Liammóir. London: Dent, 1968.

Taylor, Charles, *Sources of the Self: The Making of the Modern Identity*. Cambridge: Cambridge University, 1989.

Taylor, Richard, *The Drama of W. B. Yeats: Irish Myth and the Japanese Nō*. New Haven and London: Yale University Press, 1976.

Tennyson, Alfred Lord, *A Selected Edition*, edited by Christopher Ricks. Harlow: Longman, 1989 (1969).

Thwaite, Ann, *Emily Tennyson: The Poet's Wife*. London: Faber and Faber, 1996.

Todorov, Tzvetan, *The Fantastic: A Structural Approach to a Literary Genre*, translated by Richard Howard. Ithaca: Cornell University Press, 1975.

Tomalin, Claire, *The Invisible Woman: The Story of Nelly Ternan and Charles Dickens*. London: Penguin, 1991.

Tomashevskij, Boris, 'Literature and Biography', in Ladislav Matejka and Krystyna Pomorska (eds), *Readings in Russian Poetics: Formalist and Structuralist Views*. Cambridge, MA: The MIT Press, 1971, 47–55.

Toomey, Deirdre, 'Away', *Yeats Annual*, 10, 1993, 3–32.

— '"Amaryllis in the Shade": The Municipal Gallery Revisited', in Warwick Gould (ed.), *Poems and Contexts* (*Yeats Annual, No. 16: A Special Number*). Basingstoke: Palgrave Macmillan, 2005, 131–59.

Torchiana, Donald T., '"Among School Children" and the Education of the Irish Spirit', in A. Norman Jeffares and K. G. W. Cross (eds), *In Excited Reverie: A Centenary Tribute to William Butler Yeats, 1865–1939*. New York: St. Martin's Press, 1965, 123–50.

Townshend, Charles, *Easter 1916: The Irish Rebellion*. London: Penguin, 2005.

Turner, Frank M., *The Greek Heritage in Victorian Britain*. New Haven and London: Yale University Press, 1981.

Tynjanov, Yury, 'The Literary Fact', in David Duff (ed.), *Modern Genre Theory*. Harlow: Pearson Education, 2000, 29–49.

Ure, Peter, 'Yeats's Christian Mystery Plays', *The Review of English Studies*, New Series, 11(42), (May 1960), 171–82.

— *Yeats the Playwright: A Commentary on Character and Design in the Major Plays*. London: Routledge & Kegan Paul, 1963.

Vendler, Helen, *Yeats's 'Vision' and the Later Plays*. Cambridge, MA: Harvard University Press, 1963.

___ 'A. Norman Jeffares, *W. B. Yeats: A New Biography*', in *Yeats Annual*, 9, 1992, 323–8.

— *The Art of Shakespeare's Sonnets*. Cambridge, MA: Belknap Press, 1997.

— *Coming of Age as a Poet: Milton, Keats, Eliot, Plath*. Cambridge, MA: Harvard University Press, 2003.

— *Our Secret Discipline: Yeats on Lyric Form*. Oxford: Oxford University Press, 2007.

Wagner, Jennifer Ann, *A Moment's Monument: Revisionary Poetics and the Nineteenth-Century Sonnet*. London: Associated University Presses, 1996.

Watson, George, 'Yeats, Victorianism, and the 1890s', in Marjorie Howes and John Kelly (eds), *The Cambridge Companion to W. B. Yeats*. Cambridge: Cambridge University Press, 2006, 36–58.

Wellek, René and Warren, Austin, *Theory of Literature*. New York: Penguin Books, 1983 (1949).

Whitaker, Thomas R., *Swan and Shadow: Yeats's Dialogue with History*, revised edition. Washington, DC: Catholic University of America Press, 1989.

White, Hayden, *Metahistory: The Historical Imagination in Nineteenth-Century Europe*. Baltimore and London: The Johns Hopkins University Press, 1973.

Wilde, Oscar, *The Works*. London: Collins, 1931.

— *Salomé*. Boston: Branden Publishing Company, 1996.

Williams, Carolyn, *Gilbert and Sullivan: Gender, Genre, Parody*. New York: Columbia University Press, 2011.

Williams, Raymond, *Modern Tragedy*, edited by Pamela McCallum. Peterborough, Ontario: Broadview, 2006.

Wilson, Edmund, *Axel's Castle: A Study in the Imaginative Literature of 1870 to 1930*. New York: Charles Scribner's Sons, 1931.

Winters, Yvor, 'The Poetry of W. B. Yeats', *Twentieth Century Literature*, 6(1), (April 1960), 3–24.

Wood, Michael, *Yeats and Violence: The Clarendon Lectures in English 2008*. Oxford: Oxford University Press, 2010.

Woolf, Virginia, *The Crowded Dance of Modern Life*. London: Penguin, 1993.

— *A Moment's Liberty: The Shorter Diary*, abridged and edited by Anne Olivier Bell. London: Pimlico, 1997.

Wordsworth, William, *The Prelude: 1799, 1805, 1850*, edited by Jonathan Wordsworth, M. H. Abrams, and Stephen Gill. New York and London: Norton, 1979.

Worth, Katharine, *The Irish Drama of Europe from Yeats to Beckett*. London: The Athlone Press, 1978.

Young, David, *Troubled Mirror: A Study of Yeats's 'The Tower'*. Iowa City: University of Iowa Press, 1987.

Zuckert, Catherine H., *Postmodern Platos: Nietzsche, Heidegger, Gadamer, Strauss, Derrida*. Chicago and London: University of Chicago Press, 1996.

Index

Index

Lightning Source UK Ltd.
Milton Keynes UK
UKOW07f1133200215

246602UK00002B/114/P